USE OF LANGUAGE ACROSS THE PRIMARY CURRICULUM

Language underpins all the subjects of the primary curriculum. Children's knowledge and understanding is not only expressed in language, but also formed through language. Each area of the curriculum offers different opportunities and challenges for extending children's language and literacy experience. For learning to take root, children need to get to grips with a range of different texts. If they are to achieve their fullest potential they also need to become flexible, discriminating and independent readers, writers, speakers and listeners.

This book shows how language and literacy can be developed not just in English lessons but throughout the curriculum. In addition to the core subjects, opportunities in music, PE, ICT and design technology are examined in the context of the interrelationship between children, language and learning:

- children learning to use language
- children using language to learn
- children learning about language

Chapters describe classroom practice as well as offering reflective sections on the interrelationships and processes of language and cognitive development. An integral part of this is acknowledgement of different learning styles and special educational needs and an awareness of issues of linguistic diversity and cultural difference.

Eve Bearne has taught in schools and colleges for thirty years. She was project officer for the National Writing Project and editor of a number of their publications. She is currently Assistant Director in Research at Homerton College and is editor of *Differentiation and Diversity in the Primary School* and *Making Progress in English*.

USE OF LANGUAGE ACROSS THE PRIMARY CURRICULUM

Edited by Eve Bearne

London and New York

First published 1998
by Routledge
11 New Fetter Lane, London EC4P 4EE

Typeset in Goudy by Keystroke, Jacaranda Lodge, Wolverhampton
Printed and bound in Great Britain by
Page Brothers (Norwich) Ltd

British Library Cataloguing in Publication Data
A catalogue record for this book is available from the British Library

Library of Congress Cataloguing in Publication Data
Use of language across the primary curriculum / edited by Eve Bearne.
p. cm.
Includes bibliographical references and index.
1. English language—Study and teaching (Elementary)—Great
Britain. 2. Interdisciplinary approach in education—United States.
I. Bearne, Eve.
LB1576U74 1998
372.6'044—dc21 97–44627
CIP

ISBN 0–415–15851–6 (pbk)

CONTENTS

CONTENTS

FIGURES

CONTRIBUTORS

Helen Arnold is the author of many key books on the teaching and learning of reading, including *Listening to Children Reading* (Hodder and Stoughton, 1982). She lectures and advises widely in this country and abroad. Her career has spanned teaching, lecturing, researching and advising (as County English Adviser for Suffolk).

Eve Bearne has taught English, drama and education in schools and colleges for over thirty years. She was a project officer for the National Writing Project and editor of a number of their publications. She is co-editor of a series of books about children's literature and has written and edited several books about language and literacy, the most recent being *Making Progress in English* (Routledge, 1998). She is currently Assistant Director in Research at Homerton College, Cambridge, dividing her time between teaching students, running inservice courses for teachers, researching and writing.

Helen Bromley has taught throughout the early years range for sixteen years, most recently as deputy headteacher of Sunnymede Infant School, Billericay, Essex. She now works for the Centre for Language in Primary Education, London Borough of Southwark, as well as contributing to inservice courses in other authorities. Her publications include chapters in books about reading, most recently *Talking Pictures* (eds Morag Styles, Barbara Jordan and Victor Watson, Hodder and Stoughton, 1996), *Potent Fictions* (ed. Mary Hilton, Routledge, 1996) and *Teaching and Learning in the Early Years* (ed. David Whitebread, Routledge, 1996).

Penny Coltman gained a degree in agricultural zoology at Leeds University before originally training as a secondary science teacher. She worked as a Key Stage 1 teacher at Great Chesterford C. of E. Primary School, Essex, for eight years before becoming a science and early years lecturer at Homerton College, Cambridge. She has contributed a number of 'Project Files' to *Child Education* magazine about carrying out enterprise projects with young children.

Chris Doddington is a senior lecturer in education, teaching drama and philosophy of education within the Primary Postgraduate course at Homerton

College, Cambridge. She is a professional tutor for the initial teacher education course. Her current area of interest is in the place of the arts in education. She contributed a chapter to *Differentiation and Diversity in the Primary School* (ed. Eve Bearne, Routledge, 1996) on the principles underlying differentiation in the primary school.

Jane Edden is senior lecturer in music education at Homerton College, Cambridge. She has wide experience of working musically with children in a number of schools in this country and Trinidad. Her commitment to children's performance has led to a variety of tapes, records and broadcasts with many invitations for her group to perform publicly. She is co-author of *Managing Music with Infants* (Cambridgeshire County Council, 1989) and contributed a chapter to *Teaching and Learning in the Early Years* (ed. David Whitebread, Routledge, 1996).

Sally Elding taught in primary schools in Cambridgeshire for fourteen years before becoming the county co-ordinator for the National Oracy Project. She worked as an advisory teacher on the English team in Cambridgeshire before going freelance. She has written software datafiles for Longman Logotron and collaborated with Eve Bearne on a series of articles in *Primary English* about assessing speaking and listening. Her most recent publication is *Developing Writing with Computers* (Cambridgeshire Advisory Services).

Ian Eyres is a member of the Open University PGCE course team. He has spent eighteen years as a classroom teacher, the last five working in partnership with colleagues to support the learning of bilingual pupils. His particular areas of interest are educational drama and children's development as writers and as speakers of English as an additional language. He has contributed chapters to several publications including the Open University's *English in the Primary Curriculum* (1988) and chapters on bilingualism in *Greater Expectations* (ed. Eve Bearne, Cassell, 1996) and *Differentiation and Diversity in the Primary School* (ed. Eve Bearne, Routledge, 1996).

Noelle Hunt started her teaching career in Papua New Guinea, working with primary age children of many nationalities. For the last nine years she has worked within the Hertfordshire Minority Ethnic Curriculum Support Service as a language support teacher. She has helped co-ordinate and develop a children's publishing project which promotes children's storywriting in the form of dual-language storyboxes. She has published joint articles with Caroline Luck and also has work on punctuation published in *Making Progress in English* (Eve Bearne, Routledge, 1996).

Caroline Luck first worked in the London Borough of Newham, teaching across the primary age range with a special interest in early years. She then worked as a language support and curriculum achievement teacher with the Minority Ethnic Curriculum Support Service in Hertfordshire, teaching children in a number of primary schools. For the past three years, Caroline has been deputy head of the Reddings CP School in Hemel Hempstead and has collaborated with Noelle Hunt on various language projects in school. They have published a joint account of practice in *Differentiation and Diversity in the Primary School* (ed. Eve Bearne, Routledge, 1996) and most recently have had articles published by *Primary English* and *Multicultural Education* magazines.

Patricia Maude is head of the physical education department and director of primary school liaison at Homerton College, Cambridge. She has taught physical education for many years to children in primary schools, to students and to teachers. Her recent publications include *The Gym Kit* video and handbook (Homerton College, 1994), the gymnastics section of *Teaching Physical Education at Key Stages 1 and 2* (Physical Education Association, 1995) and *Gymnastics* for Hodder and Stoughton in 1997.

Jennifer Reynolds taught in Liverpool and Oxfordshire after qualifying from Liverpool Polytechnic in 1990 and has taught in junior schools in Cambridge-shire since 1993. She currently teaches Year 6 and is part of the senior management team at Buckden Primary School. She is particularly keen to use information and communications technology in promoting language and literacy and has collaborated with Sally Elding on a number of projects. She contributed a chapter on talk and assessment in history to *Differentiation and Diversity in the Primary School* (ed. Eve Bearne, Routledge, 1996).

Claire Saunders is a language co-ordinator in a Dorset primary school. Her interest in children's language is particularly focused on language throughout the curriculum and she has recently made a special study of children using information texts.

Bob Seberry is a senior research associate at Homerton College, Cambridge (formerly senior lecturer in design technology and science education). He is particularly interested in the art of storytelling and is developing work in these areas in collaboration with the Education Department of Kobe University, Japan.

Jane Seberry has worked as a general class teacher and also as a specialist in language, history and geography in both state and private sector schools in the UK, Bahrain and the Dominican Republic. She is keen on promoting the use of story to develop language and history.

David Somerville has taught in several primary schools in Cambridgeshire, was headteacher of William Westley Primary School and is now headteacher of St Matthew's Primary School in Cambridge.

Rachel Sparks Linfield is a senior lecturer in primary science and co-ordinator for professional studies at Homerton College, Cambridge. Before that she worked for eight years as a primary school teacher. She has published articles in *Questions, Junior Education* and *Primary Science Review* and collaborated with Lesley Hendy on two Key Stage 1 packs entitled *KS1 Science Through Stories* (Pearson, 1995) and *KS1 Science Through Stories for Special Occasions* (Pearson, 1996). Recently she joined the editorial board for *Primary Science Review*.

Paul Warwick is a senior lecturer in primary science at Homerton College, Cambridge. Before that, Paul taught in primary schools in Cambridgeshire; his last post was as deputy headteacher of a large junior school. At Homerton, Paul is involved in teaching on the B.Ed. and Primary Postgraduate curriculum science courses and on the B.Ed. professional studies course. Paul's research interests while at Homerton have focused on three main areas: the effects of using data-logging hardware and software on children's learning in science and mathematics; children's understanding of the procedural aspects of science; and the assessment of children's learning.

Sally Wilkinson taught in primary schools in Suffolk for eight years. She now works as an advisory teacher for primary English with Suffolk LEA. She has recently completed an MA in language and literature at the London Institute of Education and contributed a chapter on young children writing to *Teaching and Learning in the Early Years* (Routledge, 1996).

Tatiana Wilson is a class teacher and language co-ordinator at Redhills Combined School in Exeter. She has contributed to *Differentiation and Diversity in the Primary School* (ed. Eve Bearne, Routledge, 1996) and *Making Progress in English* (ed. Eve Bearne, Routledge, 1998).

Alison Wood is a senior lecturer in the mathematics department at Homerton College, Cambridge. She has worked there for many years teaching mathematics both to B.Ed. specialist students and to Primary Postgraduate students who follow a generalist course. She is senior tutor for the Primary Postgraduate course and has recently developed a special interest in mathematics and language and contributed a chapter on mathematics for the more able mathematician in *Differentiation and Diversity in the Primary School* (ed. Eve Bearne, Routledge, 1996).

INTRODUCTION

Language has a central role in learning; what anyone knows or understands is not only expressed through language, but formed through language. If teachers are to help children learn successfully, then attention to language is crucial. The Bullock Report, written over 20 years ago, made the point, however, that such careful attention to language needs to be integrated with learning as a whole:

> For language to play its full role as a means of learning, the teacher must create in the classroom an environment which encourages a wide range of language uses.
>
> (Bullock 1975: para. 12.3, p. 188)

This extends beyond what is usually accepted as the domain of English into all areas of the curriculum. Whenever children are being encouraged to predict or to offer hypotheses in maths, science or technology; when they are asked to reflect on the impact of a piece of music or art; when they enter into imaginative empathy with characters in history or compare people's lives throughout the world, they are using language in one form or another to hammer out ideas – whether through talk, writing or reading. Each area of the curriculum offers different opportunities and challenges for extending language experience.

The National Curriculum sees the development of language as a key element in all learning. The Common Requirements of most Orders include a specific section entitled 'Use of Language' which states:

> pupils should be taught to express themselves clearly in both speech and writing and to develop their reading skills. They should be taught to use grammatically correct sentences and to spell and punctuate accurately in order to communicate effectively in written English.
>
> (DfE 1995a: 1)

Language is not only seen as a means of learning, but as a way of demonstrating learning through *effective communication*. More recently, the School Curriculum and Assessment Authority (SCAA) have produced a series of booklets which make explicit just what 'Use of Language' should involve. The core booklet lists the principles which should apply to a common approach to use of language across the curriculum, the first of which states:

A whole school approach should include:

- developing a shared understanding between all staff of the role of language in pupils' learning and how work in different subjects can contribute to and benefit from the development of pupils' ability to communicate effectively . . .

(SCAA 1997: 3)

Each of the booklets for specific subjects offers guidance on areas where language might be highlighted.

Whilst the document is generally helpful, the new spotlight on use of language presents some difficulties. Teachers have always been concerned to develop children's fluent and accurate use of language, but the emphasis given through SCAA (and also through the Office for Standards in Education: OFSTED) imposes particular requirements which, set beside all the other responsibilities, can seem to be just one burden too many. It is also important to remember that there is more to the use of language than *effective communication*. A *shared understanding* amongst colleagues is, of course, of significant benefit to the children in any school; it ensures cohesion and continuity in the children's learning experiences and is more likely to contribute to high expectations of achievement and progression. Any consensus about the role of language in the curriculum, however, needs to be founded on a broad and informed view of language and offer a range of ways in which language development can be tackled in the normal course of teaching, rather than being just another bolt-on requirement. A genuinely successful approach will be based on a view of language as permeating learning in all areas of the curriculum. It will also go beyond the somewhat pragmatic view of language outlined in the SCAA principles. Language is more than 'communication skills' which directly 'reflect standards of achievement and help to establish whether targets have been achieved' (SCAA 1997: 3).

Traditionally, language has been seen as a proof of learning. Reading aloud has been assumed to demonstrate understanding whilst writing is often seen as the automatic end point to any learning activity – *do it, then write about it* – giving teachers the chance to check up on what children are supposed to have learned. Speaking and listening have featured in the question-and-answer format of classroom work, again as a means of confirming knowledge. Such traditional practices tend to concentrate on language as an end product rather than as a means of getting to grips with learning. Not only do such practices neglect the constructive nature of language, they also often fail to provide evidence of what children genuinely do know and understand. A full language curriculum, however, must include both the formative and performative aspects of language

2

– the processes and products. It needs to go further than simply looking at language as a proof of learning; it also needs to take into account three components of the relationship between children, language and learning:

- children learning to use language;
- children using language to learn;
- children learning about language.

Standards of literacy and language

In any anxiety over a contemporary situation there is likely to be a wistful look back to the past, with a conviction, often illusory, that times were better then than now.

(Bullock 1975: 3)

Over recent years considerable attention has been paid to standards in education. Unfounded, uninformed and unhelpful allegations have been made about 'standards falling', and the publication of school league tables and lists of 'failing schools' has added to the understandable anxiety about how well education is serving the nation. The above quotation from the major education report of the second half of the century puts current fears into perspective. The Bullock Report itself goes on to remind readers:

> Many allegations about lower standards today come from employers, who maintain that young people joining them from school cannot write grammatically, are poor spellers, and generally express themselves badly. The employers sometimes draw on past experience for comparisons, but even where they do not there is a strong implication that at one time levels of performance were superior. It is therefore interesting to find in the Newbolt Report of 1921 observations of a very similar kind. There Messrs. Vickers Ltd. reported 'great difficulty in obtaining junior clerks who can speak and write English clearly and correctly, especially those aged 15 to 16 years'. . . . Boots Pure Drug Co. remarked 'teaching of English in the present day schools produces a very limited command of the English language . . . '

(Bullock 1975: 3)

Concerns about standards are always with us. This is an optimistic sign if it means that a nation is committed to advancing the quality of education offered to young people as an investment in the future robust health of the nation. It is not so positive if it simply reflects a rosy-tinted nostalgia which insists on looking backwards rather than forwards. Education should always look towards the kind of provision which will offer the firmest foundation for future educational standards. If the new emphasis on use of language is to feed vigorous growth, then it needs to offer the fullest understanding of what kind of environment and nourishment will best support healthy development. It needs a broad and informed understanding of language in use as part of learning and as part of any individual's – or group's – meaning-making activity.

A theory of grammar in use

Part of this informed view is a theory of grammar – what it means and implies about children's language development and use. Every National Curriculum document requires that children should be 'taught to use grammatically correct sentences' (DfE 1995a: 1). There is not likely to be a teacher in the land who would argue with the general spirit of this requirement. Since standard English is the currency of examinations, and of literature, media and information texts as well as assumed as part of the writing requirements of most jobs, it is the right of every child to have access to standard forms of language. It is also general practice to offer such entitlement; there are not many teachers who would oppose the idea of children being taught 'to spell and punctuate in order to communicate effectively in written English' (DfE 1995a: 1). The reverse of this raises a bizarre picture: one morning, a teacher strides into the classroom and announces to the children: 'Today I am going to prevent you spelling and punctuating correctly. I am also going to stop you writing and speaking in grammatically accurate sentences.' This simply does not happen. One of the daily concerns of teachers is just how to get children to spell and punctuate correctly, to understand the differences between standard and non-standard forms – as well as all the myriad other things teachers want children to grasp. Suggestions that they deliberately neglect these aspects of English is ill-informed and unjust. If a positive and forward-looking view is to inform teaching approaches, there needs to be a more developed theory of grammar and how to teach it; alongside this goes a more systematic programme of progression, carefully planned to build on children's existing knowledge about language and how it works.

One of the difficulties about any discussion of 'correctness' in personal uses of language is that there is a great deal of confusion about 'poor speech', 'bad grammar' and 'proper pronunciation'. What might 'poor speech' be? And what is 'good speech'? It is very plain that attitudes to accents and dialects are permeated by social and cultural judgements about the comparative status of speakers as suggested by their home language use. It is worth clearing up some of the misconceptions here. Many of the ways of speaking which are described as 'bad grammar' are, in fact, dialect forms of speech. The National Curriculum document for English distinguishes between standard forms and 'other forms of English' and makes it clear that 'spoken standard English is not the same as Received Pronunciation and can be expressed in a variety of accents' (DfE 1995b: 3). However, it does not offer much more detail about the relationship between the grammar of English and standard forms. It is important to distinguish between 'bad grammar' and an individual's home use of language.

The grammar of any language describes the systematic way in which words are put together to communicate meaning to other speakers, writers, listeners and readers in their own language community. In short, it describes the syntax of a language. In English, I might say 'I'm going to Birmingham today'; in German I would say 'Heute soll ich nach Birmingham fahren' (Today shall I to Birmingham travel). Those are the distinctly different grammars of the two languages. If someone says 'I were that frightened' or 'Her's fair worried to death' they are not speaking ungrammatically since the syntax is recognisably that of English. The first is an example of colloquial speech with dialect use of a verb form and the second is an example of dialect use with a specifically regional way of using a personal pronoun, verb and vocabulary. In each case the speaker may well be able to speak a more standard form of English at will. If a speaker said 'Sky blue is' or missed out all the verbs in sentences, then those would be examples of incorrect grammar. However, with native speakers of a language this is so rare as to be unknown except where a speaker might have a language disorder. Studying grammar in the classroom means looking closely at the patterned ways in which language is used to make meanings in different kinds of texts. It does not mean promoting ill-informed value judgements about home language use.

The fact of the matter is that children very often write in standard forms of English even when they may speak a non-standard dialect. This is true of many adult speakers, too, and suggests that the proper emphasis for teaching standard English should be placed more on writing than on speech, where it can become a focus for fruitful discussion about shifts in register, formality and grammatical patterns. It also suggests that it is more useful to begin looking at grammar by studying its standard forms than homing in on non-standard forms, which constitute a very small amount of children's language experience. Of course, teachers need to reassure themselves that children can use standard forms when speaking – and indeed any quick experiment, like asking children to take on the role of a weather forecaster or news reader, will show immediately that they can switch into standard forms when they wish to. If an activity like this reveals any children who cannot switch in this way, then more opportunities for practice need to be provided without suggesting that a child's own language – and so, by implication, the child herself or himself – is intellectually or socially deficient.

Given the definition of grammar above, it is clear that comments about 'poor grammar' are very often nothing to do with grammar at all but judgements about the perceived value of different ways of speaking – particularly about people's accents. Whilst it is important to have a responsible approach to teaching children standard forms of English – particularly written English – it is equally important to separate judgements made about individuals on the basis of social or cultural opinion (perhaps prejudice) and judgements about the linguistic organisation of how people speak and write. Children come to school having internalised most of the grammar and communicative purposes of at least one language; much of their knowledge is of the spoken form of that language (or languages) but they will also have a reservoir of knowledge about the written system drawn from the print and media environment they live in. The media also provide them with experiences of different speech styles from groups far distant from their own homes and communities. Bilingual children, or, in National Curriculum terms, speakers of English as an additional language (EAL), are often in a position of advantage in learning. If a child is learning two languages simultaneously, or even learning a second language during the early years, the cognitive patterning is similar; the repeated experience of matching an already known word or expression to one in another language sets up a mental framework for other kinds of matching – the kind of analogical thinking which helps the development of mathematics, for example. It can also lead to the ability to reflect more analytically on language.

English throughout the curriculum

The emphasis, then, on teaching 'Effective and accurate use of language' (SCAA 1997: 3) should be less on the naming of parts or disapproval of non-standard forms and more on looking at how texts are put together – at sentence level and at the level of whole-text, or discourse, organisation. This is not a book about correctness but about how children can be helped to use the processes and texts of language to transform knowledge and experience into understanding. Part 1 begins by examining the full role language plays in learning and offering a model of English which includes the processes of language use as well as the texts (spoken and written; short and extended) which language is used to form. Part 2 takes a closer look at the formative uses of language – to generate ideas, shape thought, develop hypotheses, question and debate. This part examines the role of the teacher in planning for progressive opportunities to develop the intellectually generative aspects of language. Part 3 follows this through to consider specific uses of language for different purposes, beginning with the language of the home and tracking ways of promoting careful and thoughtful attention to precision in the use of language in learning. In Part 4 the role of narrative forms a focus for three accounts of classroom activities in different curriculum areas which describe the process of using language to shape ideas, refine them and communicate to others. This part examines the differences between narrative and non-narrative texts, between written and pictorial narratives and what all of these texts offer in terms of helping learners to select from experience and knowledge, to analyse and synthesise ideas. Part 5 takes this further by considering the role of language in evaluating learning as well as offering a means of assessment both of subject knowledge and of children's use of language itself. Talk is one of the most usual ways of reflecting on ideas and experience; however, since talk is necessarily transitory, how can it perform its full function as a means of reflection on both language and learning? This part offers some suggestions, using the less traditional ways of recording information and action – through video, information technology and drawing. New technologies offer new possibilities for using language to evaluate learning – both for teachers and learners. The final part starts with the principles of the SCAA *Use of Language* core document then expands these to suggests ways of establishing shared understandings which will help to turn principles into practice. It offers a framework for auditing and reviewing provision for the development of language throughout the primary curriculum.

The separate chapters of this book contain accounts of classroom practice and some also take a more reflective and theorised view of the interactive processes of language and cognitive and affective development. All of them examine the critical relationship between thought and language and the practical ways in which this relationship can be used to promote learning. The chapters have been selected to represent different facets of familiar classroom practice, with examples drawn from throughout the curriculum. Underpinning the work is an acknowledgement of different learning styles and special educational needs and an awareness of issues of linguistic diversity and cultural difference. The work of the teachers represented in this book bears witness to the richness of experience generated by a more complex view of the relationship between language and learning. The chapters represent teachers' experience from Key Stages 1 and 2 and include issues of assessment and differentiation, record keeping and monitoring progress as well as the important links between home and school.

Guiding the whole book is a commitment to the learners themselves; their voices are heard throughout. Sir Alan Bullock urged us to bring 'what is known' alive in every knower. He describes this as 'a formulating process' made possible through language. This book aims to recapture the best of the Bullock Report – at the very least in its honour for teachers and learners – while looking to the future. What will children need to know about? And what will they need to know about language? What meanings will they need to make and what texts will they encounter? This implies going further than using language for *effective and accurate communication*. Above all, attention to English throughout the curriculum means helping children to develop a critical view of language in all its forms; it means, in other words, creating opportunities for every child to become a fluent and assured *knower*.

References

Bullock, Sir Alan (1975) *A Language for Life: Report of the Committee of Inquiry appointed by the Secretary of State for Education and Science*, London: Her Majesty's Stationery Office.

Department for Education (1995a) *Geography in the National Curriculum*, London: Her Majesty's Stationery Office.

Department for Education (1995b) *English in the National Curriculum*, London: Her Majesty's Stationery Office.

SCAA (School Curriculum and Assessment Authority) (1997) *Use of Language: a Common Approach*, London: SCAA. The full list of principles is dealt with in detail in Part 6 of the present book.

Part 1

LANGUAGE AND LEARNING

Language is a system of sounds, meanings and structures with which we make sense of the world around us. It functions as a tool of thought; as a means of social organisation; as the repository and means of transmission of knowledge; as the raw material of literature, and as the creator and sustainer – or destroyer – of human relationships. It changes inevitably over time and, as change is not uniform, from place to place.

(DfE 1989: para. 6.18)

Language is a fascinating subject. Everybody has opinions about how people should express themselves and each of us is unique in the way we make meaning through language. One of the key functions of language in education is that it helps us to learn. We can work out ideas and reflect on them, record observations, capture and concentrate thoughts and so generate new ideas. When we give expression to ideas we are not simply clothing already existing thoughts with words, but actively shaping the slippery material of concepts, pinning ideas down and putting them together so that we are satisfied with the cut and style of our thinking.

The psychologist Vygotsky, writing in the 1930s, saw language as a tool for thinking and described the complex interaction of language and the development of knowledge as:

a continual movement back and forth from thought to word and from word to thought. In that process, the relation of thought to word undergoes changes . . . thought is not merely expressed in words; it comes into existence through them. Every thought tends to connect something with something else, to establish a relation between them. Every thought moves, grows and develops, fulfils a function, solves a problem.

(Vygotsky 1962: 125)

9

The relationship between language and concept development is complementary and dynamic; whilst thought prompts language, listening, reading, speaking and writing, in their turn, will prompt more thought – and so the cycle of learning goes on. This takes the role of language in learning beyond the communicative. In terms of classroom practice, this means paying attention to the processes of language, not simply seeing the products.

Traditionally, writing has been taken as proof of learning; tests and examinations are written and common practice in teaching often follows the model of carrying out an activity which is then written about to assure the teacher that the children have learned what they were supposed to learn. More recently, talk has also been given a place in the assessment of learning. Quite properly. Not only has talk an important role to play in allowing children to demonstrate their knowledge and understanding; teachers need to find as many ways as possible of judging what children have learned so that they can consolidate or reinforce the learning. However, Vygotsky's insights take the role of language further, seeing it as important not just as communicating the end points of learning but as an integral part of the whole process of putting ideas together to reach understanding.

Learning about language

People learn language first of all in social contexts – in the home, in the community – and children's early language is used readily and fluently without them needing to be overtly taught the rules of its use. Children actively generate the rules of language as they tussle to make their meanings clear. Whilst making meaning lies at the centre of language use, reflection and analysis are equally important processes of learning. If children are to extend their knowledge of language so as to be able to make meaning in increasingly complex ways, then studying language as a system becomes an essential feature of learning and teaching. This presents a challenge to classroom teachers: how can children be helped to know more about the structures and systems of language without separating the system from its use – in other words, without taking the texts out of context? The Language in the National Curriculum (LINC) Project offered guidance:

> Language study should start from what children can do, from their positive achievements in language and from the remarkable resources of implicit knowledge about language which all children possess.
>
> (Carter 1991: 4)

At the same time, however, it is important to be aware of the complexities of language and the ways in which it is used. The constantly shifting nature of language means that the systems which seem to govern its use are not always fixed. In other words, it is difficult to provide hard and fast rules for language use.

Both teachers and children need to understand the dynamic quality of language. Teaching rules or definitions of parts of language is not the best way to help children study language, although it is essential that they learn how to talk about language. This means developing a vocabulary of terminology – a metalanguage – which will enable them to extend their understanding of how language can be used to make more (and more complex) meaning.

Teachers, like children, have a store of valuable knowledge about language, derived from their experience as people living in social settings. The question arises of how they can best use this knowledge to help their pupils further their understanding of the structures and systems of language. Teachers create the environment in which children will succeed (or not) as learners. A large part of a teacher's contribution to developing language knowledge and use lies in the opportunities and contexts offered for learning about language. This means recognising the value and importance of community uses of language and takes into account shifts of register according to social and linguistic contexts. Rather than referring to 'sloppy' or 'incorrect' speech, classroom opportunities are provided to study the differences between spoken and written texts, between formal and informal uses of language. The next moves are to plan for deliberate and thoughtful interventions to help move the children's language use forward as part of the whole process of teaching and learning.

English as a subject

In the National Curriculum, the details of language study are mostly included in the English curriculum. However, language permeates the whole curriculum both as a vehicle for learning and as an object of study in its own right. The SCAA document *Use of Language: a Common Approach* states that 'All lessons include, and largely depend on, oral and written communication', as well as explaining that 'To be successful learners, pupils need to read in order to gain access to information and ideas from a range of texts and sources and to evaluate them' (SCAA 1997: 6). Children learn through language but they also need to learn about language:

> As pupils develop their subject knowledge and understanding, they need increasingly sophisticated and exact ways of saying what they mean. Through this they can express more subtle distinctions and more complex ideas. To do so they not only employ a more developed vocabulary, but also a range of grammatical constructions and ways of conveying shades of meaning or stages of argument.
>
> (SCAA 1997: 6)

This means paying attention not only to the processes of language but also, as mentioned above, to the structures of language – the texts, or discourses, into which language is organised for specific purposes. The diagram below is not

Texts	Processes
Study of language (includes standard English): the small shapes which texts are made of: sentences, words, phonemes, parts of speech, grammatical organisation, spelling and handwriting.	**Getting and conveying information and ideas:** reading for understanding and inference, responding to reading, writing to explain, persuade, inform, entertain, awareness of readership (audience) . . . listening and speaking for the same purposes.
Study of texts (includes media texts, spoken texts and aspects of standard English): the structures of longer texts: forms and formats, different genres of fiction, information texts, poetry, plays.	**Developing discrimination:** becoming independent, choosing what to read and what not to read, commenting on own and other people's writing (including published authors), using different registers in speaking.

A model of the English curriculum

intended to suggest that there are watertight categories, but represents both the texts and processes associated with teaching English. The processes on the right-hand side of the chart happen throughout the curriculum – including English lessons – whilst the categories on the left – the texts – are often seen as the content of the English curriculum itself. Different contributors to this book show, however, that study of language and study of texts can enter any subject area.

Since language itself is structured and systematic, teachers need to take an equally systematic and structured approach both to teaching and learning language and to teaching and learning about language. This need not, however, mean arid instruction. The accounts of classroom practice in this book demonstrate very clearly that language and understanding are best developed in contexts which make sense to the learner. The implications for structure are as much related to the planning which precedes teaching and learning as to the activities themselves. If teaching is geared towards helping children through the processes of getting and conveying information and ideas and supporting them as they gradually develop discrimination and critical sense, then teachers need to be clear about the language structures which will feed into and draw their strength from those processes.

Besides being aware of the texts and processes which comprise language, it is important to consider the different modes of language and their contribution to learning. It is equally important to look at the ways in which teachers can develop the use of listening, reading, speaking and writing. This means taking a wide-angle view of the curriculum as well as a long-term perspective on progression. It also means tackling some of the perennial classroom problems related to language and literacy. One of the most common of these is the tendency to see the surface features of accuracy as more significant than the content of what is being written about. In reality, the most successful teaching and learning happens when a balance is reached between accuracy and fluency. That is one of the long-term aims of language and literacy teaching. The growing emphasis on publishing league tables of schools based on testing has tended to shift the balance towards an overemphasis on accuracy at the expense of fluency. This can only restrict progress as it tends to reduce motivation and a willingness to be inventive and exploratory. In the opening chapter of Part 1 Sally Wilkinson takes a detailed look at the development of children's writing, starting from questions asked by teachers about how to motivate young writers. She highlights Vygotsky's view that teaching should be organised in such a way that reading and writing are necessary for something. He criticises writing which is taught 'as a motor skill and not as a complex cultural activity', stressing that 'children should be taught written language, not just the writing of letters' (Vygotsky 1978: 117–19). Sally Wilkinson emphasises the importance of the teacher's role in 'providing experiences which encourage children's knowledge of written language to develop'. This means deliberate planning for writing development as part of the general curriculum, making opportunities for working with a range of texts and paying attention to the ways they are constructed for different purposes. It also means, right from the start, an assumption that children can be discriminating language users, critical readers of writing – both their own and other people's.

In 1837 Ralph Waldo Emerson wrote that 'One must be an inventor in order to read well' (Manguel 1996: 176). In her chapter Helen Arnold points out the need for children to be given the means to become *readers*, not *lookers*, to become inventors of meaning through involvement with the texts they read. She points out that reading is more than getting information off the page; it includes making sense of new ideas, involving the affective, cognitive and textual aspects of learning. Helen Arnold echoes Manguel's assertion that 'We all read ourselves and the world around us in order to glimpse what and where we are. We read to understand, or begin to understand' (Manguel 1996: 7). She explains that reading narrative operates on a horizontal plane, linking events chronologically and sequentially, whilst reading texts explicitly designed to convey information involves operating on a vertical axis, dealing with categories of concepts arranged as a hierarchy of abstractions. Offering practical strategies for ways in which children can be helped to read information material, she looks at the smaller units of text at word and sentence level and the longer stretches of text at discourse level. She carefully analyses the differences in discourse structure between different kinds of texts, pointing out that the patterns of discourse of non-fiction texts are more complex than most fiction; the implication of this is that children need to be deliberately introduced to the differences between discourse types if they are to be helped to read in order to understand themselves in relation to the world around them.

In Chapter 3 Chris Doddington looks at oral texts, picking up several strands of thinking expressed in SCAA documents and raising questions about such notions as 'pupils' ability to communicate effectively' and 'communication skills' (SCAA 1997: 3). She argues that whilst considerations of effective speech which is adapted to purpose and audience are important, they do not give the whole picture of the part language plays in being human and becoming educated. 'It may be,' she suggests, 'that talking and listening are significant to humankind for more profound and more subtle reasons than just true reporting or calculating effect and that education should reflect and acknowledge this rather than the model of skilled or effective speech' expressed in National Curriculum documents. In taking these views further, Chris Doddington gives examples of children using language in more generative ways, including drama and using the language of philosophical enquiry.

All three contributors to Part 1 identify the development of independence and autonomy as essential in promoting learning. If children are given opportunities and experiences through which they can learn how to make their own meanings clear as well as how to make independent choices, then they are well on the way to getting to grips with the process of becoming discriminating language users. These opportunities can be provided not only through the other language process of getting and conveying information, but also through attention to the texts which children can learn to make and understand. The construction of texts, whether spoken or written, necessarily involves careful scrutiny of the smaller units – words and sentences – which make up those texts. The understanding of the texts which young readers encounter involves equally careful attention. Teachers' planning in any area of the curriculum needs to take account of both the texts and processes of the English curriculum outlined above as well as including all four modes of language – speaking and listening, reading and writing and their role in analysing and synthesising ideas. The chapters in this section offer some useful pointers for how this can be done.

References

Carter, Ronald (ed.) (1991) *Knowledge about Language and the Curriculum: the LINC Reader*, London: Hodder and Stoughton.

Department for Education and Science (1989) *The Cox Report*, London: HMSO.

Manguel, A. (1996) *A History of Reading*, London: HarperCollins.

School Curriculum and Assessment Authority (1997) *Use of Language: a Common Approach*, London: SCAA.

Vygotsky, L.S. (1962) *Thought and Language*, trans. E. Hanfmann and G. Vakar, Cambridge, MA: Massachusetts Institute of Technology Press.

Vygotsky, L.S. (1978) *Mind in Society: the Development of Higher Psychological Processes*, eds M. Cole, V. John-Steiner, S. Scribner and E. Soubermann, Cambridge, MA: Harvard University Press.

1

'WHY DO WE HAVE TO WRITE IT DOWN?'

Young children learning to write and writing to learn

Sally Wilkinson

The question in the title of this chapter is one which is asked by children of adults in many classrooms. As a Key Stage 1 teacher it was certainly addressed to me on more than one occasion by children in my class. Each time it would provide the jolt which was sometimes necessary for me to make the time to step back and reflect on my classroom practice. Since becoming an advisory teacher for English, the question still recurs as teachers ask me what I suggest they should do to help children who ask this question become more motivated to write. There are many reasons why young children are reluctant to write, as the following list compiled by a group of Key Stage 1 teachers shows:

- They may lack the confidence to 'have a go'.
- They may think that they cannot make the correct letter shapes or words.
- They may find the physical effort too great.
- They may be unsure what to write.
- They may find the classroom environment inhibiting.
- They may not have made the link between speech and writing.

So how do you help reluctant young writers become independent, confident writers who value what they write and see a reason for doing it? In this chapter, by looking at young children from nursery to Year 3 writing for different purposes and in a variety of forms, I hope to provide some possible ideas and also consider the place of writing as part of the learning process.

The need to experiment

At the heart of why we write lies reading. Whether writing is used for communicating, as art or as a record, it is meant to be read. The mark-making of

Figure 1.1 Josh's letters to his friend Toby

pre-school children shows that they understand this. Josh (Figure 1.1), writing in his nursery class, knows not only that writing is meant to be read by others, but that it exists in different formats and has different functions. He told me that each of the circular and rectangular shapes was a letter to his friend Toby, whilst the tall shape on the right was a Coke bottle, 'That has writing on'.

Evidently there is a lot that Josh knows and understands about the marks that he has made on his paper, and as Yetta Goodman says:

> It is by exploring the principles that children develop in their early writing that we can begin to see that they indeed are using their intellectual functioning to develop knowledge about written language.
>
> (Goodman 1986: 8)

Goodman suggests three principles of writing development, functional, linguistic and relational, into which she believes children's understanding and knowledge of written language can be categorised. Under her criteria of functional principles, Josh shows an understanding of some of the reasons for writing: that you can say something to another person by writing a letter, and that writing can be used to label objects and provide information about them. Josh did not attach a message to his writing, but he did tell me that he had used letters from his name in his writing.

Josh's experiments with writing show that his developing understanding is centred on the literacy events which are part of his everyday life in the culture in which he is growing up. He needs time to continue this experimentation, just as he experimented with speech when learning to talk – in meaningful contexts in which the reasons provided for writing mirror those that he sees adults and older children using in the world around him.

It is here that the distinction between writing and written language becomes important. If, as Vygotsky (1978) pointed out, young children's development as writers is only seen from a psychological point of view as the acquiring of a complicated motor skill, the need for this writing to have a meaning, which can be understood when it is read by those other than the writer, becomes secondary. The focus of the psychological viewpoint is on the surface appearance of the writing, often taking the form of the child being able to copy individual letters that an adult has written. This becomes a meaningless activity if the child is unable to read what has been written, or if they can read it, but cannot see the reason for doing it.

This focus on the surface features of writing is linked to the view that speech is all-important and writing a mere second order representation of it. This ignores how writing and speech function in different ways. Writing, unlike speech, is not dependent on the presence of an audience, nor is it linked to context as spoken language often is. If writing is seen as nothing more than speech written down, then as a child's speech becomes more complex it follows that their writing will naturally also develop. If this is the case all that needs to be taught are the written symbols that represent speech and the order in which they occur within words.

A theory of teaching writing, like the one outlined above, which considers it foremost as a motor skill, ignores the reasons why we use writing and the meanings it has for us: that is, it ignores written language. Frank Smith (1982) refers to written language as 'composition', concerned with making meaning, developing ideas and thinking through writing. Both Michaela (Figure 1.2) and Natalie (Figure 1.3), writing in their respective nursery and reception classes, illustrate the importance written language has for them. For Michaela it allowed her to record and have on public display (as she taped her writing to her jumper) the crucial information *My mummy likes me*. During the nursery session she read this to several of her friends as well as to her nursery teacher both at their request and spontaneously.

Natalie's writing came about as a result of a discussion in her reception class on how we know when something is alive. She had been quiet during the discussion, but later gave her teacher her piece of writing and said, 'I've written down what I think. [*reading*] "You are alive because you have a brain".' Both Michaela and Natalie saw a reason for recording information in writing. They had decided what they wanted to write, rather than having the content of their writing provided or edited for them by their teachers or other adults, and they had been made to feel that the shapes and letters that they used to convey meaning were accepted and appropriate. All of this meant that they were able to respond fully. They could write exactly the meaning they wanted to communicate rather than one which had been negotiated with an adult or was the result of only feeling confident enough to write words that they knew from adult praise had the right appearance.

Figure 1.2 Writing by Michaela: My mummy likes me

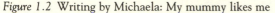

Figure 1.3 Writing by Natalie: You're alive because you have a brain

Providing opportunities for experimenting with writing

For young children to have the confidence to write independently, as Natalie and Michaela did, they not only need to feel that their attempts will be accepted, they also need to have a wide range of opportunities in which to use and develop their skills and knowledge. This can occur during writing activities initiated by the teacher, but it is also important for the children to have the freedom to choose

- the content of their writing;
- the form their writing will take;
- the materials they will write with and on.

Two ways of providing this choice are through writing boxes and through role play.

Writing boxes

One means of promoting more enthusiastic writing is to create a writing corner or area – sometimes just a table with appropriate materials. However, I often visit classrooms which, due to their size or the size of the class, make it difficult to have a permanent writing corner or role play area set up for the children. In these situations it is useful to have writing 'areas' which are portable, and can be moved to where the children are going to be. This also allows them to be used inside or outside the classroom, and if the teacher is lucky enough to have access to an outdoor area then the children can use them there as well. Figure 1.4 illustrates one possible way that materials can be stored. Other containers such as the trays of a vegetable rack or plastic tool carrier would also make good writing boxes.

Figure 1.4 The writing box

There is no need to have a great quantity of each item; a range of papers to write on and implements to write with is much more important. A box could include a selection of the following, with some kept back so that items can be changed to stimulate new ideas when the box needs revitalising.

card – various shapes and sizes	till roll
lined, plain and coloured paper cut in different shapes	chalks
pencils – lead and coloured	mini stapler
pens – biro, felt-tip	Post-its
hole punch	Sellotape
paperclips	envelopes
crayons	Blu-tac
small books – zigzag, shaped	labels
tags	appointment cards

It is important to store items in appropriately sized containers, and if these are labelled with a picture and/or word the children will find it easier to keep the box tidy.

Given the freedom to write what they would like, young children will often experiment with and make use of forms of writing that they see being used around them. A focus on letter writing in his Year 2 class provided the impetus for Gulam to explore many reasons for writing them when he was using the writing box (Figure 1.5). His three letters show that he understands three different reasons for writing them:

a   to give information (to his friend that he is going to the park);
b   to confirm a relationship;
c   to say thank you.

Dear Freddie
I am going
to the Pack
Love From
Gulam

a

To sayarun I am
youR FrenD

From Gulam

b

21

To MiS WiLKensh
Tank you for
Leting me
being on the

raiting cohar

From Gulam

c

Figure 1.5 Letters by Gulam

Learning about the reasons for writing letters had been part of the class sessions, but by providing Gulam with the opportunity and resources to write about what was important to him, his teacher had been the facilitator for further learning as well as allowing Gulam to consolidate and practise his letter-writing skills. Susan (Figure 1.6), writing a letter using the writing box in her reception class, was also able to learn something else about letter writing – that you normally receive a reply. The content of that reply may not have been the response that she wished for, but she did receive it immediately after she had written the letter. This would not have been possible if she had been writing for an audience outside the classroom, and for young children an immediate reply demonstrates very clearly that writing is read for its meaning and often needs a response. Any gap between writing and receiving a reply can mean that the impact of it is lost.

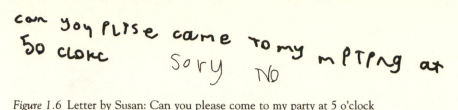

Figure 1.6 Letter by Susan: Can you please come to my party at 5 o'clock

As well as providing immediacy, the writing box can also help make links between young children's home and school literacies. Much has been written (e.g. Meek 1988; Wells 1987) on how young children's language development is influenced by social and cultural factors. It follows that the written texts they meet in the environment in which they live are likely to be significant to them and may be influential in their writing. Darryl was in Year 3 when he created the cartoon from which the extract in Figure 1.7 is taken. He had had access to comics from an early age and he spent much time at home reading, re-reading and taping these. He also wrote many stories at home, some in the comic strip format of which this cartoon is one, and he would then compile these into comics and books.

Carol Fox (1993) showed in her study of young children's oral storytelling how the written structures of the books that had been read to them influenced their oral language. Just as the children in her study had heard many stories and so were able to *talk like a book*, so Darryl was able to demonstrate his knowledge of the organisation of pictures and text in comics and their distinctive use of vocabulary first through his drawings, then orally and finally through his writing. Darryl was given the opportunity, through the use of the writing box in his class, to continue in school writing begun at home. The review of an imagined computer game (Figure 1.8) comes from a comic that he worked on at home and at school and shows a sophisticated knowledge of the syntax of the genre. Darryl's teacher valued Darryl's home literacy experiences, and provided the opportunities for him to continue learning from these through constructing his own written texts in school. By doing this he was ensuring that Darryl's knowledge of certain types of written texts was recognised and its development encouraged.

Role play

As with creating writing boxes, role play scenarios can be made portable by making up boxes which contain the props needed to provide literacy opportunities in a restaurant, veterinary clinic or library. A reception class role play box enabled the children to set up an instant post office with forms to be filled in and date-stamped, envelopes and parcels to be labelled and passports to be created and issued. These boxes can also be based on imaginary worlds or well known stories. One made up by a teacher for his Year 1 class was on the popular story of *Goldilocks and the Three Bears*. In it he included ideas for literacy

Figure 1.7 Cartoon by Darryl

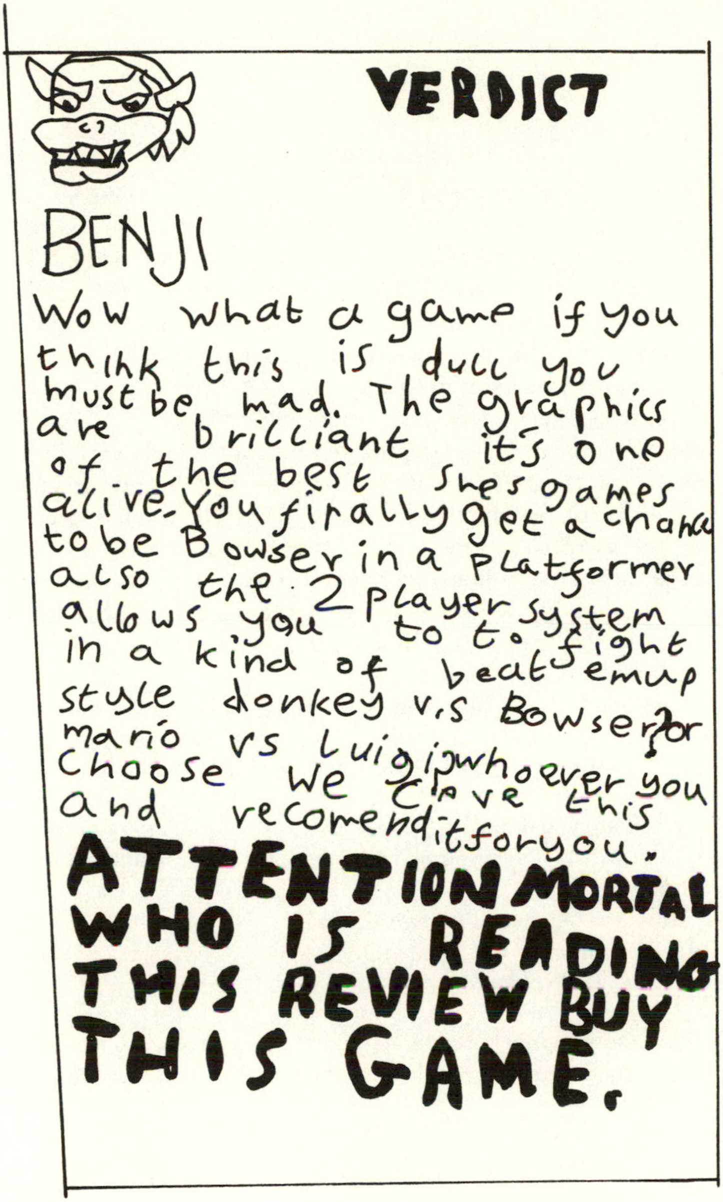

VERDICT

BENJI

Wow what a game if you think this is dull you must be mad. The graphics are brilliant it's one of the best snes games alive. You finally get a chance to be Bowser in a platformer also the 2 player system allows you to to fight in a kind of beat'emup style donkey v.s Bowser or mario vs Luigi whoever you choose we love this and recomend it for you.

ATTENTION MORTAL WHO IS READING THIS REVIEW BUY THIS GAME.

Figure 1.8 Review of an imagined computer game, by Darryl

responses to where the bears had gone to when Goldilocks arrived at their house. There was paper for writing shopping lists, letters and cards (possibly based on those from 'Goldilocks and the Bears' in the Ahlbergs' book *The Jolly Postman*), a map of walks in the woods and paper for the children to draw their own maps or write short leaflets describing what could be seen on the walks.

Linking play, oracy and writing

Storytelling has an important part to play in children's learning about written language. Many young children are excellent oral storytellers, and often their spontaneous storytelling is stimulated by play with an object such as a key, a toy animal or a feather. When several objects are placed together in a container to create a storybox most young children will opt first to tell their story orally as they manipulate the props. They may then tell it into a tape recorder, and/or record it in pictures and finally record it in writing, either on their own or using an adult scribe. All the stages in this process are important.

With older children it can be tempting to miss out the oral storytelling and ask the children to go straight into writing. However, the talk and the actions with the props are part of the process of learning. As children tell and re-tell their stories they are involved in oral drafting, improving how they tell the story as they listen to themselves telling it. Sarah, in a Year 2 class, had always preferred to tape a story rather than write it and when her teacher asked why she said it was because 'If you tape it first you can think more about it and if you get it wrong you can change it and it doesn't matter.'

Having an adult scribe also increases young children's awareness of the connection between speech and writing. Gemma was talking about an ice balloon with her nursery teacher when she noticed her teacher writing:

GEMMA: What are you doing?
TEACHER: I'm writing what you said about the ice looking like a lens, that was very interesting.
GEMMA: Why do you have to write it down?
TEACHER: To remember what you said.
GEMMA: Yes, 'cause I might forget.

This short interaction only lasted for a minute, but it gave Gemma an important insight into using writing to record thoughts and ideas and why this might be a useful thing to do.

Writing and learning

Asking young children what sort of writing they like doing best will often receive the reply that they like writing stories, and sometimes some will say poems. What is apparent is that they mostly prefer imaginative or creative writing to factual pieces. In one first school the teacher asked children in each class why they disliked factual writing. The answer was that they liked learning about topics such as the Romans or the rainforest, but having learnt about them they did not see a reason for writing about them. These children viewed factual writing as purely to do with the regurgitation of facts and felt that they were writing about a topic solely to record what they already knew. The Year 2 teacher in this school wanted to include some factual writing as part of the class topic on animals. I suggested that we give the children the opportunity to make their own non-fiction book. The authors of non-fiction material sometimes go unmentioned, unlike their counterparts who write fiction, so first I showed and read extracts from information books to the children, highlighting the fact that the author in each case was an expert in their field. We then looked at how a non-fiction book was constructed with sections on different aspects of a topic, as well as the use of contents pages and indexes.

With the purpose of their future writing established, the project began with the children talking to a partner about an animal they were interested in and that they thought they knew something about. As a class we then listened while some of the children volunteered interesting information that was possibly new to them that they had been told by their partner. The children were then asked to think of information that they would like to know about their partner's chosen animal, for example where it lived or what it ate, and in their pairs they then asked each other questions. I stressed that the person being questioned didn't have to answer if they were unsure. The talk in pairs and as a class took up most of the lesson, with much information being shared. Towards the end of the lesson I introduced writing as a way for the children to remember what they had told their partner. I asked them to write what they remembered on the left-hand side of a sheet of paper, under the heading of *I know*. On the right-hand side they made a list of their partner's questions which they had been unable to answer under *I need to find out*. It was stressed that this writing was solely for them to make a note of what they wanted to remember and that they could write single words or sentences, whichever helped them. Joshua's response (Figure 1.9) was typical of many in the class as he confidently said that he knew everything there was to know about his chosen animal, the dog.

Over the next week the children were involved in reading and looking at pictures in books and asking family members about their animal. The next piece of writing I asked the children to do was designed to illustrate the journey of learning that they had been involved in as they became experts on their chosen animal. They each had three sheets from a Post-it pad. On one they recorded something they had known about their animal from the outset of the project, on the next something which they had found out during the project and on the last something they still wanted to know. It is interesting that the information which Joshua had found out had not come from books, but from watching his grandad's dog, Lucy (Figure 1.10). He also now had a question that he genuinely wanted to find out the answer to: 'Do dogs in different countries live with humans all the time?'

JOShua W.

I know   I would like to know

dogs Can't iapm
higt as cats.

Soem dogs like Cats.
dogs like dog food.
Some dogs
Sepet in
kenalls. Some
time outdogs Direr Weter
Side. dogs like Playing.

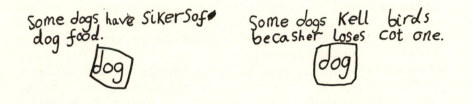

dog

Figure 1.9 Joshua's first thoughts about dogs

Some dogs have SikerSof•
dog food.

dog

JoShUa

Some dogs Kell birds
becasher loses cot one.

dog

JoShUa

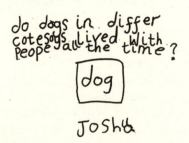

do dogs in differ
cotesogs lived with
peope all the time?

dog

JoShU

Figure 1.10 Joshua's draft for his information book

Joshua had been able to take control of his learning because he had been given the time to talk about his chosen animal, the sources to find out more – both human and in books – and an approach which included writing as a way of aiding and reflecting on learning. He was now able to research the answer to his question, redraft his text, and include the information that he found in his own non-fiction book (Figure 1.11).

Some dogs kill birds.
Some dogs eat sticks
of dog food. foxs are
Wild dogs. foxs hunt.
Some Wild dogs eat
meat.

1

Some dogs sleep
in kennels. Some
people take
dogs for their
run in the park.

4

Figure 1.11 Pages from Joshua's information book about dogs

The role of the teacher

The way in which young children's writing development is viewed by the teacher obviously has great implications for what happens in the classroom. When the goal is for young children to have command of written language, the teacher is central to the process. It is the teacher who:

*   observes the children's preferences for writing in certain forms and provides opportunities for them to write in these ways;
*   recognises the children's strengths as writers and celebrates these while aiding their development in areas where they are less sure;
*   shows the children that their home literacy is valued in the classroom and seeks to make links between home and school literacy;
*   creates opportunities where the children can make choices about their writing, both in its form and content;

29

- acknowledges that talk and reflection are important parts of the writing process and provides time for these;
- considers the real reasons why children write and acknowledges and builds on these;
- recognises the links between children's reading and writing and draws the children's attention to them.

Whilst attending an inservice course on English at Key Stages 1 and 2 in Suffolk, Jackie Maurice focused on two of the aspects of her role mentioned above with her class of Year 2 and Year 3 children. As she recorded in her journal, her project helped her to see the importance of

> allowing children to share what they know . . . I had been helping to facilitate that with paired reading, but I hadn't really tapped into using children to support and pass on their skills to one another with writing . . . Also I was not allowing space for children to write for themselves – with time to reflect and freedom to return to the same piece of writing. So I have linked the two. Children have developed ongoing partnerships with other children, commenting and discussing work on a regular basis.
>
> (Maurice 1994)[1]

Jackie also used the class conferencing techniques detailed by Donald Graves (1983) to develop the children's skills in commenting and making suggestions for improvement of their own and others' writing. She found, following her change of approach, that the children showed more commitment to the process of writing and were more confident about themselves as writers. They were now keen to begin and develop the pieces of writing which they decided on for themselves and also those which emerged as part of activities in the class.

Conclusion

I began this chapter by describing some of the reasons that teachers have found can make young children reluctant to write. Through the examples of children writing in classrooms, I hope that I have illustrated ways that these can be overcome. If writing is viewed as part of the learning process, then it is not just the physical manipulation of pens and pencils which becomes our concern. We need to provide experiences that encourage children's knowledge of written language to develop, where they see reasons for writing and are able to use writing to aid their learning. Then the questions young children ask of themselves will not be *Why am I writing this down?* but *Who is my writing for? What do I need to write down?* and *How shall I organise it?*

Acknowledgements

With thanks to children and teachers in the following Suffolk schools: Acton Primary School, Albert Pye First School, Barnham Primary School, Handford Hall Primary School, Murrayfield Primary School, Wells Hall First School.

Note

1 The inservice course required teachers to keep reflective journals of their classroom work. The extracts quoted here are from Jackie Maurice's journal.

References

Fox, C. (1993) *At the Very Edge of the Forest*, London: Cassell.

Goodman, Y. (1986) 'Writing Development in Young Children', *Gnosis* 8 (March), pp. 8–14.

Graves, D. (1983) *Writing: Teachers and Children at Work*, London: Heinemann Educational Books.

Meek, M. (1988) *How Texts Teach What Readers Learn*, Stroud, Gloucestershire: Thimble Press.

Smith, F. (1982) *Writing and Writers*, London: Heinemann.

Vygotsky, L. (1978) *Mind in Society*, Cambridge, MA and London: Harvard University Press.

Wells, G. (1987) *The Meaning Makers*, London: Hodder and Stoughton.

2

'I WANT TO FIND OUT'

What is involved in reading for learning?

Helen Arnold

Becoming literate implies being able to respond to imaginative fiction and being able to retrieve information from factual texts, both skills emphasised in the National Curriculum. But more is happening: through reading and writing we learn to think differently, not just because we are extending the ways in which we use language, but because as we learn more, the way we store experience changes. Primary school children, as this book shows, are beginning to shape their experience of the world through encounters with different areas of the curriculum. It is necessary to help them to begin to reflect on the language they are using in reading and writing – the process as well as the content.

Reading is a complex act involving the interaction of several cueing systems simultaneously: the graphophonic (matching sounds to symbols), the syntactic (using underlying knowledge about the structure of language), the semantic (predicting and confirming what the content is about) and the bibliographic (using pictures and presentation to underpin the text). In recent years much research has investigated the metacognitive processes which enable this complex ability to be achieved, concluding that awareness of what is happening is a necessary concomitant of learning to read, even though the skill itself becomes automatised later. This awareness comes about, not on the whole through direct teaching, but through the practising of reading and writing themselves, which enables children to see words on the page, distanced; to look at them in retrospect, unlike the ephemeral nature of talk.

Most of the research has concentrated on the development of phonological awareness in the early stages of reading acquisition (e.g. Goswami and Bryant 1990). Less work has been done on syntactic and semantic awareness, or on the awareness of discourse. I want to explore here what children need to bring them to this awareness, particularly regarding non-fiction reading.

What is the difference between learning to read and write in different genres? We know well what happens as children acquire a sense of story, which occurs at a very young age, usually long before they can read themselves. On holiday recently with a six-year-old, I listened to endless narratives which mixed fantasy and fact, delivered at breakneck speed, in long and rambling sentences which nevertheless managed to be cohesive and coherent. Carol Fox (1993) has analysed comprehensively the skill and elegance with which four-year-olds tell stories combining sophisticated structure with equally sophisticated plots. Narrative, as Barbara Hardy says, is 'a primary act of mind' (Meek et al. 1977: 12). The skill of young children in telling complex stories is partly dependent on the sequential nature of narrative. One event leads to another, thereby ensuring continuity.

This is not the case when children come to read information texts, which are not always sequential and where the language structure between and across sentences works very differently. I therefore want to concentrate on the less-researched aspects of using syntactic and semantic cues in non-fiction reading, and to suggest, through necessarily limited examples, how we might help children to become aware of these elements. To do this I shall rather arbitrarily separate out what happens at word, sentence and discourse level.

Vygtosky saw the spoken language of social interaction as one stream of development which fed the stream of thought. Inner speech was for him 'a regulatory process that . . . provided a means for sorting out one's thoughts about the world' (Bruner 1986: 72). In reading, the interaction is with the author, but the process ultimately will be similar especially if there is someone who can mediate between text and reader, to scaffold the new learning. What the author says will be internalised in some form. At first, recall of information for the inexperienced reader may begin rather like whole-word recognition: phrases and even sentences may be remembered as they stand, at least in short term memory, and may be reproduced verbatim. This, of course, is what the teacher is hoping to eradicate when she says *Put it in your own words*, which will be impossible if the reading has not been slotted into an existing mental schema or framework.

Word level

Young children may see reading for information as the collection of new vocabulary, the mastery of isolated words, which seems, for some, an exciting and heady achievement. This may be due partly to the belief that they are collecting 'knowledge' but also because of the look and sound of the words themselves. The attraction of dinosaurs (fairly inexplicable in its universality) may be partly governed by the seductive sounds of the long names – brontosaurus, diplodocus, ornitholestes! But to store single words is, finally, uneconomical; the memory cannot hold them. Memory must 'chunk' these delectable titles together under the word *dinosaur* to make for more sensible storage. The major difference between the storage of narrative and story and the way we hold on to information is that we tend to store the events of stories horizontally (sequentially and chronologically) whereas words about things are categorised into hierarchies – vertically – with the umbrella word at the top of the tree becoming an abstract term.

Let us take *Animals* as one of the class of things within our experience: this is a generalised term which embraces mammals, insects, fish, etc. – these also are generalised terms. We can take one example of a *mammal*, say *dog*, and break that down into *breeds of dog* – retriever, spaniel, poodle and so on. At what point in this hierarchy of terms can we picture an actual dog in our minds? Only at the lowest level where dog owners would probably picture their own dogs. But the higher generalised categories cannot be imaged. Nobody can present a satisfactory conglomerate image of *animal*.

> Each word is therefore a generalisation. Generalisation is a verbal act of thought and reflects reality in quite another way than sensation and perception reflect it.
>
> (Vygotsky 1962: 5)

Children, however, want to be able to match word with image. They are used to reading books, especially alphabet books, which match word and picture for them. So they have a very big jump to make to store hierarchically, in abstract terminology: this is much harder than picturing the events of a story with its characters. Nor will they be able to unpack the generalised terms without numerous experiences of their contributory elements.

Even simple information texts demonstrate the problem. I give one example from *Minibeasts* aimed at covering AT levels 1–3 in English and science (Butler 1991: 5). One page of text reads:

Patterns

Many minibeasts have wonderful patterns on their bodies.
Look at the way the snail shell
coils round and how the wings
of the butterfly match.
We say these patterns have symmetry.

There are two coloured photographic illustrations: a snail shell and a butterfly with outspread wings showing symmetrical markings.

To understand this, the young reader must have already, or must be able to create spontaneously, abstract concepts of *patterns*, *shells*, *wings*, *match* and *symmetry*. The pictures may help but they may also hinder because they give only two examples of specific patterns which may block association with other possibilities. The final word *symmetry* seems a particularly difficult concept to master especially as this is the only occasion on which the word occurs in the book – and there is no glossary! The word is unlikely to appear in a junior dictionary and we can hardly direct the reader to an adult definition like 'exact correspondence of parts on either side of a straight line or plane, or about a centre or axis' (Chambers 1974).

So of course we come to the conclusion, as all good teachers do, and as this book illustrates, that children learn generalised terms while experiencing countless examples of their constituents in context. In this way, the term in the book will be summing up what they already know. This is a long process, and we realise the value of Piaget's theory of assimilation and accommodation which shows how we go on adapting existing concepts to new experiences of them.

Two suggestions follow for helping children to become more aware of categorisation. Nearly all pupils keep word books, usually arranged alphabetically, to support their spelling. They could keep another type of word book to help them with their concepts, grouping entities which they have met in topics or in which they are particularly interested – minibeasts, games, trees, fish . . . Wall posters of words encountered in topics could be made by class and teacher, ready to be added to when new words are encountered and eventually, with older children, to be made into a hierarchical grid.

Second: I recently saw an account of market research analysing the reasons for successful product names. I can only remember *Kevin* body balm and cereals called *Crappies* as non-starters! Apparently, car manufacturers have moved from real words like Sirocco and Fiesta to inventing evocative words to sell their wares – Tigra, Xantia, Chimaera. Children could discuss why these names should be successful and what images are evoked by them. Wrappers for a particular food, for example chocolate biscuits, will show them how virtually the same product carries many different names like *Chocolate Chip Cookies* and *Boasters*. Children can invent their own names for biscuits. Here they will see that the properties of words do not just work cognitively: a wide network of associations trigger emotional reactions as well, even for the most mundane product.

Sentences

Single words are seldom used in isolation, and context helps even generalised terms to carry meaning. Moving to the level of syntax I illustrate the combining of words into phrases or sentences with one activity called *clustering*.

plant   water   crop

mud   grow

country   hot

months

Figure 2.1 Clustering

From a passage of about eighty words in a children's information text, I have chosen eight which I randomly display or put on separate cards (see Figure 2.1).

I have also chosen two more words from the passage, which I withhold. You are invited to cluster the words together to make small sets in any way you like. You might end up with something like this:

grow hot   mud   months

crop country   water

plant

You might do this on your own and then discuss your groupings with a partner to see whether they are similar or different. You then discuss what the passage might be about. Maybe you decide it is to do with growing some sort of crop in a hot country.

The words I withheld give the game away. When I tell you that they were *rice* and *women* you should be able to get very close to describing what is in the actual text, which you read at that point, hopefully motivated to see if you were right.

Bent double, up to their ankles in mud, women plant out the rice.

The plants were laid out in straight
lines, with plenty of space between
them so that they have room to grow.
The water discourages the weeds.
Depending on how hot the country is,
the rice takes three to six months to
grow. While they are waiting, the
peasants keep an eye on the water
level, and make sure the birds don't
eat the crop.

           (Pocket Worlds 1985)

There are many ways of using this technique. The withholding of two words developed as an excellent way of helping children to detect key words. The idea is that pairs of children should prepare the words for each other, so that they will have to decide for themselves on the key words. The styles of reading will vary, from the first close reading, to check-reading the text they are given. The activity could be done with the teacher leading a group. I have watched eight-year-olds sitting with their grouped words in front of them, their fingers darting down to the relevant word as the teacher read the full text aloud.

In carrying out the clustering activity it is interesting to note the language used by the children when they are guessing what the passage is about. Because they have grouped the words into sets they will probably relate to the sets non-sequentially, moving naturally away from chronological ordering to causal reasoning, or giving examples to illustrate. In this passage, for instance, you are likely to work out that *because* the crop grows in a hot country and needs a lot of water, *therefore* it must be rice.

The text, simple though it is, demonstrates some of the syntactical features with which readers will have to become familiar. One example is the delayed main clause in the title: to get to *women plant out the rice*, we have to wait for two adjectival clauses describing the women – *bent double* and *up to their ankles in mud*. It is not clear to me why so many information texts use this difficult construction. It means that the reader must 'hold' for understanding until the end of the sentence, not easy for those who so recently have been learning to read word by word.

The connecting function of words also becomes very important, and may have different connotations in non-fiction from when they are met in story, as Bruner shows: 'The term *then* functions differently in the proposition *if x then y* and in the narrative *the king died, and then the queen died*. The first *then* indicates logical deduction and the second an event in time' (Bruner 1986: 11–12). In our text *so that they have room to grow* indicates 'in order that', not as 'a result of' (e.g. 'The soldiers were cowards *so* they were beaten'). *Depending on* is an important but difficult phrase to understand fully, again placed before the fact that it is describing. Obvious as the inference is to us, will all children work out that rice grows quicker in hot countries?

Amazingly, many children show awareness of syntactical links at an early age. My prime example of this is Jessica, aged five, in reception class. The teacher introduced the topic of polar bears, showed them different books, and put key words and phrases on a flip-chart. Each child was then given a five-page booklet in the shape of a polar bear and asked to make their own texts. I watched Jessica from afar while she wrote her book. She had no further input from the teacher. This is how it went:

Page 1 polar bears live in caves
Page 2 polar bears hunt for fish
Page 3 polar bears walk on ice
Page 4 polar bears never meet penguins

The class had been particularly interested in this last bit of news and the reason for it. At this point, however, there was a long pause. Jessica had come to the end of what she knew about polar bears. And there was a page left to fill. She did not seek advice. At last she picked up her pencil and triumphantly wrote:

Page 5 and penguins never meet polar bears

I was entranced by her ability to transform the sentence to make good sense, and to supply the wonderful connecting *and*!

For those who are not so aware, underlining or highlighting is one of the most satisfying ways of helping children to see relationships between phrases. In the rice passage we might suggest using two colours to underline, first words and phrases which show what *helps* the rice to grow and another colour to show what might *hinder* it. There should be discussion here; mud helps the rice but hinders the workers. Water is a help as long as there is not too much of it. The originators of this technique, one of the DARTS (Directed Activities Related to Texts) recommended by the Effective Use of Reading project (Lunzer and Gardner 1979), insisted that these should be group activities centred round talk.

Discourse

We have moved almost imperceptibly into the patterning of the whole text, which is as it should be, since words are part of sentences which are part of the whole read. And the readers need to be aware of this, to know why they are reading and what kind of text it is.

Non-fiction reading serves two main purposes. If the reader wants to find the answer to a direct question and knows exactly what to look for, it can be done as quickly as possible using an index and chapter headings, and retrieving the information rapidly through scanning. This is fine as long as there is an index – and as long as there is an answer to the question. One of my most irritating memories is of encouraging two boys who were researching butterflies to look up how long a butterfly lives (I thought it was only for a day). We went to the library to find the answer, but even a book entitled *The Life Cycle of a Butterfly* did not tell us. Enough to put the three of us off research for life!

The other kind of non-fiction reading is much more leisurely, involving skimming interesting-looking material to find something which takes the fancy. Unfortunately, while many information texts look attractive on the surface, with beautiful illustrations, the text is often less accessible. The result is that readers become lookers, which happens with adults and children. Children's books often mix up expository and procedural texts (directions to carry out an activity) so that instead of enjoying an inspiring read, the child is suddenly thrust into finding impossible-to-obtain materials and using a high-level skill in order to make a bird bath or a camera or an aeroplane. Children's information books also tend to ask rhetorical or unanswered questions. The rice page ends with a question in very small print following the quoted paragraph: *Did you know that there are thousands of varieties of rice in the world?* It is hard to see why this fact is put into question form, particularly as it has nothing to do with the context.

The patterns of non-fiction discourse are far more complex than most fiction. To give one more example, the relationship between author and reader may vary in distance from page to page. The present chapter illustrates this. Sometimes I have used the personal approach of *I*, which then changes to *we*, supposedly intended to include the reader more closely in a chummy partnership, but probably antagonising her/him because of association with the royal *we*. I have tried to avoid passive sentences and delayed main clauses, but I am sure they have crept in; and maybe the most annoying part for you, the reader, is where I describe clustering and demand that you carry out an activity. I would wager that most readers at that point did not actually pick up a pen and do what was demanded of them!

Similarly for children, where this mixture of expository and procedural text interleaved with rhetorical questions occurs, it is natural to miss out most of the reading. It is important that ways of coping with the words on the page are carefully modelled, which implies choosing and using a few information books in depth rather than sending children off to look for likely material before they are quite sure how to handle it.

I have emphasised the differences between reading fiction and non-fiction, in order to show how children need to be weaned on to the latter. There is another way of looking at all this which can be equally important. Non-fiction *can* be read for enjoyment – to satisfy deep curiosity, to inspire and to awaken latent interests. Some books do this well, often because they bridge the gap between fiction and non-fiction. Purists feel strongly that information texts should be kept within their own boundaries, and certainly gratuitous fantasy built round facts is often confusing. Margaret Meek believes that the boundaries should be more flexible:

> From time to time we catch glimpses of writers who want to share their accumulated understanding with their readers, and who offer them learning in a different sense by *lending their minds out*. Then a reader begins to see that coming to understand the world is a single enterprise, with many books, many different kinds of texts and different versions, which no single account can encompass.
>
> (Meek 1996: 119)

Bruce Chatwin's *Songlines* is an example of a book which inspired and taught me. David Macaulay's *Pyramid* and Jeanine Baker's *Where the Forest Meets the Sea* would, I think, do the same for many children. We should be collecting these rare and beautiful books to read to children just as we use beloved fiction.

I end as I should perhaps have begun, with a reader who is having difficulties. Jo, aged seven, read an information passage to me with singular lack of success – achieving 37 correct words out of 70 and showing no idea of independent strategy. One of the words he did read correctly, though, was *invented*. The ensuing conversation went like this:

H.A.: You were very clever on one word. How did you know that word? Some of the little words you didn't get, but you got that long word there.
JO: Because I knew I had it in my reading books.
H.A.: What – *invented*! In your reading book?

JO: Yes, I have some books about things.

H.A.: Ah – so you like reading about things. And you remember that word *invented*? Would you *really* rather read about things than stories?

JO: Yeah.

H.A.: What particularly interests you?

JO: About armour.

H.A.: What sort of armour?

JO: Army armour.

H.A.: Old armour? Metal armour?

JO: Yeah.

H.A.: I wonder what made you interested in that?

JO: The kind of way they look . . . and they show about the weapons –

H.A.: I wonder how you got interested in the first place?

JO: Because I go to this library and they have all this war stuff and once I found a book what really interested me, so I kept on getting books like that.

H.A.: And then what do you do? Some of those books have very hard words in them, don't they?

JO: I don't read them – I just look at the pictures.

Jo is at the crossroads. At the moment he does not know the fundamental difference between reading and looking. He can go one of two ways. He can climb into mastery of the text through his curiosity, or he can become disillusioned and reject the written medium. Many children like Jo, often boys, are in a similar position. I believe that they can be encouraged and supported but they need to be shown the ways very carefully.

References

Baker, J. (1989) *Where the Forest Meets the Sea*, London: Walker Books.

Bruner, J. (1986) *Actual Minds, Possible Worlds*, Cambridge, MA and London: Harvard University Press.

Butler, D. (1991) *Minibeasts* (Take One series), London: Simon and Schuster.

Chambers (1974) *Twentieth Century Dictionary*, Edinburgh: W&R Chambers.

Chatwin, B. (1987) *The Songlines*, London: Picador.

Fox, C. (1993) *At the Very Edge of the Forest*, London: Cassell.

Goswami, U. and Bryant, P. (1990) *Phonological Skills and Learning to Read*, Hillsdale, NJ: Lawrence Erlbaum Associates.

Lunzer, E. and Gardner, K. (1979) *The Effective Use of Reading*, London: Heinemann.

Macaulay, D. (1988) *Pyramid*, London: HarperCollins.

Meek, M. (1996) *Information and Book Learning*, Stroud, Gloucestershire: The Thimble Press.

Meek, M., Warlow, A. and Barton, G. (eds) (1977) *The Cool Web*, London: The Bodley Head.

Pocket Worlds (1985) *The Story of a Grain of Rice*, London: Moonlight.

Vygotsky, L. (1962) *Thought and Language*, Cambridge, MA: MIT Press.

3

SIGNIFICANT SPEECH

Chris Doddington

To develop effective speaking and listening pupils should be taught to:

- use the vocabulary and grammar of standard English;
- formulate, clarify and express their ideas;
- adapt their speech to a widening range of circumstances and demands;
- listen, understand and respond appropriately to others.

(DfE 1995: 2)

At the base of what is prescribed for education lie assumptions about the nature of what is valued in our everyday lives. To learn to speak and to listen are among the most significant achievements of the young child and to do this well continues to mark out the most able of adults in a variety of contexts. The television presenter and politician are obvious examples of people judged in part by the way they speak and we applaud the rousing speech or the stimulating live talk in its various forms. We value the good priest, teacher, manager or doctor who attends and communicates appropriately and effectively. We also praise those whom we judge to form good relationships in their personal and public lives because they *express themselves well* or are *good listeners*. People are often judged to be *funny*, *clever*, *caring*, *witty* or *warm* on the strength of their ability to talk and listen. On purely commonsense grounds then, the development of our capacity to speak and listen has considerable value for us as social beings.

True to life

One obvious strand of general value is accuracy and truthfulness. We value a correct account in various contexts. The doctor or car mechanic diagnosing what is wrong, the policeman or eyewitness giving evidence, or the surveyor evaluating a house for a mortgage can all be blamed, if not penalised, if their testimony is judged to be false. In some areas the notion of 'truth' however can be problematic. The journalist, the salesperson and the politician make claims to truth but in reality what they offer us is interpretation. Success is frequently

41

measured here by their skill in being *effective in their communication*. So we move from the value of accuracy to the value of effect. If speech can be more or less effective within given contexts, there is a need to attend closely to how we achieve 'effect' and one obvious consideration could be attention to the perceived needs of the audience. Numerous business- or workplace-oriented courses hail the power of effective communication as an empowering skill. The person who can speak, listen and be aware of the effect they have in a variety of situations will undoubtedly have more control and power than one who does not have this awareness. To teach children how to be effective communicators can therefore be justified as an important aspect of their education which will be of great value in later life.

All judgements about 'good' speaking are, of course, forms of assessment. Speaking and listening are overt behaviours which are relatively open to assessment. Listening to someone talking is a frequent occurrence and on the strength of what people say listeners will often consciously or unconsciously judge those who are speaking. Explicit and implicit judgements can be made about a whole range of personal and cognitive traits when we speak. We may wish to argue that the grounds for making these judgements are far from adequate; nevertheless many of us engage in making them, and this appears to strengthen the argument for educating children to consciously speak and listen well.

Speaking with skill

In the current National Curriculum model, there is a particular stress on 'adapting to purpose', 'effectiveness' and 'audience', which reflects the ideas outlined above:

> Pupils should be given opportunities to consider how talk is influenced by the purpose and by the intended audience.
>
> (DfE 1995: 4)

Even from an early age, the thrust of a child's progress will depend on the teacher making children more conscious of how they talk and how the audience responds:

> pupils should be taught the importance of language that is clear, fluent and interesting . . . pupils should be encouraged to speak with confidence, making themselves clear through organising what they say and choosing words with precision . . . taking into account the needs of their listeners.
>
> (DfE 1995: 4)

Closer examination of this model shows that it assumes that talk can be seen as a tool that we can learn to use skilfully. The analogy of a 'craft' is often cited.

Attention to *effectiveness* and *audience* will supply the criteria for selecting what to say:

> Pupils should be given opportunities to communicate to different audiences and to reflect on how speakers adapt their vocabulary, tone, pace and style . . .
>
> (DfE 1995: 11)

The effective speaker will be able to devise and select the best means of achieving the desired end. This implies that the outcome can largely be predetermined and that practice, or even rehearsal, might exercise and strengthen skills and the ability to speak well.

Within the general purpose of the National Curriculum, this description of the role speech plays in life has an additional attraction. Speech which is effective according to purpose and audience is also one of the more straightforward forms of speech to assess. A competent teacher can decide if a child has satisfied a particular purpose, such as delivered a message accurately or bought some bread at the role-play corner 'bakers'. It is relatively easy to align oneself with a particular audience or seek their verdict and thereby make a reasonable judgement on effectiveness. It could be claimed that it is also easy to assess speaking that corresponds to actuality. Reporting and describing can be judged by how detailed or accurate the account is.

However, there remains a significant question about whether this gives a picture of the full story of a child's development, or reflects the central role language plays in being human and becoming educated. The model embraced by the National Curriculum rests on the idea that it is possible to treat language and human behaviour as predominantly systematic and scientific. This means that explanations can confidently be given for cause and effect in much the same way that we can explain the processes of cooking or forces such as magnetism. The question is whether this is the best model for understanding language and making curriculum decisions. It may be that talking and listening are significant to humankind for more profound and more subtle reasons than just true reporting or calculating effect and that education should reflect and acknowledge this rather than the model of skilled or effective speech sketched above.

The power of words

It will be useful at this point to step back from the classroom context and into adult behaviour to consider when our own speaking or listening experiences as adults become significant to us or worthy of comment. Many instances of speaking and listening soak invisibly into the fabric of our day-to-day lives. Everyday speech is often instrumental or provoked by a straightforward purpose and when woven smoothly with our actions and behaviour, we converse, tell and listen to stories and make enquiries or answer questions all barely conscious of the processes involved. Sometimes we only become aware of the significance of speech when it is notably successful or when words fail us. At times we struggle:

I was so excited I just couldn't take in all of what was said.

It left me lost for words – I just didn't know what to say.

Alternatively, we can become aware of how potent language can be when spoken words effect change in us that is meaningful:

Once she had talked me through it, I really understood it.

His story really moved me.

As I tried to explain the problem, it suddenly fell into place – it all became clear to me.

Superficially, it would seem these examples can simply be classed as talk that is either effective or not. However there are a number of features that do not fit comfortably with a systems-based model with its emphasis on calculated efficiency. The 'effective' examples do not all depend on premeditation and selection. In particular the first, and especially the third, call attention to the value of interaction or process which cannot be fully predetermined. They describe moments of enlightenment and could be seen as clear illustrations of education in process. They may also signal an important general point:

One cannot determine in advance the efficacy of one's words and deeds. Efficacy turns out to be a form of influence; it lies not so much in one's own operation as in the co-operation of others. The nature and extent of this co-operation cannot be counted on beforehand and even afterwards one cannot be sure just what it has been.

(Dunne 1995: 359)

If we accept this as a more accurate insight into how speech generally operates in conversations and discussions, the model described earlier is somewhat undermined. This can be endorsed by reflecting on the statement *His story really moved me*. Here, speech has considerable power but the idea that someone would set out to 'move' an audience with a story may seem appropriate in a theatrical context but would ring untrue in real life. If the idea of deciding the end and choosing the means were retained in this instance, suspicion of manipulation and accusations of a lack of sincerity might follow. To complete the point, if we reverse the coin, it would also seem absurd to claim that the examples offered where speaking and listening has 'failed' could have been retrieved by rehearsal or rational pre-selection.

I am developing my argument through consideration of particular statements but these could of course be placed within variable contexts which might alter their meaning considerably. This draws attention to another flaw in the idea that speech can be exercised as if it were simply a rule-governed activity. Human interaction is notoriously unpredictable and it would be impossible to furnish a complete list of rules to cover every situation. Children learning to *be kind* (whatever we might decide counts as being kind) do not do so by applying rules systematically. Although general ideas like *being kind means not consciously hurting someone* can be useful as a guide, each particular situation needs active interpretation by each individual involved. What counts as being scrupulous, conscientious and fair-minded cannot be specified in detail in advance. Decisions about kindness will depend on the circumstances together with judgement by those involved. In the same way, speaking and listening is locked into the particularities of each occasion. It is not uncommon to find individuals who try to operate from generalised rules without close attention to the situation and therefore speak and listen in ways that appear wooden or unresponsive. In this context we might judge someone unfavourably for appearing rehearsed or insincere.

This point leads on to a third feature of the examples cited, for they are based on judgements that are not made by reference to an 'audience', but to oneself. There is no need to seek public agreement in order to determine what moves us. Whether we understand or not is a judgement we make for ourselves. This is not to say that discussion does not help this process, but there is an important sense in which speaking and listening has to be self-determined. In a very fundamental way our speech has to express what we want to say. Care and attention to our own sense of what is right rather than what appeals to an audience is not an unusual idea. *I want to say what I really think – not what I think you want me to say* highlights a value that many would consider vital to personal life and various public domains.

Expression

The argument has now moved into an area which is barely visible in any account of talk as a communication system in which one can receive technical training. The vocal word is in reality only the most obvious feature of a whole realm of expression which grows from and includes bodily action, facial expression and gesture. Yet it is rather telling that the only mention of 'expression' within the Attainment Target for speaking and listening occurs at levels 5 and 6. Here the word refers to vocal production and is largely a technical term evaluated again in the context of satisfying an audience:

> [Pupils'] talk engages the interest of the listener as they begin to vary their expression and vocabulary.
>
> (DfE 1995: 26)

'Expression' is seen in essence as cosmetic, a superficial acquisition which can be added on to speech. However, 'expression' can have a far richer meaning in relation to speech. R.G. Collingwood in his book *The Principles of Art* sees the realm of expression as fundamental to human communication and calls it the 'language of total bodily gesture'. He goes on to proffer an interesting conceptual analysis of the expressive nature of language which contrasts sharply with the technical view of speech outlined earlier:

> beneath all the machinery of word and sentence lies the primitive language of mere utterance – the controlled act in which we express our emotions.
>
> (Collingwood 1938: 236)

Collingwood's ideas can be summarised in this way: within the flow of sensation which surrounds us, we focus on sights, sounds, events and feelings, all of which carry for us an emotional charge. The moment we give attention to some of the sensation that surrounds us we bring that focus into our consciousness, but in order to form or know that feeling or emotion we need to express it.[1] When we speak, we bring into consciousness our feelings, emotions and ideas. For Collingwood, the value of this is clear and should not be underestimated. He continues:

> Self-consciousness makes a person of what, apart from that, would be merely a sentient organism . . . The discovery of myself as a person is the discovery that I can speak, and am thus a persona or speaker; in speaking, I am both speaker and hearer; and since the discovery of myself as a person is also the discovery of other persons around me, it is the discovery of speakers and hearers other than myself.
>
> (Collingwood 1938: 248)

This view is shared and extended by more recent writers who offer significant claims that language is the means by which both personal and cultural identity is forged:

> It is through [speech] that one discloses and achieves the unique identity that distinguishes one as a person; at the same time it reveals the depth of one's interdependence with others.
>
> (Dunne 1995: 359)

Accounts which rest on these views can be sharply distinguished from talk seen as a means to predetermined ends. They suggest that talk enables me to have ideas, to find out what I want to say, as I say it. It involves the expression and sharing of thoughts and emotions. The prime value of speech is that it is vital for personal meaning, human interaction and all thought:

No one really *uses* language; no one, that is, constructs thoughts within his or her subjectivity and *then* employs words which can best convey these thoughts to a public. Rather thinking itself is already within language; even when, as a creative or radical thinking, it does not fall into the obvious pathways of the language (i.e. its clichés) but strains to cut fresh paths.

(Dunne 1995: 360)

Quality talk

Put together, the above points alert us to vital qualities of talk that are neglected in a systematised view of language. These can be summarised as follows:

- Language in its fullest sense is important as the prime form of expression for each individual.
- Talk is the means of developing thought and one's sense of self for it enables personal engagement with others and with ideas. This requires that practice in speaking and listening should seek to support talk that is authentic rather than contrived.
- Speakers need to be versatile rather than programmed. Genuine talk is not practice of a rule-governed social action but expressive and purposeful engagement with others.
- The conception of talk as simply a process which can be engineered towards predetermined ends is inadequate. Each instance of talk relates intrinsically to the particular speech situation in which it is embedded.

If these aspects are seen as significant for speaking and listening in the classroom, it implies less emphasis on the criteria of *accuracy, effectiveness and performance*:

One does not first acquire a language and then use it. To possess it and to use it are the same. We only come to possess it by repeatedly and progressively attempting to use it.

(Collingwood 1938: 250)

The aim in schools would be for children to engage in rich language experience where the context and the process are seen as important, rather than the outcome.

Attention to context and process takes us to the heart of what kind of practice might follow if we espouse this account of the value of talk. If talk is to sustain vibrant thought and be authentic, the practice must in some sense be open-ended and genuinely expressive rather than prescribed. Much of the day-to-day talk in the classroom involves specified outcomes. Even discussion groups are often set up with clear outcomes in mind – the problem to be solved or the answer found.

Now while there is undoubtedly a place for this, a richer conception of the value of language means that talk in the classroom needs broadening beyond this narrow practice and other activities need to be considered.

Drama

Drama offers opportunities to develop speaking and listening, particularly in practising roles and improvising in a range of contexts. Within a technical version of developing talk, role play can be seen as encouraging conscious selection and use of appropriate structures, styles and registers. However the aesthetic nature of drama means that it is an area which can also offer richly expressive language experience. Children of primary age engage in imaginative play from an early age. This involves speaking and listening as if they are someone else – a mother or father, a shop assistant or a doctor. Teacher-led drama in school can build on this, taking children into fictional frameworks where their imagination and emotional involvement is high.

A teacher can use a variety of dramatic conventions to build belief and commitment to a fictional context. As emotional commitment to the situation grows, the children can face dilemmas and predicaments in role as the characters they have 'become'. Villagers who seek help from the wizard, or archaeologists who try to persuade an island official they are experienced and knowledgeable enough to dig for Roman remains, face language demands which are genuine rather than theatrical if there is emotional commitment to the fictional context. This is not to say that children are duped into believing the context is real, merely that they are able to engage in the aesthetic procedures of drama much as we can become aesthetically and emotionally involved in a film or a play or a novel. If aesthetic involvement is developed, we care about what is occurring. There is a particularly strong challenge to express your emotions and ideas when in role you feel concerned about issues that you have become involved with.

Once children are empowered to intervene as participants within the fictional context of drama, listening becomes vitally important in ways it is difficult to replicate in normal classroom interaction. You may have learnt a great deal about life in ancient Egypt, but when you and others have at last earned a formal audience with the Pharaoh (the teacher-in-role) and can ask questions, then listen to the answers, the experience has a quality of intensity that can rival the tension and suspense felt during a powerful performance of *Macbeth*.[2]

Picture books and talk of philosophy

Another area that is rich in language opportunity is discussion. One focus of discussion for children which has received some recent attention in both America and Britain is philosophy for children of primary age. Karen Murris in her folder *Teaching Philosophy with Picture Books* makes a promising claim:

> Philosophy begins in wonder . . . Philosophical questions are thought-provoking. They open up enquiry, rather than closing it down with a single answer.
>
> (Murris 1992: 1)

She suggests that young children frequently 'wonder why' and that they can be helped to make distinctions, connections and comparisons, to seek problems and find questions beyond the literal:

> Reasoning comes naturally to children, but can be improved greatly by regular practice in having to put ideas into words, in justifying beliefs by giving reasons, and in working out their own thoughts.
>
> (Murris 1992: 4)

Her analysis is interesting, for again this could be seen as merely a skill which requires practice. Other advocates have offered similar advice for the development of what is sometimes referred to as 'critical thinking'. Murris however makes an important further point:

> This sort of questioning is a skill which can be taught, but effectively only if this coincides with [development of] a philosophical attitude, that is, the attitude of open-mindedness.
>
> (Murris 1992: 7)

Murris chooses to begin this voyage with children through picture books which can be available in every primary classroom. She selects those she feels are intense and powerfully thought-provoking and which have the sensual qualities to stimulate the imagination. Her folder offers lists of the kinds of questions which might arise in discussion with the teacher where that discussion is planned to allow children to express their ideas and move beyond the author's overt meaning. She suggests that familiar books such as *Not Now, Bernard* by David McKee or *Where the Wild Things Are* by Maurice Sendak can provoke discussion of identity, gender roles, the nature of punishment and powers of the mind as well as discussion of emotions such as anger and sadness. Some questions relate directly to the book: *Do you think Max could help behaving the way he did?* while others move beyond: *Do you think a group of people can live together only when there is punishment?*

Experienced teachers will be sensitive to the way in which questions of this nature would need to be paced and introduced carefully within discussion, but they can also be used successfully by teachers-in-training with small groups of children.[3] What is important is that the context is congenial to open-ended discussion. This means careful planning of the physical context such as seating arrangement and location as well as establishment of a conducive atmosphere, appropriate attitudes and attention to language and timing. Teachers who are new to this way of working will also need to be conscious of the principles which underlie the procedures in order to help children openly respect and respond to each other's views. Children often need help to move away from the assumption that questions can only provoke right and wrong answers.

Discussions of this nature appear to weave and move between three stages. The first stage tends to focus quite literally on the story – children can be asked questions, or they themselves ask questions which establish a common understanding of what happened. Because they relate so closely to the story these questions tend to be rather closed, having answers which are broadly right or wrong. They also tend to be the kind of questions in which both children and teacher feel secure, for the answers and areas covered in the discussion can largely be predicted. The second stage allows for children to make personal connections with the story, to become involved and wonder beyond the literal content. *Why did the monster eat Bernard? Do you think Bernard is an only child?* It is here that the discussion becomes more interesting, as the process begins to draw genuine expression and ideas from the children. The third stage moves into broader issues. Questions such as *Is an only child, a lonely child?* asks those in the discussion to generalise beyond individual experience.

This level of abstraction and intellectualisation may seem beyond primary-aged children, but the experiences of teachers-in-training and those who have used Murris's materials have shown that, with support, children can speak and listen at this level:

> I was astounded at the comments children made and the depth and extent of their thinking. Although their feelings of being alone happened in very different circumstances they empathised strongly with Rose and also with the jealousy felt by John Brown.

> My group enjoyed the freedom – once they realised that nobody was going to give them the answers, they enjoyed thinking things through, out loud.

> The discussion began to range over wide areas as they thought about loneliness and old age, why we have pets and our relationships with animals. They really seemed to enjoy opening out the discussion and everyone wanted to 'chip in'. We even got on to thinking about the differences between humans and animals.[4]

Murris quotes an exchange between nine-year-olds based on *Not Now, Bernard*, which illustrates movement from particularisation to generalisation:

> One child raised the question: 'Why did Bernard go to the garden, if he knew there was a monster who was going to eat him up?' His reasoning that Bernard knew about the monster, was that: 'Bernard told his Mum, so he must have known what was going to happen.' One classmate was puzzled: 'Why would Bernard want to be eaten by the monster?' Two

others suggested that: 'His parents don't want him' and that 'They are ignoring him.' Another child introduced the concept: 'Perhaps it was suicide, because nobody loved him . . . ' another classmate [commented] 'Killing yourself is not always suicide, because you might be a baby or something, and you might electrocute yourself, but because you don't want to die, it is not suicide' . . . All sorts of reasons were offered for wanting to kill yourself: 'Being bullied; Running out of money; Copying mother; Mum is annoying him; If you are not allowed to become what you want to be; If there are only a few of you left in the war'; and even 'When you realise you have killed your friend; When you have to live in cardboard boxes.'

(Murris 1992: 4)

Drama and philosophical discussion, as I have briefly outlined them, are related oral practices. One dimension they have in common is that effective practice rests less on the clarity of predetermined outcomes and more on attention to the procedures in use. Each experience of discussion or drama is unique and distinctive for the teacher and the participants. While there should be no formulas or predictable patterns of oral outcomes, the procedures in use are nevertheless structured and principled. One principle that would underpin this kind of practice and guide how the discussion or drama should proceed is a concern that children are able to express what they feel and think within the clearly defined constraints of either the particular fictional context of the drama or the collaborative, open-minded context of the discussion.

These practices can be seen as educationally valid on a number of counts and could simply be argued for within a technicised view of speaking and listening. However, they can offer a richness which goes beyond this. The most significant common feature is that these practices can encourage authentic expression in areas which genuinely concern those who are engaged in the practice. I have tried to argue that this is a more worthy educational aim than is offered by a view of language which emphasises development as the technical acquisition of skilful ways of using speech. I have also attempted to show that this reflects a fundamentally richer view of the value language holds for humankind.

The significance of speaking and listening is enormous in modern life. It is the glue of our relationships to others and the way we articulate our situation in the world. Children deserve opportunities to be fully empowered in this deeply personal and yet public behaviour. Impoverished and narrow-minded conceptions of what language is, do not serve children or teachers well in this vital task. With a fuller and more thoughtful understanding, language practices can be implemented in ways that allow children to articulate themselves and bring themselves into being in relation to others. In this way, imaginative and exciting classroom practices can be valued for what they significantly offer – not oral exercise, but a chance for children to communicate genuinely with others and in the process find a voice of their own.

51

Notes

1 Collingwood later explains that intellectual thought also has emotional charge which determines expression. He cites Archimedes' excitement on his discovery and conceptualisation of specific gravity which drove him to run naked through the streets crying 'Eureka!'

2 Various accounts of how drama can work in this form can be found in a range of curriculum drama books and various collections of materials for use in primary schools. See in particular *The Drama Box* by Lesley Hendy and Patricia Broadsmith (London: HarperCollins, 1995), and for a list of drama conventions and (a fuller) explanation of the 'teacher-in-role' strategy see *Drama 7–11: Developing primary teaching skills* by Neil Kitson and Ian Spiby (London and New York: Routledge, 1997). An official version of the educational potential and worth of drama can be found in *Curriculum Matters 17: Drama 5–16* (DES, 1989). This is a fuller and more enlightened outline than is found in the current National Curriculum English document, which merely summarises skills and the range of activities for a programme of study along with attainment levels.

3 Part of the Primary Postgraduate course at Homerton College, Cambridge, requires students early in their professional placement in schools to undertake discussion with small groups of children. The discussions are conducted with a view to trying to broach philosophical issues arising from poems or picture books chosen by the student with reference to the class teacher. The Murris folder and sets of suggested books/ questions/materials and videos are available to the students for support and reference.

4 This is from a discussion between Helen Brown and Val Dufour, together with other teachers-in-training, following a classroom discussion conducted by pairs of Homerton postgraduate teachers-in-training in 1995. The classroom discussion was with six ten-year-olds and arose out of a reading of *John Brown, Rose and the Midnight Cat* by Jenny Wagner (London: Kestrel Books, 1977).

References

Collingwood, R.G. (1938) *The Principles of Art*, Oxford: Clarendon Press.

DfE (1995) *English in the National Curriculum*, London: HMSO.

Dunne, Joseph (1995) *Back to the Rough Ground*, Notre Dame, Indiana: University of Notre Dame Press.

McKee, David (1980) *Not Now, Bernard*, London: Andersen Press.

Murris, Karen (1992) *Teaching Philosophy with Picture Books*, London: Infonet Publications Ltd.

Sendak, Maurice (1963) *Where the Wild Things Are*, Harmondsworth: Puffin Books.

Part 2

GETTING IDEAS GOING

The work described in this part explores ways of using language to generate ideas, find things out, explore, research, hypothesise, plan . . . This involves children researching spoken and written texts, listening carefully and responding to other people's ideas and combing carefully through written texts to select material for their own purposes. One of the key points made by the three teachers whose work is included here is the importance of models and examples. This in itself implies a need for thoughtful and informed planning of classroom activities and raises some critical points about theories of teaching and learning.

Written models are recognised as essential for children's developing understanding of different text structures and genres. Even developed writers faced with an unfamiliar writing task turn to an example of the form they have to emulate. It is equally well recognised that children's successful reading is founded on the sounds and rhythms, not just of words and sentences but of longer stretches of text, too. However, as Helen Arnold points out in Part 1, whilst children will absorb some of these models from experience alone, such knowledge is transformed into understanding when teachers plan for children to pay careful attention to the ways in which language is structured for particular effects. Children's implicit knowledge about language deserves to be made explicit if they are to build on and extend their knowledge of language structures. It is also important for the development of knowledge and understanding in the different areas of the curriculum.

Once again, the Bullock Report, *A Language for Life*, provides some helpful guidance:

> It is a confusion of everyday thought that we tend to regard 'knowledge' as something that exists independently of someone who knows. 'What is known' must in fact be brought to life afresh within every 'knower' by his [sic] own efforts. To bring knowledge into being is a formulating process, and language is its ordinary means, whether in speaking or writing or the inner monologue of thought.
>
> (Bullock 1975: para. 4.9, p. 50)

53

This section of the report concludes with a summary of the relationship between language and learning:

> (i) all genuine learning involves discovery, and it is as ridiculous to suppose that teaching begins and ends with 'instruction' as it is to suppose that 'learning by discovery' means leaving children to their own resources;
>
> (ii) language has a heuristic function; that is to say a child can learn by talking and writing as certainly as he can by listening and reading;
>
> (iii) to exploit the process of discovery through language in all its uses is the surest means of enabling a child to master his mother tongue.
>
> (Bullock 1975: para. 4.10, p. 50)

The first point of this summary succinctly expresses the role of teacher intervention in promoting learning. Contrary to common usage of the word, often interpreted as face-to-face interaction, intervention properly begins before a teacher even reaches the classroom. Thoughtful and planned intervention is part of the planning process where a teacher identifies learning objectives and sets out a programme of activities to help children get to grips with them. Each lesson will involve a set of teacher–pupil and pupil–pupil interactions using a range of resources all of which are designed to move the learning forward. The learning will be observed and progress monitored so that at the end of the series of activities the final interventions will be to use assessment and evaluation to plan for the next set of learning objectives to be reached.

Point (i) also suggests that current (sometimes deliberate) misunderstandings about progressive methods of teaching are no new phenomenon; the use of the word 'suppose' makes it clear that Bullock was familiar with misconceptions about active approaches to learning. It is a peculiarity of some of the recent attacks on methods of teaching that they signal very clearly that progression (as expressed in 'progressive methods') is seen as unacceptable whilst more conservative approaches (which suggest standing still, or even going backwards) are seen as preferable. This is ironic at the end of a century when the language and technological demands of the following century mean that it is critical to adopt more forward-thinking ideas. For Bullock, writing in the 1970s, a sensible balance between what a teacher offers and what learners can work on for themselves forms part of productive pedagogy.

The second point in Bullock's summary sets out very clearly the role of language in learning, emphasising the productive modes of language as well as the receptive modes. The third point is perhaps the most telling, although understated here (and expressed in the gendered style of the time). The most *effective* way of developing language (or English, as is our job in the UK) is, indeed, in its *use*.

Asking and answering questions

One of the commonest forms of language used in teaching and learning is the question. Much formal education in the United Kingdom (and in many other places) is based on what is often referred to as 'the Socratic method'. It is worth examining just what the original method used by Socrates means and implies for modern educational practice. In Socrates' own dialogues, questioning was part of a collaborative quest for greater knowledge and understanding. Very often, teacher and pupil were engaged in a shared endeavour to reach a point which was unknown to both partners in the dialogue. The dialectical process rolled on, moving from thesis to antithesis to a newly developed synthesis which in itself became the new thesis, and so the process of argument advanced. Classroom uses of questioning do not often follow the dialectical process. Very often questions become like a test of mind-reading where learners have to second-guess what is in the teacher's mind in order to provide the 'right' answers. Such practices suggest a view of learning simply as knowledge-getting where teachers are repositories of information and pupils simply have to get it out of them. As Bullock emphasised, learning is much more complex than that – and, indeed, teachers recognise the complexities, yet often fail to break out of the historically encrusted mode of teacher questioning which assumes a straightforward relationship between knowledge and understanding.

There is nothing wrong with teacher questioning, of course. At times it may even be appropriate to stimulate children's ideas by asking them to *guess what I'm thinking*. As a regular form of pedagogy, however, it does not lead to the transformation of fact-gathering into sure and enduring understanding; it does not bring knowledge to life. If the aim of questioning for Socrates (and many other great teachers of wisdom) is to stimulate, shape and maintain the learner's thought processes, then modern teachers need to find ways of using questions to do just that. This often involves developing a different pace for question-and-answer sessions; it may even mean using written as well as spoken means for children to work through their developing ideas. The other major and significant move which a new approach to questioning suggests, is a shift from teacher questioning towards the pupils themselves asking the questions. Anyone who has lived or worked with young children knows that asking questions is often second nature to them – many of the questions stumping the adults who are being called upon to provide answers. Experience in parrying children's questions about the world they live in often leads to the development of an approach where, instead of attempting to come up with answers, adults participate in the process of hypothesising. This can offer some helpful pointers for classroom question-and-answer sessions.

Questions in the classroom are not always likely to offer children an equally open set of opportunities for forging their own understandings about experience and about the natural world. Gordon Wells gives this example:

A small group of children are looking at colour slides of India. The teacher has selected a slide, looked at it through the viewer and passed it to Rosie:

T: They're Indian ladies, and what else?
R: [*Looks though viewer*] I can see something.
T: What can you see?
R: And they're going in the sand.
T: [*Fails to understand.*] Mm?
R: You have a look.
T: Well, you have a look and tell me. I've seen it already. I want to see if you can see. [6 *second pause.*]
R: [*Looks through viewer*] Oh they're going in the sand. They're going in the sand. [20 *second pause; T doesn't hear as she is attending to other children.*]
T: What's behind the men? Can you see the men in the red coats? [2 *second pause; R still looking*] Can you see the men in the red coats? What is behind those men? [4 *second pause*] Can you see?
R: [*Nods*]
T: What is it?
R: They're walking in . . .
T: Pardon?
R: They're walking.

(Wells 1985: 230–1)

The questioning continues with the teacher trying hard to get Rosie to give answers which are so obvious that she can't understand what she is supposed to say. To the teacher the activity is straightforward and Rosie is giving the wrong answers. It is interesting to surmise just what the teacher did want to find out from the questioning. Rosie's teacher, no doubt for all the best reasons, shuts down possibilities. This is particularly problematic when considering the fact that she has probably at least 30 children to have conversations with. They not only get little of her time as conversation, but her approach to questions and answers means that these very precious exchanges have little or no value and may even seriously impede the child's learning. Gordon Wells comments:

> This sort of impasse can only be avoided if teachers become more aware of the interactive nature of conversation and hence the need for them to adopt a more negotiatory attitude in their talk with pupils.
>
> (Wells 1985: 232)

Each chapter in this part of the book considers the role of questioning as well as taking a careful and critical view of teacher intervention and models for language and learning. All three chapters begin by considering the role of speaking and listening, moving later into reading and writing. In Chapter 4 David Somerville focuses on common areas of English and mathematics as outlined in the document *Mathematics and the Use of Language*. In mathematics children are expected to 'Discuss their work, responding to and asking mathematical questions; collect, represent and interpret data', and in the Speaking and Listening attainment target of English they should be taught to 'Explore, develop and explain ideas when reporting observations to a variety of audiences' (SCAA 1997: 2). Somerville looks at issues relating to recent criticisms of the level of attainment in mathematics in England and Wales. By drawing on research and theoretical insights into the nature of teaching and learning, and in particular of the nature of the dialogue between pupils and teacher, he identifies ways that the language used in the classroom may help or hinder this process. He illustrates this with reference to observed classroom interactions, in particular considering the nature of teacher questioning as a means of promoting genuine mathematical enquiry. He gives examples from the early years to Year 6 to argue that language and thought necessarily develop together. This leads him to identify ways in which recent calls for more whole-class mathematics teaching can be responded to in a way which has educational validity.

Whilst David Somerville considers the process of mathematical thinking, Noelle Hunt and Caroline Luck describe how they made opportunities to develop pupil questioning as a means of transforming information into understanding. Their history project allows them to focus particularly on one group of children, several of them bilingual learners at different stages of confident English use, confirming that the best way to develop standard forms of English is to use the language in a range of registers and contexts. They show that if children are to learn how to interpret information in order to understand it, they need to be in a position to make connections between what they know and what they can come to know. This involves using language in its most inventive and generative ways, including imaginative role play as well as direct information gathering. Chapter 5 describes a carefully planned series of activities deliberately designed as a progressive set of interventions and experiences to help children use questioning to scaffold learning.

Claire Saunders shifts the debate about valid forms of questioning a little further by looking at the more experiential areas of the curriculum involved in personal and social education. There is no established body of knowledge to be learned here; this area of the curriculum involves the development of personal opinion based on balanced and careful examination of the relevant issues. As well as 'expressing themselves confidently and clearly' (DfE 1995: para. 2a, p. 11) Claire Saunders found that her Year 6 class had explored 'the kinds of language modelled effectively for them by others'. In the process, they certainly gained from experiences which allowed them to study language itself. In both the spoken debating activities and in the associated writing, her pupils were

given opportunities to develop their understanding of the similarities and differences between the written and spoken forms of standard

English, and to investigate how language varies according to context and purpose and between standard and dialect forms.

(DfE 1995: para. 3a, p.12)

Claire Saunders's chapter provides an opportunity to look at persuasive and argumentative uses of language and highlights the importance of having a clearly worked out theory of teaching and learning. Intervention in these sensitive areas implies a view of equal opportunities for learning and an examination of the balance of power between teacher and learner. As mentioned earlier, genuine learning will arise from a learning partnership between teacher and pupil where the teacher's thoughtful interventions do not cross the line into interference with the learner's development of independent thought. Language is not just the medium for the development of discrimination; it needs to be carefully scrutinised so that learners can detect and use language specifically chosen for particular effects.

References

Bullock, Sir Alan (1975) *A Language for Life: Report of the Committee of Inquiry appointed by the Secretary of State for Education and Science*, London: Her Majesty's Stationery Office.

Department for Education (1995) *English in the National Curriculum*, London: Her Majesty's Stationery Office.

School Curriculum and Assessment Authority (1997) *Mathematics and the Use of Language*, Hayes, Middlesex: SCAA.

Wells, G. (1985) 'Pre-school Literacy-related Activities', in D.R. Olson, N. Torrance and A. Hildyard (eds) *Literacy, Language and Learning: the Nature and Consequences of Reading and Writing*, Cambridge: Cambridge University Press.

4

'BRITISH MATHS FAILS TO ADD UP'

David Somerville

BRITISH MATHS FAILS TO ADD UP was the headline on the front page of the *Times Educational Supplement* on 15 March 1996. Reporting findings from a research project carried out by Professor David Burghes at Exeter University, it indicated that secondary pupils in England and Scotland 'trail far behind their international peers'. Professor Burghes stated that:

> maths in other continental countries is characterised by the teacher playing a central teaching role, not a management role as we see so often in the UK . . . Whole class interactive teaching is the norm with teachers adept at bringing everyone into a discussion.

Before teachers had had time fully to consider the implications of this report for classroom practice, Professor Reynolds of Newcastle University had produced his *Worlds Apart* report. This study looked at mathematics teaching and the attainment of pupils in Taiwan; it concluded that Taiwanese pupils were well in advance of their British peers in important aspects of mathematics, and linked this to differing styles of teaching. Once again, the prevalence of interactive whole class teaching was noted, coupled with a core belief that *all can succeed*. It was suggested that the widespread use of differentiated work in mathematics in primary schools in this country could actually be a contributory factor to the acknowledged existence of a long tail of low-achieving children in mathematics.

Professor Reynolds's research achieved national prominence through an edition of the BBC's documentary programme *Panorama*. The national press took up the debate eagerly. Inevitably, some of the subtlety of the analysis that Professors Burghes and Reynolds had presented was lost as the stories were prepared for mass consumption. Teachers who first heard of the debate through the national press can be forgiven for feeling disaffected by this latest round of 'teacher bashing'. Dedicated mathematics teachers who have devoted themselves to the implementation of the vision of mathematics teaching and learning that such seminal documents as the Cockcroft Report (*Mathematics Counts*, 1982) encapsulated will have felt once again that the foundations of their philosophy were being attacked, and will probably not have been much heartened by Professor Burghes's caveat that 'we are not blaming teachers – in the main they have been trying to implement, in difficult circumstances, the advice being given by educationalists, administrators and the Government'. The Cockcroft Committee, which reported to the Government in 1982 on the state and future of mathematics teaching in England and Wales, had said, for example:

> We are aware that there are some teachers who would wish us to indicate a definitive style for the teaching of mathematics, but we do not believe that this is either desirable or possible. Approaches to the teaching of a particular piece of mathematics need to be related to the topic itself and to the abilities and experience of both teachers and pupils. Because of differences of personality and circumstance, methods which may be extremely successful with one teacher and one group of pupils will not necessarily be suitable for use by another teacher or with a different group of pupils.
>
> (Cockcroft 1982: para. 242)

The Report went on, in what has become a seminal paragraph, to outline the range of activities that should be present in an effective mathematics classroom:

> Mathematics teaching at all levels should include opportunities for
>
> * exposition by the teacher;
> * discussion between teacher and pupils and between pupils themselves;
> * appropriate practical work;
> * consolidation and practice of fundamental skills and routines;
> * problem solving, including the application of mathematics to everyday situations;
> * investigational work.
>
> (Cockcroft 1982: para. 243)

This statement received widespread support at the time, and indeed helped act as a catalyst for change in classrooms where a very traditional approach was still the dominant mode of teaching. The importance of discussion and the role of language in the mathematics classroom was touched on:

> The ability to 'say what you mean and mean what you say' should be one of the outcomes of good mathematics teaching. This ability develops as a result of opportunities to talk about mathematics, to explain and discuss results which have been obtained, and to test hypotheses . . . Pupils need . . . extended discussion.
>
> (Cockcroft 1982: para. 246)

The importance of the role of language in all aspects of learning has long been recognised, and the Cockcroft Report says nothing on this subject that, for instance, the authors of the Bullock Report, *A Language for Life*, would have disagreed with seven years earlier. For example, a mathematics teacher is quoted as saying:

> It is not just that language is *used* in mathematics: rather, it is that the language that is used *is* the mathematics.
>
> (Bullock 1975: para. 12.10)

In establishing criteria for judging whether a primary classroom is providing a rich context for language use, the Report suggests that we should ask, among others, the following question:

> How much opportunity is there for the kind of talk by which children make sense in their own terms of the information offered by teacher or by book?
>
> (Bullock 1975: para. 12.3)

How true it is, as Burghes suggests, that teachers have been striving to use these pedagogical perspectives to improve their classroom practice. A generation of teachers has grown up with these ideas central to their own understanding of the nature of teaching and learning.

In the months that followed the *Panorama* programme on Reynolds's study, other educational issues stole the limelight and it was possible to stand back and consider in a calmer atmosphere what these reports were telling us. It is widely acknowledged how difficult it is to make comparisons between educational systems in different countries and to establish reasons for their relative successes and failures. Cultural factors clearly play a role, and their significance is hard to assess. There is no guarantee that transplanting elements of one country's educational system into another country will produce improved teaching and learning.

And yet these reports are too important to dismiss in this way. Teachers have a responsibility to consider their own practice in the light of such comparative studies, and to consider what can be learnt from them. As I pondered their significance, I returned to the descriptions of *interactive whole class teaching* and of the importance given to this by the reports' authors. Professor Reynolds was careful to distance himself from those who might link the return of (to parody an extreme viewpoint) whole class teaching, grammar schools and the cane as keys to a return to the educational glories of the past. Taiwan's 'interactive whole class teaching is an intensive, rapid, demanding and involving style that is far removed from the past British whole class teaching' (Reynolds and Farrell 1996). Certainly the classes shown on the *Panorama* programme seemed to be full of alert, actively involved young people.

Nearly a year later it became clear that those in charge of educational policy in this country had been attracted by what these reports are saying. The new national curriculum for teacher training will require trainee primary teachers to learn how to use interactive whole class teaching, and in particular to use 'questioning that elicits answers from which pupils' mathematical understanding can be judged'. It would of course be extremely worrying if trainee teachers were not learning how to use questioning for this purpose, but now it appears that for the first time a teaching method is being made statutory, despite promises over the past decade that the National Curriculum would prescribe knowledge, skills and concepts, but *not* teaching methods!

In the light of this development, the need to understand what exactly such methods comprise is given greater urgency. The findings of Burghes and Reynolds must make teachers return to looking critically at what it is they are doing in classrooms. If there is something in the classroom practices observed in Taiwan that makes for better learning of mathematics, we need to understand in both theoretical and practical terms what this actually is. Only in this way will there be a chance of raising children's attainment. The key may lie in a report David Reynolds and Shaun Farrell wrote:

> In Britain we have systematically reduced the constant of the teacher to maybe 20 per cent of total lesson time, and shifted the burden of learning to children and their achievement-differentiated groups . . . High-quality whole class interactive teaching – not the whole class teaching that is the mantra of some – gives children their teacher. We give children mostly themselves.
>
> (Reynolds and Farrell 1996: 4)

We can ask some simple questions about mathematics classrooms. What kind of classroom do the pupils experience? What expectations do pupils have of mathematics lessons? Do they expect to be involved and excited, or do they expect to work in isolation from a textbook or worksheet and then spend substantial amounts of time waiting to see the teacher to have their work marked? When they have time interacting with the teacher, is the teacher partly distracted by the other children waiting, or is the teacher fully engaged in the discussion? Teacher and pupils together create the culture of the classroom, its practices, its expectations, its ethos. And it is through language that this complex process is mediated.

Language and the development of the culture of the classroom

In 1969, James Britton wrote:

> We teach and teach and they learn and learn: if they didn't, we wouldn't. But of course the relation between their learning and our

teaching isn't by any means a constant one. From any bit of teaching some learn more than others: we teach some lessons when everybody seems to learn something, and other lessons when nobody seems to learn anything – at all events, not anything of what we are 'teaching'.

(in Barnes et al. 1969: 81)

There now exists a substantial body of work which analyses the complex interactions that take place between teachers and pupils and between pupils themselves, which has crucial implications for furthering our understanding of how learning takes place, and which helps give a clearer understanding of why it is we find ourselves in the situations so eloquently described by Britton. The work of Margaret Donaldson (and subsequently many others) has shown how inadequate are the ideas of Piaget in understanding how children develop their understanding (see for example Donaldson 1978). Piaget's view of the child's thinking developing mainly as a result of its direct interaction with its physical environment (in which the role of the teacher then has to be that of the creator of an appropriately rich and stimulating learning environment) fails to take into account the rich and complex role that language plays in the development of thought. Nor does it account for the importance given by young children to developing meaning out of the social situation they find themselves in. Donaldson, quoted by Davis, has shown

> how context-bound young children's thinking is. Their ability to solve problems depends on a variety of factors over and above the children's skill: the way in which problems are presented, the language used in 'testing' children, the children's interpretation of the task and the interpersonal relationship between adult and child.
>
> (Davis 1991: 23)

That this implies a very different role for the teacher and a different notion of the nature of teaching hardly needs to be spelled out.

Piaget's notion of the child as an 'egocentric' being, incapable of taking the point of view of another, has been shown to be incorrect. First and foremost the child sees itself as a social being, and its learning is mediated through the social interactions that it is immersed in. For most children, of course, these interactions operate through language:

> Thus we may say that we become ourselves through others ... Any function in the child's cultural development appears on the stage twice, first on the social plane and then on the psychological.
>
> (Vygotsky 1991: 39)

Judy Dunn, in her book *The Beginnings of Social Understanding*, has studied the way in which the social context and the way the very young child views and understands the emotional dimension of this context are crucial determinants of the extent to which learning will take place. She concludes simply:

> Children can learn very fast about rules when the context is emotionally urgent.
>
> (Dunn 1988: 173)

The insights of Vygotsky have led to many valuable analyses of children's thinking. The activities called teaching and learning take place in what he called the zone of proximal development, which he describes as being 'the distance between the actual developmental level as determined by independent problem solving and the level of potential development as determined through problem solving under adult guidance or in collaboration with more capable peers' (Vygotsky 1978: 86). Bruner (quoted in Edwards and Mercer 1987) described as 'scaffolding' the process by which the teacher helps the child to do that which, without such help, s/he would be unable to achieve. Bruner also described the process of handover, where children come to take control of learning for themselves. Translating these ideas into the reality of everyday classroom practice is far from straightforward, but there is an obvious connection between these ideas and the notion of dynamic and interactive teaching. (The extent to which it is possible to achieve this in a whole class setting is beyond the scope of this chapter.)

In *Common Knowledge* Edwards and Mercer analyse a range of observed classroom situations. They see teaching and learning as being about

> the induction of children into the academic world of knowledge and discourse inhabited by the teacher. It is a process of cognitive social-isation through discourse, a process akin at least as much to general behavioural and ideological socialisation as to the cognitive psycho-logical notions of mental growth or development.
>
> (Edwards and Mercer 1987: 155)

They indicate the difficult balancing act teachers have to perform as they struggle between the needs of society (as expressed implicitly or explicitly in the content of the curriculum) and the needs of the pupils as dynamic seekers of sense from the social, cultural and intellectual world they are immersed in. In their very detailed analysis of classroom interactions between pupils and teacher, they identify a number of ways in which the teacher attempts to retain control of the process of establishing common knowledge, of enculturing the pupils into the world of school. These include, for example, elicitation of pupils' contributions, significance markers (for example, special enunciation by the teacher to show that a word, a phrase, an idea has extra value), joint knowledge markers (using 'royal plurals' to make it clear to the pupils what is expected of them), cued elicitations (in which the teacher provides heavy clues to the information required), paraphrasing and recapitulating pupils' contributions in order to 'redefine these things as altogether neater, nicer and closer to the intended lesson plan' (Edwards and Mercer 1987: 146), and so on. At best these strategies contribute to the exploration of the pupil's zone of proximal development and the dialogue between pupil and teacher can contribute to the process of scaffolding the concept being worked on. At worst, they amount to little more than a game of *Guess what the teacher wants us to say*. Edwards and Mercer point out that such strategies can fool us. For example:

> The danger of cued elicitation is that . . . it can give a false impression of the extent to which pupils understand, and are ultimately responsible for, what they are saying and doing. It can easily mask rather than bridge the gap between teacher and child that is the basis of Vygotsky's developmental process.
>
> (Edwards and Mercer 1987: 146)

They differentiate between procedural and principled understanding:

> saying and doing what seems to be required, rather than working out a principled understanding of how and why certain actions, expressions and procedures are appropriate or correct.
>
> (Edwards and Mercer 1987: 130)

Acknowledging that 'education is inherently concerned with introducing children and adults into a pre-existing culture of thought and language' (Edwards and Mercer 1987: 157), they argue that a significant part of the problem for pupils is that much of the process remains mysterious to them:

> Pupils have to divine as best they can the unspoken and implicit ground-rules of the system, and must learn how to extract meaning from the teacher's hints and clues, how to play the classroom game. The child-centred ideology needs to be replaced with one that emphasises the socio-cultural and discursive bases of knowledge and learning . . . Some things that could usefully be explicated remain unspoken.
>
> (Edwards and Mercer 1987: 168–9)

The importance of these insights is that they give us the tools to analyse classroom interactions, and to identify the shared meanings being created through the medium of language. They allow us to see that the culture of a classroom is not a fixed immutable thing, but is subject to constant renegotiation. And they allow us to see that the nature of this culture will have a critical effect on the type and quality of the learning that takes place in the classroom.

Creating the culture of the classroom

Children expend great effort in the struggle to understand how the social context in which they are operating works. What are the rules, both explicit and implicit? Who is in charge of the rules? How much flexibility and negotiation is possible? What is the nature of the social reality in which they find themselves? Watching four-year-old children in their first few weeks of formal schooling shows how successful most of them are in grasping these issues. That they should be prepared to do this is not surprising – their 'survival' depends on it. Most do not want to be told off, but want to be accepted as part of the group, to conform. Parents are often astonished by how well their four-year-old can sit in assembly, and see levels of concentration that are rarely found outside this special context. But the child knows it is a special time, and very quickly learns what is expected.

If the culture of the classroom is a key determinant of how and what children learn, then as teachers we need to look closely at what it is we do that adds to or detracts from the culture, that makes it a more or less successful learning environment. What do children learn from being in the company of their teacher for five or more hours each day, for a thousand hours a year? How do teachers use the power and control that they have? Do they create the conditions for principled rather than procedural understanding?

Let us now return to the issue of *dynamic, interactive mathematics teaching* and consider the following exchange in a class of Year 5 and 6 children who are doing some mental arithmetic as a whole class. The examples that follow are drawn from recent observations in my own school.

Interaction	Commentary
TEACHER: What is 99 add 99? Don't call out, just have a think, OK?	*T indicates that an instant answer is not expected, that time to think is allowed. The choice of question itself is, of course, important. T clearly expects that not only is it at a suitable level for the children, but that it can lead to some interesting discussion.*
[*There is a pause of about 10 seconds. Some hands go up. Towards the end of this time some whispering starts.*]	*T indicates that this is to be private thinking time. The child who gets the answer quickly is not asked straight away. Other children are given longer to think.*
TEACHER: No, don't say anything. Thinking time. Don't even whisper.	*T stresses this point. T is indicating a type of working which he considers to be valuable – it is not competitive, but everyone is expected to join in.*

[*The pause continues for about another 10 seconds. More hands go up.*]

TEACHER: OK, let's see what you ... Jane?

JANE: 198.

TEACHER: Jane thinks it's 198. Sam?

The teacher's intonation is as flat and neutral as possible. T gives no indication as to whether Jane is right or wrong. There is still everything to play for, and the question still 'belongs' to the children. T is not yet using his authority as arbitrator of correct and incorrect answers.

SAM: 199.

TEACHER: Sam thinks 199, Jane said 198. Zoie?

Again the intonation is neutral. T sets up the possibility of doubt in children's minds. Each child will have to decide how committed s/he is to her/his answer.

ZOIE: I think it's 198.

TEACHER: OK, Zoie agrees with Jane. Now Stephen, you've been waiting, OK, now what do you make it?

T still refuses to use his authority to give correct answer.

STEPHEN: I think it's 198 as well.

[*Several more children are asked. Most say 198.*]

TEACHER: Anyone think anything else? Anyone got a different answer?

T still maintains a neutral and unstressful context in which a child could still present an alternative answer.

[*No response from children.*]

TEACHER: OK, we've had different answers ... can they all be right, or only one?

T indicates that there is an important distinction to be drawn between questions with unique answers, and those with multiple possibilities.

JO: No it's only one, it's 198.

TEACHER: OK, hands up if you agree with Jane, that it's 198.

A chance for children who might not yet have contributed to be included in the discussion.

[*Most hands go up.*]

This interaction is much more than doing a small piece of mental arithmetic. Through implicit and explicit linguistic features and also through essential para-linguistic features, the children are learning that they are expected to engage in the intellectual struggle of working towards an answer, that they will be given time to do this, that their contributions will be accepted and not be evaluated instantly, that alternatives will be sought, that mistakes are tolerated, that this question is actually worth spending valuable class time on. In this section it is the teacher who is doing almost all the teaching. The children's verbal contributions are short and limited in complexity, but behind the utterances is a degree of emotional commitment, even urgency, that arises from the refusal of the teacher to arbitrate. The observed body language of the children indicates that involvement is generally high.

The discussion now moves on to a more challenging level:

Interaction

TEACHER: OK, it's 198. Who can explain how they did it in their heads, I mean you didn't just know that it was 198, did you, it's not like knowing that 2 and 2 is 4, is it? Penny?

PENNY: Well, I said that 100 and 100 is 200 and then I took away 2 to get 198.

[On the board T writes:
100 + 100 = 200
200 − 2 = 198.]

TEACHER: Why did she take away 2?

KATHLEEN: Because each 99 is 1 less than 100.

TEACHER: OK, good, that works, is that right, Penny?

PENNY: Yes.

TEACHER: Anyone else got a different way?

JAMES: Yes, well I took 1 from one 99 and put it on the other so it's 98 and 100.

Commentary

T indicates that there is more that is of interest here, that the maths is worth looking at in its own right as pure maths. T also indicates that there are different sorts of sums – ones you just know, ones you have to calculate.

T shows a way to express symbolically the operation Penny has performed in her head.

T asks for further explanation in order to check whether other children are following.

Penny is now given the authority to arbitrate between right and wrong.

T indicates that this is a different kind of question, that alternatives are to be welcomed.

[*On the board T writes:*
    99 + 99
    98 + 100 = 198.*]

TEACHER: Like that, do you mean?   Again, T gives the child authority.
    Is that right?   Child is being told that disagreement
    with teacher is acceptable.

JAMES: Yes.
TEACHER: Hands up if you did it like
    James.
[*Some children put up hands.*]
TEACHER: Hands up if you did it   Again, ownership of the mathematics is
    Penny's way.   given back to the children.
[*Other children put up hands.*]
TEACHER: Anyone got a different   The search for alternatives is not yet
    way?   over.
TOBY: Yes I did 90 and 90 and that's
    180 and then 9 and 9 and that's
    18 and so I put them together . . .
    that's 198.
[*On the board T writes:*
    90 + 90 = 180
    9 + 9 = 18
    99 + 99 = 198.*]
TEACHER: OK?   Again, T indicates that he too can
    make mistakes and expects children to
    tell him if this happens.

TOBY: Yes.
TEACHER: Right, we've got three   T makes explicit the point of this part of
    different ways, and they all work.   the activity.
    Well done.

On another occasion the teacher might give the pen to the children and ask them to write on the board to show how they have manipulated the numbers. This would reduce the level of support given to the children, reduce the level of scaffolding that the teacher provides. The teacher would be looking to see if the children can start to make that move to the symbolic representation more independently.

There are moments in the interaction described above that depend crucially on acceptance of shared knowledge between those participating. For example, the discussion depends on the acceptance that changing the sum from 99 + 99 to 98 + 100 is a valid transformation that will not alter the final outcome. The teacher could have decided to linger on this point and to explore it in greater depth, to explore why it works, to help the children find the language to describe and explain the transformation and how it can be represented symbolically, but

69

in this particular exchange it was allowed to pass without comment. If there were children in the group who did not share this understanding, then the activity probably taught them little. The activity would be outside their zone of proximal development. We often see children making using of shared understanding and knowledge to explain and justify something. For example, a younger child would typically justify the fact that 5 add 5 makes 10 by saying 'I've got 5 fingers and 5 fingers and that's 10.' The child's statement does not *prove in a mathematical way* that 5 add 5 makes 10, but it shows that the child can relate the mathematics to knowledge that can be taken for granted and relied on to work and to be accepted by others. It is, perhaps, a different type of proof.

The example does not prove that this kind of dynamic interaction meets the needs of all the children in the class. Mathematically more able children are being encouraged to make explicit what they find relatively easy, and less able children are sharing in an exchange from which they can learn. But the teacher will have to assess whether the needs of the most able and least able are being met in this type of activity, or if adjustments to content and ways of organising the class are necessary. Are there children in the class who ought to be explaining how to do 99.9 add 99.9 in their heads?

The same teacher was observed working with a class of Year 1 children. The teacher had a rod of 10 Multilink cubes (interlocking cubes) in his hand. The rod had been made using two white cubes, two black, two white, two black, two white in order to draw attention in a very visual way to the even numbers. He told the children to watch, saying *You need to use your eyes for this sum.* He hid the rod under his jersey, and then brought back out four of the cubes. Important features of the part of the lesson described above can be seen in what follows:

Interaction	Commentary
TEACHER: How many cubes am I hiding?	*Many children clearly assumed the question would be 'How many cubes can you see?' and hands that had gone up went down. T wants the children to visualise the operation just performed.*
TEACHER: Have a think . . . don't say anything!	*Once again, thinking time is being given. A long pause follows. Hands go up. Some whispering starts, but is stopped by T. Children are observed looking at their fingers and counting.*
TEACHER: OK, what do you think, Sam?	
SAM: 6.	*T does not indicate whether this is right or wrong. Intonation and body language are carefully controlled.*
TEACHER: Charlotte?	

CHARLOTTE: It's 6.
TEACHER: Timothy?
TIMOTHY: 5.

Although this is wrong, it is accepted in exactly the same way.

[*Several more children have their say, with a variety of answers given.*]
TEACHER: OK, let's have a look and see if you got it right.
[*Remaining cubes are taken out from under T's jersey, and together they count in twos: 2 . . . 4 . . . 6.*]
TEACHER: OK, it's 6, 6 and 4 make 10. Now who can tell me the take-away sum we've done.
[*T puts the rod of 10 back together, then slowly takes off the 4 to leave the 6.*]
ALICE: 6 take away . . .
TEACHER: No, not 6 . . .

Stress on 6. T wants to draw attention to a particular aspect of formulating subtractions, and is prepared to take authority here.

ALICE: 10 take away . . . 10 take away . . . 4 . . . is . . . 10 take away 4 is 6.
TEACHER: Well done, that's right, 10 take away 4 is 6.
[*The activity is repeated several times, with careful emphasis being put on the formulation of the sum in words. On a small whiteboard, children also write down the sum using numbers. They are keen to have their turn using the special pen.*]

As Alice slowly puts the sum into words, T repeats the taking apart of the rod for the children to look at.

Two weeks later, the same activity moves much more quickly, and the teacher is now making use of questions such as *Has Chris got it right, do you think, Edward?*, thus handing over authority to the children to arbitrate on the accuracy of their ideas.

In both these exchanges, there is evidence of the teacher attempting to create (and indeed succeeding at creating) what he considers necessary aspects of the culture of a successful mathematical classroom. Through the scaffolding process evident in both examples, he is helping the children relate the activity to existing knowledge and understandings. He reacts carefully to the children's responses

71

– it goes without saying that if none of the children had been able to work out 99 + 99, the activity would have proceeded in a very different way! Within the zone of proximal development the teacher is probing for ways in which to move the children's thinking to new stages, and to find ways to help them subsequently cope with similar activities with less support.

Orton, in *Learning Mathematics*, discusses the problematic nature of teacher-led discussions. Such discussion

> often allows only the teacher to ask the questions . . . [which] are almost inevitably carefully sequenced to lead towards a defined objective . . . When pupils are allowed to ask questions of the teacher, the response given effectively kills off the likelihood of contributions from other pupils at that point . . . It is inevitable that the teacher will take up some contributions from pupils and will reject and subsequently ignore others . . . Finally, it is also inevitable that some contributions from pupils will be received in a complimentary manner by the teacher, clearly indicating that these were the correct answers, the ones the teacher wanted all along, and preventing other pupils from subsequently suggesting alternatives which might have highlighted their particular difficulties.
>
> (Orton 1992: 139–40)

This, I would suggest, is an accurate description of passive whole class teaching. The lesson extracts analysed above indicate that it is possible to be aware of the dangers that such an approach poses, and to generate through whole class (or at least large group) discussion meaningful and purposeful mathematical activity. But this can only be achieved through a clear understanding of the nature and complexity of the classroom dialogue.

Children who are exposed to approaches such as those described above come to see the types of questions being asked as normal, and soon they become part of the children's approach. Children who are asked to explain how they did sums, and who are challenged in this way, come to look for alternatives as a matter of course. Their mathematical understanding is then enriched. They have become encultured into an enquiring, active, dynamic mathematical classroom.

Conclusion

In *Investigating Mathematics Teaching* Barbara Jaworski reports on a research project looking at the way several secondary teachers from different backgrounds tackled the challenge (with varying degrees of success) of developing a classroom culture in which investigative approaches were firmly established. She comments:

> Evidence showed that an investigative approach resulted in classrooms with a very particular social ethos. The . . . teachers indicated that they

had to work hard for a significant period of time to create the ethos in which an investigative approach could succeed. Indeed, [two teachers] indicated that they had other classes with which they needed more time to achieve their goals. It is likely that without a sound basic philosophy and sufficient clarity of vision (which includes a recognition of the influence of pervading cultures), changing to an investigative approach might have little chance of success.

(Jaworski 1994: 184–5)

Jaworski has identified critical components relating to any teacher's attempts to influence the culture of their classroom: a sound basic philosophy, clarity of vision, and an understanding of the existing and pervading cultures of the school and the wider community.

We have seen above the central role that language plays in the development of the culture of the classroom and in the process of teaching and learning. Attempts to change practice in classrooms and to raise levels of attainment and understanding that do not give due attention to this central fact can only fail. Teachers who are able to interpret new initiatives of the sort discussed at the beginning of this chapter through a clear understanding of the place of language in the learning process are likely to find that their classrooms, their teaching and their pupils' learning all improve.

Acknowledgements

The author would like to thank staff and pupils of William Westley CE Primary School, Whittlesford, for their assistance in the writing of this chapter.

References

Barnes, D., Britton, J. and Rosen, H. (1969) *Language, the Learner and the School,* Harmondsworth: Penguin.

Bullock, Sir A. (1975) *A Language for Life,* London: HMSO.

Cockcroft, Dr W.H. (1982) *Mathematics Counts,* London: HMSO.

Davis, A. (1991) 'Piaget, Teachers and Education: into the 1990s', in P. Light, S. Sheldon and M. Woodhead (eds) *Learning to Think,* London: Routledge.

Donaldson, M. (1978) *Children's Minds,* London: Fontana.

Dunn, J. (1988) *The Beginnings of Social Understanding,* Oxford: Blackwell.

Edwards, D. and Mercer, N. (1987) *Common Knowledge,* London: Routledge.

Jaworski, B. (1994) *Investigating Mathematics Teaching,* London: The Falmer Press.

Orton, A. (1992) *Learning Mathematics,* London: Cassell.

Reynolds, D. (1996) 'The Truth, the Whole-Class Truth', *Times Educational Supplement,* 7 June.

Reynolds, D. and Farrell, S. (1996) *Worlds Apart? A Review of International Surveys of Educational Achievement involving England,* London: HMSO.

Vygotsky, L.S. (1978) *Mind in Society: the Development of Higher Psychological Processes*, London: Harvard University Press.
Vygotsky, L.S. (1991) 'Genesis of the Higher Mental Functions', in P. Light, S. Sheldon and M. Woodhead (eds) *Learning to Think*, London: Routledge.

5

WHO'S ASKING THE QUESTIONS?

Year 4 pupils extend their question and answer skills while studying the Tudors

Noelle Hunt and Caroline Luck

Pay attention! Listen carefully! I'm going to ask you some questions.

> In the classroom, who asks questions at an average rate of one every twelve seconds? Yes, perhaps a little uneasily, we should all have our hands up as we know the answer to be ourselves – the teachers. Not only do teachers take the major role in asking questions, but these tend to be low-level questions which only require recall of factual information.
>
> (Reid et al. 1989: 53)

We all acknowledge the importance of acquiring factual information as a base on which to build further learning; but for that learning to be applied usefully, creatively and effectively, individuals must also develop investigative skills and the confidence to explore and argue ideas. This chapter gives an account of a history project with Year 4 pupils which aimed to shift the emphasis away from traditional question and answer sessions towards providing opportunities, in varied contexts, for children to practise and develop their own expertise to phrase questions, respond appropriately to the questions of others and make statements. Our objectives are briefly summarised below.

We wanted our pupils to develop their skills in the following areas:

- asking appropriate questions, either 'open' or 'closed' according to the learning context, in order to gain maximum information from any given task;
- devising questions which keep in mind the intended objective and diverge only where it is useful to do so;
- following a line of questioning, i.e. predicting responses and phrasing a series of questions which solve a problem;

- articulating clear and appropriate responses to questions and, in writing, constructing answers that are written in well punctuated sentences;
- using the information gained from question and answer activities to complete other tasks which may include representing this information in a variety of ways.

These clearly focused language objectives sat neatly within a historical topic about the Tudors. Activities were planned which presented pupils with new information and this was subsequently reinforced through discussion, negotiation and further investigation. In planning to work in this way we had high expectations of our pupils and their potential to develop questioning skills both in writing and in speaking and listening. With Irena Cassar we assert that our children 'are capable of making valid choices about their own learning and setting their own questions' (quoted in Brierly et al. 1992: 227).

Our working relationship as class teacher and language support teacher was most important to the success of the project. Planning time, as always, was limited so it was helpful that we brought to the task shared ideals and understandings as well as the beneficial experience of previous collaboration which included work with the same class. A shared sense of humour was also an asset!

In planning our project, we did not imagine that a *laissez-faire* approach, where we sat back, hoped for the best and let the children take the floor, would be successful. It sounds simple: stop asking so many questions and see if the children ask correspondingly more. But, as with any language skill, the teaching needs at some stage to be quite specific. What is important is the context in which the skill is taught and the opportunities provided for purposeful reinforcement. However, consideration of contexts and opportunities would be pointless if the classroom ethos was not conducive to supporting this shift in relationship between pupils and teachers. Children must feel safe to venture opinions, to take risks with their ideas and be confident to challenge and question others. As far as possible, we felt that the Year 4 classroom did indeed offer a safe climate for children to talk but we were always aware of the limiting social factors to which Laura Brierly refers: 'children exposing their thinking to a powerful and possibly judgmental adult . . . as well as a demanding and potentially critical peer group' (Brierly et al. 1992: 234). Even the best-intentioned adult can sometimes be unpredictable in responding to a pupil. Not every child feels confident to take the risk despite encouragement. We work hard to make a class group gel but it would be unrealistic to expect children not to show occasional intolerance towards each other. Our reaction to these problems is what matters.

A history topic seemed a good choice through which to encourage investigative skills. Children are introduced at an early age to the difference between fact and opinion and issues relating to the reliability of evidence. Undisputed facts provide a backbone of knowledge which is fleshed out by evaluation of different sources of opinion. Children enjoy playing the part of historical detectives, seeking clues to people and places from the past. In half a term of work, we planned our collaborative teaching (one session a week) to cover those main aspects of Tudor history identified in the National Curriculum. The core of our planning included a profile of Henry VIII, six great Tudor explorers, ways of life in town and country, houses great and small, a skim through Elizabeth I and the Armada and a taste of Shakespeare. Quite often, the work planned for Monday afternoons served as reinforcement for information introduced at other history sessions in the timetable.

Near the beginning of the project we planned to include a visit to Knebworth House, near Stevenage in Hertfordshire, an historic house originating from the Tudor period and not too far away from school. Although it is now greatly altered, it still includes many original features and offers educational visits for schools. We hoped that by planning the visit at the start of the project rather than at the end, as is more often the case, it would inspire, motivate and stimulate the children to investigate this period of history with heightened awareness.

Organising activities

Having agreed on the length of the project, the number of sessions, shared responsibilities and a clear underlying focus, we tried to construct a programme of work which would fulfil our original aims and objectives. A basic principle was that each session would explore and develop a specific type of language usage in a way that was inspirational rather than prescriptive and predictable. Our intention was that every pupil would have an opportunity to participate and develop skills as an historian. We also decided that one of us would be responsible for the preparation and initial delivery of each session and the other would take on a supportive role. In reality we worked so well together that these distinctions were often blurred!

Week 1

Generating ideas/finding out

This aims to give pupils the opportunity to look at historical evidence at first hand. They will bring something old from home as a basis for considering types of questions used to find out about the past. We will also look at a variety of artefacts in this session and ask pupils to consider questions of what counts as historical evidence. Pupils will think of questions to ask during the visit to Knebworth House which would be helpful in finding out more about the Tudor period. After the visit, a follow-up session will allow pupils to examine the results of their questions.

Week 2

Using language to explore ideas

This session will follow on from the knowledge gained from the Knebworth House visit to look at ways of life in town and country. Both teachers will use role play, one as a rich and the other as a poor Tudor, and 'hot-seating'. The children will be asked to think of different types of questions before the hot-seating. These activities will allow pupils to develop questioning techniques following a line of enquiry which does not rely on yes/no answers and from which they can gain most information. Pupils will then play the *Rich Man, Poor Man* game to practise categorising statements about Tudor life, carefully considering the criteria contained in each one and deciding whether it best fits *rich/country*, *poor/country*, *rich/town*, *poor/town*. From this information, pupils will write *A Day in the Life of* . . . (suitable Tudor name to be chosen by each pupil). They will use a simple planning sheet for guidance.

Week 3

Using language to research

Pupils will be divided into groups, each group choosing from a list of six explorers. (Choices range from Christopher Columbus, familiar to most of us from school days, to the less well-known Estevanico, a North African adventurer who accompanied expeditions to Florida and the Gulf of Mexico.) Given an information sheet about the explorer, members of the group will find out six key facts to pass to another group. The second group's task is to formulate questions for which the facts fit as answers. Questions and answers are then returned to the original group.

Weeks 4 and 5

Using language to plan, hypothesise and design

Each group is to be given the task of devising a game which incorporates all the information gained during the preceding session. There will be whole class discussion about the different facets which a game might include as well as suggestions for making the game both interesting and enjoyable. All pupils will be given the same A3-sized base board, divided into squares, on which will be drawn an explorer's ship (product of a previous art session). Members of each group collaborate to plan a game including considering the form it could take and the jobs which it will involve for each pupil. Specific responsibilities within the group will be legitimised by a mini-contract which each member has to sign. Games will be produced, played, evaluated by other groups and, if necessary, revised.

Week 6

Using language to generate/explore ideas

This session will introduce the pupils to William Shakespeare and some of his work. They will watch A *Midsummer Night's Dream*,[1] analyse and discuss the style of language used, and work in groups of four to devise a short playlet of about two minutes in length to include some kind of magic and transformation scene (in response to Bottom et al. in the *Dream*). The playlets will be performed and shared.

Week 7

Using language to question/research/report

This final session should help us assess the skills we have been trying to develop in our pupils. Using the 'jigsaw' collaborative learning technique, pupils will be initially organised into 'Home' groups then reorganised into 'Expert' groups, each set up to provide information on one aspect of the life of Henry VIII.[2]

Expert groups will have a set of statements to consider and decide whether they are true or false. An answer sheet will help each group to check responses and reorganise statements if necessary. Experts then return to Home groups to help compile a profile sheet of Henry VIII.

Focus on the pupils

With the programme of work planned we began to consider groupings that would work together successfully. We wanted as much interaction between as many pupils as possible in order to increase their opportunities to ask and respond to each other, so it was essential that we created the best possible mixes. Inevitably we had the usual considerations which occur in most primary classrooms: there were children we knew would work well together, those who would be likely to disrupt others, those who would be too dominant and those, perhaps through natural reticence, who would sit back and let others do all the work. The children were already seated in mixed-ability groups; but for paired work we considered partnerships which would be mutually supportive, giving scope for individual contributions. For the jigsawing activity, we chose one group leader from each table group who was a fluent reader and not too dominant within the group.

We decided to focus the development of our work on ten key pupils and monitor their progress at each stage. These pupils represent a cross-section of the class in which this work has been focused.

Douglas[3] is a quiet, reserved boy who is always willing to try an activity. He is less confident in reading and writing but he has a good general knowledge and is offered a wealth of valuable experiences at home. When prompted and encouraged he can be quite articulate.

Anna has a bright and bubbly nature which is apparent in any task she undertakes. Anyone who works with her cannot fail to find her enthusiasm catching. She is happy to work on her own or share her ideas with others. Anna will work supportively with any other member of the class. During the course of this project, she once volunteered to work with an early-phase beginner bilingual because she felt she could help.

Michael is a bright, capable boy whose achievements are limited by his severe behavioural problems. He finds concentration difficult and is easily distracted when not himself distracting others. Working individually or in groups is virtually impossible for him but, with a carefully chosen partner, he has produced some excellent work. This was to prove the case when he and a partner produced an imaginative explorers' game and similar successes have been observed in other areas of the curriculum.

Darryl is an enthusiastic and sensitive boy who particularly enjoys science and maths. He has fixed ideas about what he wants to do and finds it hard to tolerate the views of others if they do not conform with his own. On one occasion, during group working, we were surprised to find Darryl reduced to tears when the other members did not agree with him. Adult intervention was needed to resolve the situation.

Sadia is a bilingual pupil who speaks Punjabi as her first language. When spoken to she initially appears to understand what has been asked of her. However, if questioned more persistently, she clams up and will not answer at all. Strong-willed by nature, if she has decided not to speak, she cannot be persuaded otherwise. Recently we have devised the tactic of asking her a question, waiting for a response and, if none is forthcoming, explaining that we will return to her in a few minutes by which time we would expect some kind of a response. This works quite well and seems to prevent her feeling threatened by having to give an immediate answer.

Rachel is supportive of all who work with her. Capable of asserting herself in discussion, she is equally receptive to the ideas of others. She is mature in her approach to her work and to both adults and other pupils in school. She can hold caring and thoughtful conversations. Rachel proved to have the qualities of an excellent group leader in several of the planned activities.

Susan appears a quiet girl who, unless prompted, would be happy to let life pass her by in the classroom. When assigned to a group whose members were similarly quiet, she showed she could take the lead when necessary. Susan speaks Cantonese as her first language.

Rosheen, a moderately fluent bilingual pupil, has recently joined the class having attended three other schools in a comparatively short period. She is very willing to try but often misunderstands what is expected of her. She needs instructions to be repeated on an individual basis. She has specific learning difficulties and receives both learning and language support.

Finally, **Mustapha** is a capable boy whom a teacher needs to make a point of including. Fluently bilingual, he has a good vocabulary in English and is very articulate but tends to opt out if given the chance.

A step back in time

Most teachers who work with primary-aged children appreciate the enthusiasm and spontaneity their pupils can bring to work in the classroom. Before the half-term holiday, in preparing for our topic on the Tudors, we had asked our pupils to bring something to school which they considered as historical evidence. We suggested examples such as old books, photographs, coins and so forth. That first Monday morning, we were delighted when about two thirds of the class streamed excitedly through the door tightly clutching something treasured from home! Everyone wanted to explain immediately:

This was special to my mum because . . .

My uncle sent my auntie this letter in the war . . .

My grandma kept this to remind her of . . .

My friend found this Tudor coin in London Colney . . .

The level of response exceeded all expectations and we certainly considered the preparation session before half-term as time well spent! This initial level of enthusiasm created a positive and receptive ethos in the class towards the Tudors topic, and generally this was maintained throughout the course of the project.

With all our historical evidence in front of us, we began by sitting in a large circle. (The children are used to doing this as we put a strong focus on Circle Time sessions in this class.) Each pupil and teacher had the opportunity to tell others about what they had brought and why. They could then ask questions of each other. This prompted some discussion of which types of questions gained most useful information and allowed us to encourage individuals to pursue lines of enquiry about those artefacts which they found of particular interest.

Following on from this, we asked children to prepare questions to ask at Knebworth House. We acknowledged that this was a difficult task when few (if any) pupils had prior experience of visiting Tudor houses, but perseverance in the form of adult support and paired and whole group discussion yielded at least one question from each pupil.

What next?

One of the advantages of hot-seating the teacher (or teachers) is that they have some control over the information imparted and, if sufficiently skilful in their responses, can steer their pupils towards asking more appropriate questions. Prior research is important, especially as some pupils need no prompting to ask quite searching questions. One of us was once caught out in role as Christopher Columbus by not being more diligent in finding out his domestic set-up. Having denied being married, a fudged response was called for when an accusatory questioner asserted that she had read about his wife in a book! However, as an imaginary rich and poor Tudor, we were not quite so vulnerable. By this stage of the project, several pupils were doing extra research at home, which was evident during the role play exercise.

In the *Rich Man, Poor Man* game we used the base board shown in Figure 5.1.

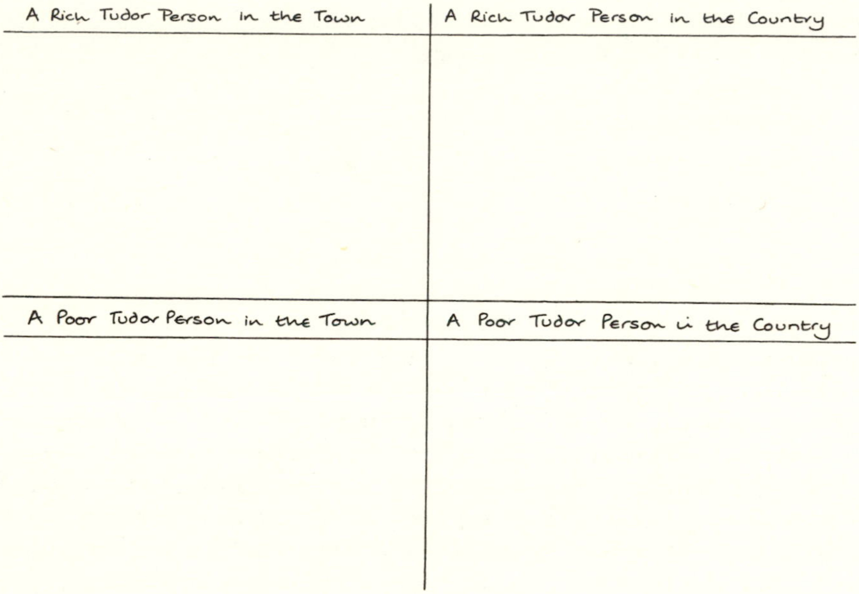

A Rich Tudor Person in the Town	A Rich Tudor Person in the Country
A Poor Tudor Person in the Town	A Poor Tudor Person in the Country

Figure 5.1 Base board for *Rich Man, Poor Man* game

Pupils, in small groups, were given statements to consider and place in the appropriate squares. Some could fit in more than one place, which encouraged further discussion. All of this was intended to stimulate ideas for writing *A Day in the Life of . . .* , for which the planning sheet in Figure 5.2 was used.

Having completed the plan, the pupils, who had chosen suitable Tudor names and lifestyles, were asked to write a sequenced account of a typical day. We made some suggestions of ways to start the writing in the hope of avoiding a glut of *One*

A Day in the Life of.........

Tudor Name : _____

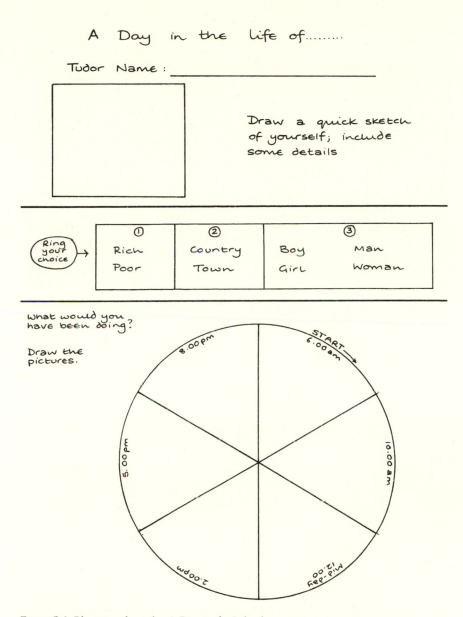

Draw a quick sketch of yourself; include some details

Ring your choice →

①	②		③
Rich	Country	Boy	Man
Poor	Town	Girl	Woman

What would you have been doing?

Draw the pictures.

8.00 pm

START 6.00 am

5.00 pm

10.00 am

2.00 pm

Mid-night 12.00

Figure 5.2 Planning sheet for A Day in the Life of . . . game

day . . . and *Once upon a time* . . . As always, some pupils followed our suggestions very closely while others extended them.

From the following week we changed tack (to borrow a nautical term) to research Tudor-age explorers and their intrepid sea voyages. We had collected as many books on the subject as possible but, though some books are well illustrated and simply presented, others available had too many features which could deter less experienced readers. In consideration of this we prepared information sheets on six explorers with a glossary on each to explain unfamiliar words. Exploration in the Tudor Age had been discussed elsewhere in the timetable so our introduction to this session was quite brief. Pupils, in groups of four, were asked to write six statements of key facts about their chosen explorer. The emphasis was on *key facts* and not on copying large chunks of information from the sheet. Having swapped with another group, the task was then to devise questions for which each statement would fit as an answer. These were then returned to the original groups as the basis on which to devise a game. We have already briefly described how pupils went about this task but it is useful to point out that each group's mini-contract proved a good device for ensuring that all pupils shared some responsibility in the process and that each job identified was important to the completion of the whole. For the teachers, it provided a useful checklist to ensure every pupil remained on task (see Figure 5.3).

After two weeks of producing games, we devoted one whole session to William Shakespeare. We found the BBC 'Animated Tales' version of *A Midsummer Night's Dream* an invaluable resource and the outcomes of this session are more fully described later on.

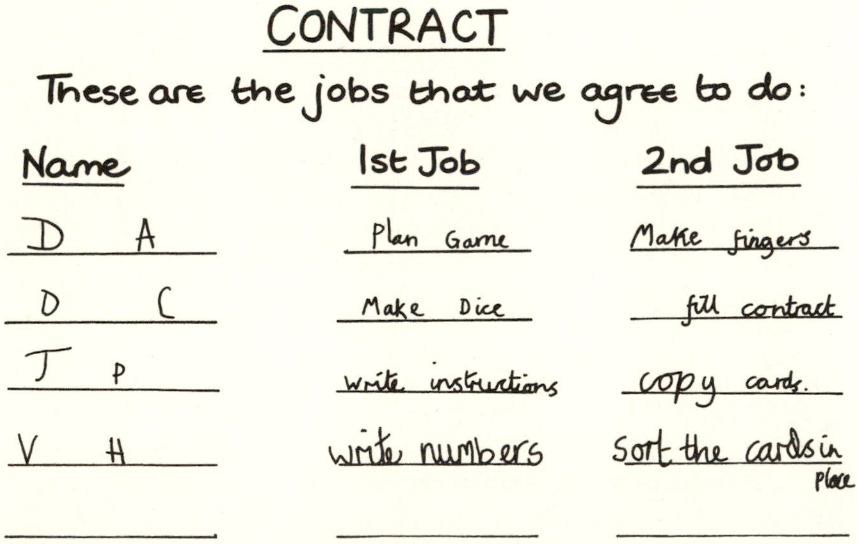

CONTRACT

These are the jobs that we agree to do:

Name	1st Job	2nd Job
D A	Plan Game	Make fingers
D C	Make Dice	fill contract
J P	write instructions	copy cards.
V H	write numbers	Sort the cards in place

Figure 5.3 Contract to keep pupils on task

To bring several strands of the topic together and to serve as a form of assessment, we planned the last session carefully so that we could observe how pupils' techniques for questioning had developed. This involved allowing for small group discussions in which we could participate only as attentive observers. We found that jigsawing the groups provided an impressive strategy for achieving these aims.

Outcomes

We have already described the range of ability within the class and other factors which contribute to the diversity of the group. We had to consider the needs of a near-beginner bilingual as well as other bilingual pupils who are moderately fluent in English. We also needed to take account of the range of pupils in the class – some confident, articulate pupils and a few showing below-average achievement, including one boy with special educational needs, another with emotional and behavioural problems and a third with dyspraxia. In short, the class represents the range of achievement typical of many primary classes. In evaluating the outcomes of this project we recognised that its range of achievements would be correspondingly wide. While we could certainly make general comments relating to the whole class it is important, and illuminating, to identify individual successes. In this, we also include our own learning experiences, for example finding new strategies to cope with the unexpected. Focusing our observations throughout the project on ten particular children highlighted their individual progress and raised issues relevant to the whole class.

In the first session pupils were faced with two main tasks; the first supported by handling and looking at real objects and the second, more abstract discussion in preparation for the trip to Knebworth House. The combination of these two tasks reinforced the concept of historical evidence and pupils were asked to glean as much information as possible from the evidence they had. This provided a good opportunity to consider whether open or closed questions would be more useful. In looking at old objects brought from home, **Martin** and **Rachel** quickly latched on to the idea of asking questions which prompted a 'story' from each owner. They realised that *Is it . . . ?* invariably led to *yes/no/don't know* answers whereas *Why is it . . . ?* yielded a more satisfying response. We were pleased to see that these two, among a few others, had remembered related discussion from a previous research project. A small number of the group, including **Sadia, Susan** and **Rosheen**, sat quietly and unobtrusively. This was not untypical. Other pupils were keen to try phrasing what one described as 'suitable questions' but were obviously anxious about the form of words need to gain the intended response. Sometimes we would interject by giving a statement and suggesting pupils work back to the question but, at this stage, it proved a skill beyond many of them. Our general observation was that when using artefacts as prompts for investigation many questions were woolly and undefined, some perhaps hastily phrased without predicting what kind of response was likely.

As may be expected, preparing questions prior to the Knebworth House trip was still harder as many pupils had too little prior experience to draw upon. We still felt it was a useful exercise as it helped to focus pupils' thinking. Those who did pluck up courage to ask their questions of the guide during the house tour were generally good at noting responses. Pupils especially favoured information giving facts and figures. As we progressed from room to room, one enthusiastic boy thoroughly tested a tour guide by requesting the birth and death dates of every Lytton forebear, which he noted down assiduously.

By our second session together, the pupils had been able to digest their experience of Knebworth House and had also done some work on the lives of rich and poor people in Tudor times. Firmly reversing our traditional roles in question and answer sessions, we prepared ourselves to be hot-seated. This time we were pleased to find that more of the class wanted to participate and that we were put on the spot with some quite thoughtful questions. We were glad that our planning was sufficiently flexible (deliberate when experimenting with new ideas) to allow the oracy work to continue for most of the session. Each pupil had the opportunity to ask a question and sufficient time beforehand to prepare it. This encouraged some of our quiet minority to take part. Initially, **Rosheen** misunderstood the task, probably because her level of fluency in English often demands individual reinforcement of instructions. She thought she had to answer, not ask, questions but, when it was explained again to her she was happy to volunteer the first question. **Susan** needed some prompting but given the single word *clothes* as a suggestion was able to phrase a useful question. When, after the role play, one of us asked how more could have been found out about family life, she suggested asking 'Are you married?' A good step forward. **Mustapha** also contributed a question when his turn came up but **Sadia** posed a problem. Moderately fluent in English, she has no problems with the everyday social demands of the language; in fact, she can be quite talkative especially when she is not supposed to be! However, as previously stated, she often resists all attempts and encouragement to make her answer teacher questions even when we are certain that she understands the question and knows the answer. We had already decided, in the interests of developing these important language skills, that we did not want to give children an opt-out clause from any activity. We aimed to encourage every child to contribute something, however tentative, when called upon to do so. Sadia remained stubbornly resistant. We could not decide whether there was a language problem, a lack of confidence peculiar to this kind of activity or whether this was attention-seeking behaviour, not unusual for Sadia in other class contexts. We presumed that she did not like to be put on the spot and tried the strategy of giving her warning that we would come back to her for a contribution after a couple of minutes. This worked well and, when we returned to her, she immediately asked 'How did you wash your clothes in Tudor times?', later followed by 'What do you like eating?' A breakthrough and a worthwhile strategy which has proved successful in other sessions. It should also be noted that Sadia often provided first language support to the beginner bilingual girl in the class. She coped very well with this considering that they did not share a perfect language match and were also not personality types who would naturally come together. We tried not to presume on Sadia too often to support this other girl. At a later session, we were grateful for the support of a bilingual classroom assistant.

As a counter-balance to intense questioning in the first part of the session, pupils enjoyed forming into groups to play the *Rich Man, Poor Man* game which was devised by Caroline and successfully used in another school. In considering where to put each statement, it was rewarding to hear groups arguing quite vociferously as pupils sought to justify ideas and disagree with those of others, sometimes politely, sometimes less so. One or two groups managed a more refined and reasoned discussion. This kind of activity throws up another skill: learning to be assertive while tolerating the opinions of others. The *A Day in the Life of* . . . writing activity which followed was very successful. Some pupils produced personal bests in terms of well-sequenced extended accounts. Several thoughtful contributions reflected the information derived from our role play.

Two sessions followed (and a few finishing-off slots at other times!), when pupils devised questions from given statements and decided how to incorporate these questions and answers about explorers into an informative and enjoyable game. At this point **Darryl**, who had earlier contributed thoughtful questions to whole group activities, showed that he had problems. He had very set ideas about how to make a game and was happy to collaborate only so far as others agreed with him. When dissent arose, he was quickly tearful and accused others of not listening to him. Careful teacher intervention was necessary to resolve any upsets. A clear division of tasks legitimised by the written contract was helpful and Darryl proved more tolerant as his group's game took shape. A turning point (no pun intended) was when he was able to show the other children how to use a pair of compasses. **Susan**, assigned to a group where we had deliberately put quiet but capable children, surprised us by taking the lead, firmly and competently organising the others. By contrast, the week following, she was badly affected by hay fever and took barely any interest at all. **Michael**, so often disruptive in carpet sessions, was inspired by the thought of making a game. A bright boy, he brought excellent ideas to a game which was quite different to the usual 'throw the dice and move round the board' variety. He was so motivated that he not only stayed on task but was also happy to support his weaker partner and together they produced a game of which they were both very proud.

The facility to argue a case and discuss options is often under-represented in the curriculum (Woods 1996: 51). We felt that as well as reinforcing essential language skills like arguing and discussing, small group collaborative working addresses a wider range of individual needs than is possible in whole class activities.

It was generally noticeable that the children were becoming more skilled in the art of argument and all its essential attributes. As we circulated among groups, we heard pupils being assertive, persuasive, posing questions and solving problems. A rather indistinct tape recording of one session identified some examples of question starters now being used:

When was he . . . ?

Well, what question can you think of?

How about . . . ?

What about . . . ?

What one . . . ?

What do you mean . . . ?

Pupils were now demanding specific information and putting forward ideas. They were more successful because they were more often asking focused relevant questions. **Rachel** entered into lively debate with **Martin** over where START should be. Should it be at the edge of the board or in the centre? This was the gist of it. **Mustapha**, a quiet member of the group, did not enter into the discussion but always listens carefully to talk around him and, when prompted, often surprises us with his profound comments and extensive vocabulary. Collaborative working allows **Anna** to shine as a bubbly supportive team member. In a later session, she volunteered to work with the beginner bilingual pupil in order to help her as much as possible. **Douglas**, who is less confident, finds small group work a more supportive forum in which to share his thoughtful ideas. After three sessions, the games were completed, with tempting titles like *The Great Shipwreck*, *Ropes and Ladders*, *Tudor Marines*, and ready to play.

And now for something completely different

We now wanted to give the children just a taste of Shakespeare. Our aim, as earlier described, was to ensure the session was sufficiently enjoyable for the children to gain some insight and enthusiasm for the Bard now, but not so intense that they were put off returning to him when they were older. Here we found the 'Animated Tales' a real boon. Not too long with plenty of cartoon effects, the annotated version of *A Midsummer Night's Dream* proved quite captivating. The children particularly enjoyed the mischievous exploits of Puck, Bottom transformed as an ass and the plight of the star-crossed lovers. Even eight- and nine-year-olds enjoy romance. After the video, the children were so appreciative and interested that the discussion (with far more questions coming from them than from us!) went on longer than we intended. They wanted to know about the change in language use and were amused at how 'poppet' was once a term of abuse. **Darryl** was particularly interested in the language of

Shakespeare and later attempted a snippet of his own in the improvisations that followed: 'And behold . . .' Shakespeare was variously described as 'exciting', 'very imaginative' and (from **Mustapha**) his writing was very 'describable'. A wonderful word!

Pupils spent the rest of the session working on their own improvisations. Nearly all showed key features from the Shakespeare play they had been shown. Regrouped following the three previous sessions, they worked very well in the limited time available to prepare their scenes. There was very little dissent and they showed themselves much more ready to listen to each other's ideas. After some rehearsal time, they were given five minutes to work in groups and suggest ways of making improvements. They were more than happy to do this and it was quite difficult to stop the discussions when it was time to perform. Putting magic drops into people's eyes to bewitch them proved popular, as did a Puck-like character weaving mischief in a number of settings. In an all-boy group, one actor caricatured the part of a girl in a lovers' scene, little realising how authentic that would have been in Shakespeare's day.

What did we learn?

Our final session was intended as an assessment of many of the skills we had been working to improve. We found it quite a challenge to plan something so all-embracing and decided on the jigsawing strategy to ensure that every pupil would have a role to play as an Expert. The activities and groups were all organised as described earlier in the chapter and we were initially despondent about the likely outcomes on a day in the last week of term which proved to be the hottest and stickiest so far. Despite a very fidgety, wriggly start, we were delighted that the class responded very well and became absorbed in the activity. Even so, one Home group was disadvantaged by having a sulky Expert who refused to divulge any of her knowledge. Her group was left with a significant gap on its Henry VIII profile sheet. On that hot day she was beyond caring but the peer group pressure might, in other circumstances, have been enough to have brought her round.

Another group had to sort Henry VIII's wives into the order in which he married them. Each statement contained clues which required a logical approach to order them correctly. Here we were testing real detective work – following a line of enquiry! It was rewarding to hear questions start like this:

If we put Anne Boleyn second where will . . .

If Jane Seymour goes there can we . . .

Logical discussion achieved the correct result, which was confirmed by one child who remembered the old rhyme: 'Divorced, beheaded, died, divorced, beheaded, survived.' A good show of initiative.

Other groups had to organise statements into two piles, those they thought were false and those they considered true. More lively discussion ensued. Could it really be possible that Greenwich Palace had a toilet so large it could seat 28 people at once or was it more likely that it had two small toilets outside somewhere? They quickly decided on the latter. **Michael** read 'Henry VIII was tall and handsome when he was young' and proclaimed that that was a matter of opinion, not a fact. Eventually, despite the heat, groups had made good progress in compiling profiles of Henry VIII and, apart from the one exception, everyone had been actively involved.

The term has ended now and we can stand back to consider what has been achieved. We know that we have made progress with individual pupils; the reticent children are generally less so, the intolerant children generally more tolerant. These kinds of outcomes are always hard to quantify as they relate to personality and behaviour which can be unpredictable and certainly varies according to context. However, we can say with confidence that most pupils now ask better questions; they know that there is more to asking questions than just starting sentences with *who, what, why* etc. and ending with a question mark. As teachers we know that the art of questioning is a powerful tool in deepening knowledge and understanding, and perhaps these pupils are just beginning to see that for themselves. Next term, with the new Year 4, we will try to be more conscious of who asks the questions, when and how often!

Acknowledgements

We should like to thank all staff at Reddings CP School, Hemel Hempstead, for their support and Elaine Green of Tudor JMI School, Hemel Hempstead for her help with the original *Rich Man, Poor Man* activity.

Notes

1 The version of A *Midsummer Night's Dream* that we showed the children was contained in the 'Animated Tales' video produced by the BBC.
2 'Jigsawing' is a group-work technique which involves children switching from 'Expert' to 'Home' groups to share information. It is explained in greater detail in The National Oracy Project (1990) *Teaching Talking and Learning in Key Stage 2*, York: National Curriculum Council.
3 Pupil names have been changed to protect confidentiality.

References

Woods, C. (1996) 'The Creative and the Critical – Argument Reconsidered', *English in Education* 30 (2), pp. 50–6, National Association for the Teaching of English.

Brierly, L., Cassar, I., Loader, P., Norman, K., Shantry, I., Wolfe, S. and Wood, D. (1992) 'No, We Ask You Questions', in K. Norman (ed.) *Thinking Voices*, London: Hodder and Stoughton.

Reid, J.A., Forrestal, P. and Cook, J. (1989) *Small Group Learning in the Classroom*, Perth, Australia: Chalkface Press.

6

RIGHTS AND RESPONSIBILITIES

Persuasive language and points of view

Claire Saunders

Few teachers would question the assertion that talk is a valuable tool in developing children's learning. At least, I never have – in theory. Yet in practice I am only too aware of how often I may have stifled talk in my classroom as the clock ticked away and the pressure to produce required written work dissolved all my good intentions. Thus, when my scheme of work challenged me 'to develop persuasive language and debate' with my class of Year 6 children I determined to explore fully the value of talk in the classroom. Here was an opportunity to consider how effectively carefully planned talk activities might both challenge the children and move them on in their understanding.

At Key Stage 2 the National Curriculum Programme of Study for Speaking and Listening demands that children 'should be encouraged to qualify or justify what they think after listening to other opinions or accounts, and deal politely with other points of view' (Department for Education 1995: 11). In its Programme of Study for Writing, we note that children should be 'taught to use the characteristics of . . . eg argument in their writing' (ibid.: 15).

Hidden in these almost throwaway lines is a huge challenge. For if we truly develop these aspects of our children's learning, we will be doing immeasurably more than fulfilling National Curriculum requirements. What we will be about is developing children who are critical thinkers, who can assimilate a range of points of view, reach their own informed conclusions and clearly communicate their own opinions in both spoken and written form. Critical thinkers shape societies; we are about nothing less than this.

This is a long-term ideal. At Key Stage 2, we need to reach the children where they are now, to develop in them these skills of critical thinking by finding contexts that relate to them in a very real way. Both the projects I undertook with the children to try to develop persuasive language and debate provided such a context. First we considered the issue of school uniform, discussing, debating and recording the different points of view. Second, we considered smoking, and ways of persuading peers and parents to never take up, or to give up, smoking. Both issues were underpinned by the moral question of rights and responsibilities

– who has the right to decide what children should wear to school, what rights do smokers and non-smokers have? Two different written outcomes were planned – a piece of discussion writing which assimilated opposing points of view from the school uniform work, and a piece of purely persuasive writing aimed at a specific audience from the work on smoking.

Whilst the written outcomes of the work were somewhat different, there were some important common elements in the two projects:

- an issue with which the children could clearly identify;
- a series of structured talk activities, which characterised both the pre-writing and the writing stages;
- written outcomes which were an integral part of, but not the sole purpose of, the work.

The great school uniform debate

My key objective was that the children should be able to analyse the arguments for and against school uniform. I planned two outcomes of this work: a piece of discussion writing weighing up both sides of the argument; and a whole class debate on the issue, with speakers for and against the motion *This house is in favour of school uniform.*

I hoped that, by the time a piece of writing was required from the children, it would be seen by them not as an end product – the debate was that – but as another way of presenting the issues. I wanted to give the children the opportunity to present both sides of the argument for two reasons. First of all, to allow the issues to be clear in their heads ready for the debate; anyone who can understand another's point of view has a greater chance of successfully challenging an opponent in debate. Second, to enable me to assess the depth of the children's understanding of the key issues.

Preparation – the modelling of adults

Initial discussions revealed that the children could identify a whole host of arguments against the wearing of school uniform (we had recently been doing some work on children's rights, and they were keen to express their right to decide what clothes they wanted to wear!). At this stage it became obvious that more information was needed to develop the discussion and provide a balanced view.

We talked about the people who might be in favour of school uniform, and identified the head and deputy and parents as likely supporters. Here was an issue where we had no information books to turn to. Our source of information was adults to whom we had easy access. And so began a project which demonstrated the power of talk in generating ideas for writing.

We began our research into the various arguments by each child talking at home with their parents about the arguments for and against school uniform. Two results emerged from this work. The children returned to school with many of their arguments against school uniform clarified and developed. I suspect that the opportunity to present their own thoughts in the safe and familiar context of a conversation with a known adult was one which allowed the development of ideas. Many of the parents supplied their children with a range of arguments in favour of school uniform. The children's thinking had been challenged as they began to consider issues of expense, peer group pressure to be 'trendy' in casual clothes and so on. One child's father wrote down the argument 'no financial discrimination' under the column in favour of uniform. This child had asked his father to explain the phrase, and was able to communicate this to the rest of the class. At this very early stage the use of language was becoming more sophisticated, and appropriate to the task. The parent had modelled a use of language which his child had taken on board. And so the children's learning began to develop.

A brainstorm of the main arguments for and against school uniform which followed these parental interviews showed just how much further forward was the children's understanding of the key issues.

However, because many of the children had presented similar points we needed to refine the brainstorm until we were satisfied that we had clarified the key arguments. The ensuing class discussion was essentially a redrafting activity. But, because the writing aspect was my responsibility the children were free to explore and refine their ideas, speaking them out loud and redrafting them until they sounded right. There was a very real purpose to this activity – we needed a summary of the key arguments, expressed in easily accessible language, to refer to throughout the remainder of the work. I wanted the children to be immersed in the arguments, able to express them in their own words, and understand the counter-arguments for each statement – all this before any writing took place.

Developing the argument – the use of role play

In the informal context of a drama session, the children took on the task of role-playing proponents of the opposing sides of the debate. In the initial stages these role plays took the form of simple reiterations of two unrelated arguments, but this soon developed into challenging an argument with a related, but opposing viewpoint – and diverting the opponent with new arguments when the going got tough.

Some of the conventional language of debate began to emerge quite naturally from this work. This language came from the children as they got to grips with the genre, and my role was to support their use of language with further examples of appropriate vocabulary, and discussion about the formal register of the language; we discussed the appropriateness of the word 'kids' in the context of the discussion, and it was soon replaced with 'children'.

The class were fired up now, and plans were made to interview the head and deputy to establish their views. All the children were involved in drawing up and agreeing the questions for interview, and I talked with the chosen 'interviewers' about being prepared to present their anti-uniform stance in order to challenge their interviewees. Armed with tape recorder and interview questions they set about their task with more than a mild attack of nerves. The results of the interviews showed how rapidly the nerves evaporated once the task was under way. These children knew the arguments inside out; we had discussed them in a range of contexts, refining them as we went. The children were now more than a match for their adult interviewees.

What follows is a transcription of part of the taped interviews. Both the head and deputy were asked the same set of questions, and the children's analysis of the results gave them a fascinating insight into the ways in which debate can be shaped and developed.

JOHN: One of our arguments is that school uniform is too expensive. What is your opinion?

MR M: Well, it's no more expensive than having to wear other clothes which can often wear out just as easily. At least with school uniform you know exactly what it's going to cost, you know exactly what you're going to have to wear to school and so any other clothes you wear outside of school are probably going to last longer.

SAM: But once you've bought the trousers, the shirt, the tie and the jumper, it would cost slightly more than a tracksuit.

MR M: Well, you don't wear a tracksuit to school for a start. You're going to have to buy trousers, shirt and a jumper whichever school you go to, so surely it's best to buy school uniform stuff and feel you're a part of the school.

The same question was put to Mrs J:

MRS J: Well, I'm going to answer you both as a teacher and as a mother. I've got two children who have needed school uniform over the years. One of the things that I think is that your everyday clothes actually cost quite a lot of money . . . and at least during school time, if you're wearing school uniform, it can actually be bought quite cheaply. It's cheaper than fashion clothes, so as a mother I actually think I found it cheaper to put my child in school uniform during school time. As a teacher, I actually think it does look smart, don't you?

SAM: Yes, it does.

It is not possible here to convey the tone of voice of the two interviewees, but this was the first thing the children seized upon. Mr M's tone, they noted, was more aggressive, whilst Mrs J was very reasonable in tone. From here, a little careful analysis clearly demonstrated which tone was most likely to be successful in debate. The children had felt able to challenge the more aggressive response which, they noted, also demonstrated a less coherent argument. Their challenge was greeted with the defensive response about not being allowed to wear tracksuits, and from here on the interview developed in the children's favour.

As well as responding more calmly, Mrs J also demonstrated a clear and reasonable argument, simply and persuasively presented. The children noted that she had cleverly manipulated the conversation so that the children agreed with her final statement, and this too set the tone for the remainder of the interview. The children consistently agreed with Mrs J's views and often said so. Whilst the transcription of this interview contains evidence of the children challenging and extending Mrs J's views, it also shows their anti-uniform stance being gently challenged.

The interviews were another instance in which adults were used to model talk, and the children were able to analyse it critically. This analysis gave the children important information about how to construct and develop arguments, something which was to prove invaluable in the subsequent debate. Above all, the children's confidence was boosted by the knowledge that their peers had successfully presented their arguments to an adult audience, and had even achieved a degree of success in challenging adult opinion. The arguments they had developed really were effective.

All of this work took place over two weeks or so – and the only writing which had taken place was in the form of occasional notes in draft books. The quality of language work which had taken place was undeniable. The children were fully immersed in the issue; in particular, children whose literacy was insecure were released from the strain of having to record their work in written form, and I hoped that this would be reflected in the quality of their eventual written work.

My aim had been to allow the children to extend and challenge one another's ideas in a range of supported frameworks. Even the least confident children were happy to talk through their ideas at home with parents, and this in turn gave them greater confidence when they presented arguments in class discussions. They had tried out their ideas in a safe context, and the higher-threat activity of sharing ideas in class became more manageable as a result. The more confident children were keen to try out their newly formed arguments on the head and deputy. The supportive environment provided by the role play activities increased their confidence further.

The key factor influencing the subsequent success of virtually all the children in written work was the fact that they came to the task with the ideas firmly in their minds. They knew all the arguments for and against school uniform. They could express them orally, and even respond to adults who challenged their views. Some children were already beginning to support the idea of uniform – the original vote had been almost unanimously against. With all these ideas clarified in their minds, creating a piece of discussion writing was something many were keen to do, rather than a chore.

I was aware at this stage that it was vital to maintain this enthusiasm. Asking for a piece of discussion writing was presenting them with a written genre with which they were unfamiliar. They knew the arguments, but I wanted them also to achieve success in presenting them within a clear written structure. Here the EXEL project, based on research at Exeter University, was invaluable. It offered the same supportive environment for writing that I had tried to offer for all the talk activities. Some of the writing frames offer starting points for opinion writing such as *People who think . . . claim that . . .* or structures designed to help children look at both sides of an argument like *If . . . then . . .* [1] The talk had generated the ideas; I hoped that the writing frame would generate writing of an equally high quality.

Joe is a child who consistently struggles to organise his ideas, either in verbal or written form. The writing frame offered him an ideal vehicle to present all that he had gained from the preceding discussion activities. The following example from his finished work shows two key aspects of his learning:

> People in favour of school uniform, such as myself, claim that you don't have to go into your wardrobe in the morning for clothes that match to wear. I also claim that this saves arguments between parents and children on what they are going to wear to school that day.

Joe has clearly understood one of the key arguments in favour of school uniform – and has developed the argument in two ways. He has adopted some of the conventional language of the genre in which he is writing. His use of the word 'claim' as opposed to simply using the word 'say' is evidence of this.

Michael's writing also contains evidence of adopting the genre of discussion writing with some confidence. He presents an argument in favour of school uniform, and immediately challenges it with an opposing point of view. Framed around the sentence structure of *It is true that . . . but . . .* he has successfully used a common linguistic device:

> It is true that school uniform is cheap, but you can only buy it in two shops, and it is poor quality.

In his presentation of the arguments against school uniform, Alex's writing demonstrated another sophisticated technique:

> If there is no uniform, then people will wear their own clothes. This may not seem like a problem, but some people will have better clothes than others. This could lead to teasing and bullying about whose clothes are best. This won't happen with uniform.

The use of the phrase 'this may not seem like a problem' challenges the reader to think beyond the surface of an apparently simple argument to its deeper implications. The simplicity of the final statement makes clear the power of this particular argument.

These are just three brief examples. The overriding impression the children's writing left me with was one of sophisticated language use which had not been evident at the start of the project. The talk activities had given the children the confidence – and the ability – to express the arguments clearly on paper.

Debate – the modelling of peers

Hannah had received a great deal of support from home in the writing of her speech, and her presentation was astounding, both in terms of the content of the speech, and her delivery of it to her peers:

> you must agree that the uniform we have . . . with its modern style, is very functional and inexpensive. I also believe strongly that if there were no uniforms people would be judged simply by what they wore . . . This would quite obviously lead to teasing which would not happen should we retain school uniform . . .
>
> . . . We have presented our basic arguments, and I'm sure that you can all think of many more. So, if you are truly free-thinking individuals, not swayed by the crowd, the only conclusion that you can come to is that school uniform must be retained.

Her subtle manipulation of the audience both in tone and content had a significant effect on the eventual outcome of the debate. My only fear was that the support she had received from home had given her an unfair advantage over the opposition. Initially this proved the case; none of the other main speakers in the debate could match her. But as it progressed, the other speakers drew on the style of language and delivery Hannah had adopted in their responses to opposing arguments from the floor. The debate took on a more sophisticated tone, and the quality of language use from all participants, both main speakers and contributors from the floor, was enhanced. One of the less academically able children received a spontaneous round of applause from his classmates on delivery of his persuasive and succinct contribution:

> We have a good quality uniform which is not expensive. Our casual clothes are protected. Of course we should keep school uniform.

The debate ended in an extremely close vote. The result was a victory to those in favour of uniform by a margin of two votes. Recalling the original almost unanimous anti-uniform stance two or three weeks previously, this alone stood as evidence of the children's learning; whichever view they held, it was based on careful consideration of the arguments.

What learning had taken place?

The children had undoubtedly moved on in their understanding in a number of ways. In relation to the issue of school uniform itself, every child had developed a greater awareness of the main issues on both sides of the argument. They could express them verbally and in written form. In terms of specific language learning they had also absorbed a great deal. They had developed their understanding of a number of conventions in relation to the discussion genre. They understood the formal register of language required for the debate they had engaged in, and they had begun to learn how language could be manipulated to persuade others of an opposing point of view. They were, quite simply, empowered users of language. With a firm grasp of the issues at their fingertips they could engage in debate both with their peers and with adults.

But that was not the only learning that had taken place. I had learned a great deal about the power of talk in generating and exploring ideas. Above all, the children had moved on most in their understanding when they were given opportunities to explore for themselves, in a structured and non-threatening environment, the kinds of language modelled effectively for them by others.

Further persuasion – the great smoking issue

Part of our personal and social education (PSE) work required us to look at the issue of smoking and its effects on health. Here was another issue about which the children had a general understanding. They knew it was bad for them. They had some vague ideas as to why exactly this was the case. But, asked to present the arguments they would use to persuade an existing smoker to give up the habit, they realised they did not have enough information at their fingertips. Thus we were presented with another opportunity to develop our arguments to the point where we could effectively persuade others of a point of view.

Of course, I had my own PSE agenda here. I did not want to simply promote a discussion of both sides of an argument about smokers and their rights. I wanted to leave the children in no doubt about the dangers of smoking, and, in helping them to develop the kind of language use which would persuade others of this point of view, I wanted to persuade the children themselves that to take up smoking in the first place was a bad idea.

National No-Smoking Day is an annual event which always provides schools with a wealth of material for such work. Our PSE co-ordinator made available to me all the material collected from these events over the past four or five years, and this was a valuable starting point for our work. Along with a wealth of hard-hitting statistics, the slogan for each campaign provided a valuable insight into the way language might be used in advertising to manipulate the consumer. Since some of the children were to produce an anti-smoking leaflet at the end of this work, the persuasive language of the slogans seemed a good place to begin.

I wanted the children to identify for themselves what made a good slogan. A group discussion task encouraged them to do this. Presented with a No-Smoking Day poster, the group discussed the following questions:

- What is the AIM of the poster?

- How does the ILLUSTRATION try to get the message across?

- What is the SLOGAN on the poster?

- How does the SLOGAN help to get the message across?

One group's poster had the slogan KICK THE HABIT with an illustration showing a large boot kicking a cigarette way. The following contributions to the discussion of the above questions came from a mixed-ability group of children:

> They've made it so the person really is kicking the cigarettes.
>
> It's kicking it away – you don't want it.
>
> Like a football, you kick it away before someone gets to you.
>
> They've used short words and a short phrase to make it easy to remember.
>
> The slogan is short and snappy.
>
> The main thing is, the person is actually kicking the thing that is the habit.

This was just one group. Others engaged in similar discussion, and the slogans they made up themselves were valuable evidence about the kind of learning that had taken place:

DON'T SMOKE YOUR HEALTH TO HELL

PLAY SQUASH WITH A KILLER

DON'T LET YOUR LIFE GO UP IN SMOKE

THERE'S NO JOKING ABOUT SMOKING

COUGH UP THE HABIT

The children had picked up some key messages here. They had begun to see the importance of coming up with a slogan which lent itself to a powerful illustration, they had created slogans which relied on metaphor, they had understood the power of a short, snappy slogan and had used such linguistic devices as rhyme and alliteration to create slogans that were easy to remember. All of this learning had taken place as a result of a structured talk task. The children themselves at this stage were unaware of the specific learning which had taken place. They had simply discussed the given slogans and used them as a model for their own.

In itself this was valuable, but there was more learning to take place. The children deserved to have made explicit to them the specific language devices they had used. It is true that children remember best what they have discovered for themselves. These children had discovered a great deal, but as yet were unaware how sophisticated that learning had been. We discussed each slogan and identified the devices they had used. Many of the technical terms for the devices they had met in other language contexts. Helping them to see that they had used them here developed their understanding and surely made it more likely that they would apply such devices in a wider range of contexts in future. At this stage, the only writing that had taken place was in jotting down their slogan in draft. But the quality of learning that had taken place was huge.

From the knowledge children already had about the arguments against smoking, we were able to categorise three main 'dangers'. This formed the basis of the next section of the work, which involved investigating the many anti-smoking leaflets already provided by the PSE co-ordinator, and others the children themselves had collected from other sources. We were in fact inundated with leaflets, and the wealth of information needed to be categorised. This was a vital part of my planning. The children needed a clearly defined and manageable task – and they still needed the opportunity to talk. I asked them to find at least two pieces of information for each of three categories which highlighted the negative aspects of smoking. The categories were:

Health
Money
Passive smoking

As one of the children said at the outset of the task:

'Why should they give up? That's what we need to answer.'

This clear focus was intended to enable the children to be selective in the information they jotted down from the leaflets. In pairs they grappled with the mass of information, gradually becoming confident enough in the task to reject what was unnecessary. A common sequence of talk involved:

- reading aloud the information as it was in the leaflet;
- working together to thrash out the meaning of unknown words;
- rewording the information in language they understood;
- deciding whether to reject or note down the information;
- writing the information in note form.

Here was quite a complex sequence of events in which talk played a vital part; it allowed the children to make and extend meanings of unfamiliar text, applying them to their own purposes. At the same time, the reading aloud and rewording of text meant that the children became immersed in the language of the leaflet, consequently developing a clear understanding of the kind of language which would be appropriate for their own writing. They soon grasped the need for hard-hitting facts to support their arguments, and gradually began to adopt the device of using rhetorical questions to enhance their power of persuasion, as these examples from their posters show:

Nicotine: You wouldn't inhale poison, so why nicotine?

Do you want to be a killing machine?

Have you thought how unhealthy your smoking is for other people?

The more competent readers and writers grasped the process of sifting information and began to use a range of language devices with very little adult intervention. Again it was important to make explicit to them the devices they had used. The academically less able children needed greater support in the initial sifting process, but again the legitimising of almost constant talk enhanced their learning immensely. My observation notes record two significant occasions:

> Ben and Luke are both less confident readers, and the leaflet presented to them fell into the category of literature not written specifically for children. With no prompting they set about using a paired reading approach to make sense of the leaflet. With this valuable use of peer support they succeeded in an almost entirely accurate reading of the leaflet.

In the case of Alex and Jon, adult intervention was need to kick-start the whole process. Both lacking in confidence, they were initially overwhelmed by the task. In this case teacher modelling of the process for sifting information, including modelling of the kind of talk they would need to engage in together, enabled Jon to take on the role of trying to guide the discussion. Alex, whose writing difficulties so often hamper his success with language, was relieved that Jon was prepared to take on the note-taking role, and began to respond to the task with greater enthusiasm. He began to identify information, and to explore its meaning verbally, with Jon writing down the final outcome. It was a slow process, but one which allowed them ultimately to succeed in the task.

Yet again peers and adults alike were contributing to the children's language development.

Some of the children produced their own anti-smoking leaflets. With all the necessary information at their fingertips, and a vast range of leaflets available as models for their own work, the supportive framework for their writing was further enhanced by explicit discussion about sub-headings, use of artwork, captions etc. The resulting work was characterised by the use of a range of the linguistic features they had encountered and explored in the talk stages of the project.

Other children produced a piece of persuasive writing, again using a framework offered by the EXEL project. At this stage it was as important as ever to keep the motivation for talk high. Yet again the strategies of peer and teacher modelling could be exploited. Teacher modelling of the writing frame makes explicit to the children the appropriate structure for their writing. In this case, the structure required them to produce an introductory paragraph, outlining the theme of their writing, three subsequent paragraphs each containing a different argument against smoking, and a final concluding paragraph to sum up. Simply explaining this to the children and giving them the writing frame as a 'worksheet' to complete would undeniably have given the children the opportunity to write down three of the pieces of information they had researched. But teacher modelling and supported talk meant that they learned so much more.

I wanted the children to aim for two key elements in their writing: a clear argument which developed through the piece, and an argument that was supported by facts. The very nature of the paragraph starters suggested by the writing frame offered an opportunity to discuss how an argument is constructed. The layers of the argument are built up through each paragraph, and the importance is thus placed on saving the main and most persuasive argument until last. They had already acknowledged that the use of factual information gave extra weight to their argument. The children had the tools for the task; now a supportive writing environment would ensure their continued success.

Smoking

I want to argue that smoking is a dangerous and dreadful habit. I am going to high-light the issues of health, money and passive smoking.

Firstly, smoking can damage your health badly, you'll find that if you looked in a smokers' lungs you would find some lung, but mostly tar. More smokers die of heart attacks than a non-smoker, so you can kill yourself by carrying on smoking or you can stop.

Another important point is that cigarettes can cost a fortune nowadays, so not only are you wasting money, your life can be snuffed out like a candle for £2.81! You, if a smoker, could save up for six months the amount of money you spend on cigarettes, you would have enough money to buy a holiday. That would be worth the money instead of buying killing machines.

Furthermore there is 'Passive smoking'. Have you thought that not only are you damaging your own health, you might be damaging someone else's health at the same time? Non-smokers die of smoking diseases because they have inhaled smokers' smoke. So you can stop killing your health and someone else's!

Therefore, don't let your life go up in smoke, but stop. If you want to carry on smoking you might as well jump off a cliff, because sooner or later you'll die, because you didn't stop.

Figure 6.1 'Smoking': Jack's final draft

Talk was still a key characteristic of classroom activity at this stage. The two key elements I wanted the children to achieve were made explicit to them at the outset. These then became the basis for subsequent discussion at the drafting stage. In this way the talk opportunities maintained a clear focus. The talk involved discussing one another's drafts in relation to the key elements. The continued sharing of ideas helped to develop and extend the writing.

Jack's initial draft contained three central paragraphs of two short sentences each – a sentence to explain the argument, and one fact to support it. Whilst it was clear and concise, his peers did not think the writing persuasive enough. Trained by now to make positive comments first, they identified that he had made three clear points and encouraged him to expand upon them. The final draft contained the rhetorical questions and paragraph punchlines which transformed the tone of his writing altogether. Jack is a child of average ability who had previously struggled to organise his ideas on paper. As Figure 6.1 shows, the tasks he had undertaken in relation to this piece of writing had provided a positive and constructive environment which contributed to his success.

Conclusions

These two writing projects involved very different subject matter, but they shared some important factors which contributed to the quality of learning which took place.

Above all, talk activities preceded any formal writing task – not just in the limited sense of a short discussion before writing took place, but in that clearly focused tasks were planned and undertaken over a series of sessions, with minimal note-taking serving simply as an *aide-mémoire*.

The writing task came later – another day, another week even – when the children had become immersed in the subject through talk. It was only then that they had understood the facts, the key arguments and the linguistic devices and genres appropriate to the task. They had explored their initial ideas to the point where they were well informed – experts in the field, almost. All of us prefer to write what we truly know – how often do we give children that same opportunity?

Also important was that the talk did not stop when the writing began. The tried and tested response partner method was crucial to the development of the writing. Early adult intervention in the drafting stage was also essential. Teacher response to a confident child, prepared to read out their work and subject it to scrutiny, allows the less confident child who has listened to the constructive criticism to make adjustments to their own work in the light of such comments. Yet again, the modelling process is so valuable here – teacher modelling of response to a child's writing makes the response partner relationship between peers more explicit.

This question of explicitness emerges time and again – and rightly so because it is vital. Once fully aware of the issues they are exploring, children need to know what it is they are required to do with the information – who are they presenting it to? How are they to present it? What kind of linguistic genres and devices might they employ? What does successful writing in the appropriate genre look like? Here the teacher's role is critical. Talk generates ideas, there is little question about that. To truly deepen children's understanding of language we need to move children on from there, making all that they have learned themselves explicit to them, and giving them the technical language to talk about their language work with confidence.

Above all, writing must be seen as a whole experience – to write about a subject with conviction and clarity, the children need first to immerse themselves in it; to talk and to read, and to keep talking and reading until they understand the issues – and only then to write.

Note

1 The EXEL project was set up in 1994 at Exeter University by Maureen Lewis and David Wray. The work of the project is written up in Maureen Lewis and David Wray, *Extending Literacy: Developing Approaches to Non-fiction*, London: Routledge, 1997.

Reference

Department for Education (1995) *English in the National Curriculum*, London: HMSO.

Part 3

LOOKING CLOSELY AT LANGUAGE

Part 1 outlined a model of English which combines study of texts with the processes of developing discrimination and getting and conveying information. Part 2 raised issues of teacher intervention and classroom organisation in using those texts and processes to shape learning. The emphasis was on the longer stretches of discourse. This part combines issues of curriculum content and pedagogy by focusing on children's construction of texts which are specific to particular subject areas. This means paying special attention to choice of words as well as the forms of longer texts which best support learning. Whilst all three chapters share that common theme, each introduces another facet of the use of language in learning. The part begins with a chapter looking at children's experience of mathematical language and how this relates to work in the classroom. Alison Wood and Penny Coltman give a range of examples of children's mathematical talk in the home, stressing the importance of the contribution which parents and carers make to the development of mathematical language.

It is fascinating to see how young children take on the language of their community. Gordon Wells refers to 'compelling evidence that children actively construct their own hypotheses' about the way language is patterned and used (Wells 1986: 43). They do not just imitate adult speech; they use it as a model for innovation and further generation of new meanings. However, children are not just active language users in terms of acquiring the vocabulary and syntax of their language community. In taking on the forms of language, children also take in the meanings and concepts carried by the language. While learning to use language they also learn through language; implicitly, also, they learn about language. Talk is an everyday act as children learn to make their meanings clear through conversations with members of their family or community. In the classroom, however, language is not only the means by which the daily business is carried out; it is an object of study in itself. However, children's experience of using language cannot easily be put into separate compartments labelled 'home'

107

and 'school'. Since language is so central to a child's whole experience of learning – both at home and at school – it is important to find ways of identifying just what children can do with language when they come to school, and what they understand about language, so that teachers can build on that experience.

As Part 2 shows, if teachers are to help children learn as efficiently as possible, equally attentive response from adults is crucial. It is also sensible to use ways of supporting language development which are similar to those used in the home since the child's home experiences of language are the bridge between home and school learning. As children grapple with language, in genuine conversation with adults, they begin to construct a complex inner set of rules which means that they can generate an infinite number of sentences which follow the grammatical pattern of the language of their community.

Deficit views of language

Educational writers have in the past identified differences between home and school uses of language as 'problems'. There were commonly held beliefs that the language used in some children's homes (particularly in working-class homes) was deficient or restricted. However, Barbara Tizard, Martin Hughes and Gordon Wells, amongst others, set up extensive experiments with children aged between three and a half and four and a half where they recorded and analysed their language at home and in the nursery, paying attention not only to the children's language but also to the language of the adults who interacted with them (Tizard and Hughes 1984; Wells 1985). Their results began a move towards a much more informed way of thinking about home language – seeing it not as deficient but as complex and challenging. Indeed, these researchers found that children's home experiences of extended conversations or stories were rarely replicated in the classroom. In the following extract Jonathon is helping his mother polish his wardrobe:

J: Do you think this is lovely?
M: I think it's a bit smeary
J: Why do you think it's a bit smeary?
M: Because you put far too much polish on [*two words unclear*]. Right, now you can put the things back on there . . . and I'll put the carpet sweeper over the room.
J: Well why can't I put the carpet-sweeper over the room?
M: Because that's my job, OK?
J: What is my job?
M: You've done your job. You've polished the furniture

[*a little later*]

J: It doesn't matter if the polish goes in your eyes, does it?
M: Oh it does yes, it makes them sting.

J: [*unclear*]
M: It makes them sting very badly
J: Well just now some of that polish waved in my eye
M: Did it?

(Wells 1985: 33–4)

The conversation continues . . .

This brief exchange is a clear example of a three-and-a-half-year-old using language to construct meanings and knowledge for himself. His mother answers his questions as part of a genuine exchange of ideas. This is a very different kind of conversation from Rosie's conversation with her teacher in the introduction to Part 2. Jonathon's mother is able to engage in genuine dialogue of a kind which helps him to develop his use of questions.

This conversation between an adult and a child, in contrast to Rosie's with her teacher, strongly suggests that whilst teaching is often seen as adult talking and children listening there are very good reasons – linked with the development of thought – for teachers to listen rather more to children. In this way teachers will be able to detect what children already know and will be more likely to extend, rather than deny or restrict, children's language and learning. Alison Wood and Penny Coltman argue that the style of learning and teaching mathematics in the classroom over the past thirty or so years has tended to silence children's hypothesising and so impoverish their way of communicating and exploring mathematical concepts. By paying more attention to children's precise use of language in maths the role of language in promoting learning can be fully used.

Talking and learning

In Chapter 8 Rachel Sparks Linfield and Paul Warwick continue this theme. They use their observations of children writing and talking about scientific concepts to argue not only that close attention to language is essential for developing scientific understanding but that overemphasis on the products of learning can stand in the way of children developing procedural understanding in science. Language plays a part in helping children to learn from their very early days, but it is important to draw a distinction between school learning and home learning; according to Vygotsky (1962) home learning is more spontaneous and unplanned and school learning is more systematic and analysed. He emphasises the importance of the creation of authentic contexts for language learning through teachers' deliberate, planned and explicit attention. The implication for any teacher, then, is to make sure that in the course of work throughout the curriculum, reading, writing, speaking and listening are seen as having genuine purposes.

For many years, writing (and speaking) were seen as ways of proving that children had learned what they had been taught. This meant an overemphasis on

109

writing as a thing – a noun or a product. In recent years there has been a shift from looking only for the products of learning towards considering the processes which contribute towards those products. The National Curriculum for English requires that children are taught how to draft their writing – how to get from early plans and jottings to final product. This puts more emphasis on writing as an activity – a verb or a process. Although people use writing every day to shape thoughts, note ideas, reflect and plan – in other words, to help them in processes of thinking – these kinds of writing are often given less value in the classroom. The account, the story, the explanation – all of them products – are seen as more important than speculative and formative kinds of writing. But the product or outcome of thought is more than that. The activity of composition is a powerful mental process and the product, or outcome, involves making meaning which we had not realised (that is, made real) until the act of writing (or speaking). That is just as true of scribbles, jottings and aids to memory as it is of more extended pieces of discourse. And its accompanying product, or outcome, is an extension of experience – a combination of previously held ideas and new ones. In this way, process and product are not seen as opposites but as complementary, and learning is perhaps better referred to as *a process of production*.

Writing can, of course, be for anything or anyone. The varieties of writing which children and adults engage in during the course of any week are extensive, including: lists, notes (some passed illicitly in class; others left on the kitchen table), birthday cards, letters, diary entries, and more lengthy pieces of writing – accounts, stories, reports, poems, essays. The recipients or readers of those different kinds of writing include ourselves, friends, members of the family, teachers, travel agents, the bank manager, governing bodies of schools . . . and so on. Both the purposes of writing and the readers will influence the way the texts are constructed. It is an enlightening exercise to ask children in the classroom about the purposes of writing. Responses range from 'We write to remember enjoyable things' and 'I write to my gran to keep in contact' to 'Teacher makes us' or 'Punishment' or, perhaps more worryingly, 'We write because if we didn't write we would waste paper' (Bearne 1998: 76). In all the investigations made by the National Writing Project, the overwhelming sense from children was that writing at home was enjoyable while writing at school attracted more negative comments (National Writing Project 1991). This is understandable if writing is seen as the end point of learning – the product. Rachel Sparks Linfield and Paul Warwick argue that the more formative kinds of writing – jottings, notes, reflections – accompanied by talk, are essential to procedural understanding in science. If teachers judge learning only by attention to written products, then they are likely to miss evidence of genuine scientific understanding. Their chapter stresses the importance of careful attention to language at all stages of learning.

In writing about language and music, Jane Edden agrees. *Music and the Use of Language* (SCAA 1997) makes explicit links between the National Curriculum requirements for English and music. In speaking and listening pupils should:

Listen carefully and show understanding of what they see and hear, making relevant comments.

Extend vocabulary through activities that encourage an interest in words. Use more imaginative and adventurous choice of words; evaluate and make reasoned judgements.

In music they should:

Listen with concentration, recognising the musical elements.

Describe in simple terms the sounds they have made, listened to, performed, composed or heard, including everyday sounds.

Express ideas and opinions about music, developing a musical vocabulary and the ability to use musical knowledge to support views.

In reading:

Materials should stimulate the imagination; they should include language with recognisable repetitive patterns, rhyme and rhythm, structural and organisational features.

whilst in writing children should 'write in response to a variety of stimuli'.

The music curriculum requires that they should 'compose in response to a variety of stimuli, eg written texts and respond to musical elements and the changing character and mood of a piece of music by means of . . . writing' (all extracts taken from SCAA 1997: 2).

Jane Edden, in Chapter 9, does not confine herself to the requirements of National Curriculum documents, however. For her, 'Language is the enabling vehicle.' She picks up on issues about children's early learning of language and how it relates to school learning as well as asserting the need for teachers to take a more facilitating role in learning. The traditional ways of inducting children into music can not only be counter-productive, but can take up space and time which would be better used in helping children explore what they already know. For Jane Edden, however, knowledge and understanding are not simply confined to the cognitive domain; much learning depends on developing the affective aspects of learning and experience.

The importance of affective as well as cognitive aspects of learning links directly back to the points made in Chapter 7 about early language. As Jerome Bruner points out:

Obviously children quickly and painlessly master syntax without crisis. With somewhat more difficulty, but still easily, the child also 'learns how to mean' – how to refer to the world with sense. But children do not

111

master syntax for its own sake or learn how to mean simply as an intellectual exercise – like little scholars or lexicographers. They acquire these skills in the interests of getting things done in the world: requesting, indicating, affiliating, protesting, asserting, possessing and the rest.

(Bruner 1986: 113–14)

He goes on to point out that 'Cognition is not a form of pure knowing to which emotion is added' (Bruner 1986: 117). This echoes Vygotsky's comments on the relationship of thought and language 'as a dynamic system of meaning in which the affective and the intellectual unite' (Vygotsky 1962: 8). In a chapter rich with practical detail of how music and language work together, Jane Edden demonstrates the importance of providing children with opportunities for choice and experimentation, playing with sound and language as well as paying scrupulous attention to how language can be used to describe sound. To make all of this possible, the teacher need not be a musical expert, but a thoughtful organiser of opportunities for children to pay attention to the construction of texts – both musical and linguistic.

References

Bearne, E. (1998) *Making Progress in English*, London: Routledge.

Bruner, J. (1986) *Actual Minds, Possible Worlds*, Cambridge, MA: Harvard University Press.

National Writing Project (1991) *Perceptions of Writing*, Walton-on-Thames: Nelson/National Writing Project.

School Curriculum and Assessment Authority (1997) *Music and the Use of Language*, London: SCAA.

Tizard, B. and Hughes, M. (1984) *Young Children Learning*, London: Fontana.

Vygotsky, L.S. (1962) *Thought and Language*, trans. E. Hanfmann and G. Vakac, Cambridge, MA: Massachusetts Institute of Technology Press.

Wells, G. (1985) *Language at Home and at School*, Cambridge: Cambridge University Press.

Wells, G. (1986) *The Meaning Makers: Children Learning Language and Using Language to Learn*, London: Hodder and Stoughton.

Wells, G. and Nicholls, J. (eds) (1985) *Language and Learning: an Interactional Perspective*, Lewes, East Sussex: The Falmer Press.

7

TALKING MATHEMATICS

Alison Wood with Penny Coltman

Michela was three years old and confused. Many times we had counted the steps down from the hallway to the kitchen and, on this occasion, she had decided to put a milk bottle on each step. She knew there were *five* steps down (see Figure 7.1) but she only appeared to need *four* milk bottles (Figure 7.2). Fortunately Michela was used to talking about numbers. She had what I now realise to be an exceptionally good mathematical vocabulary for a child of her age: she frequently counted things and had a firm grasp of the concept of one–one matching when dealing with numbers less than ten. She was able to articulate her problem: 'Look, there's five steps but only four milk bottles and there's a bottle on every step! Why?'

I was in my first year of teaching as a mathematics specialist in a secondary school and lived as a lodger in Michela's house so I had ample opportunity for engaging in mathematical discussions with her. This time I had to think very carefully about my answer to her question. Had Post-it pads been available at the time I might have used them to label the five vertical risers; they weren't, so I didn't. First we found five pieces of sticky paper. Michela put one dot on one of them, two on the next, etc. and I wrote the numerals below her dots. (Yes, she could read them; perhaps there are some advantages in having mathematicians as lodgers!) We walked down the stairs counting as we went and put the labels in order on the four milk bottles. We were, of course, left with a spare label 5. This Michela put on the kitchen floor, saying, 'We need another bottle.' Another was found, placed at the foot of the stairs and duly labelled (see Figure 7.3). Her problem was solved – or was it?

Risking the possibility that I might confuse her again but selfishly wanting to exploit the situation, I asked her what would happen if we walked *up* the stairs. She did this, counting up to five as she went. She then said 'The milk bottles are wrong.' I asked why and she said 'The numbers are different from the stairs.' We collected up the five labelled bottles, she walked up the steps again and placed the appropriate bottle on each stair (see Figure 7.4). She pointed out that now there was no bottle on the kitchen floor but there was a bottle on the hall floor.

I resisted the temptation to ask further questions.

113

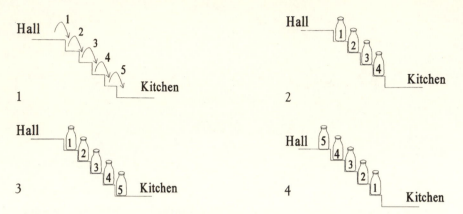

Figures 7.1–7.4 Michela's milk bottle problem

It is difficult to overemphasise the importance of verbal communication in the development of children's mathematical understanding. Without a vocabulary to express ideas and the confidence to use it, children can be trapped in their own mathematical muddles and have no adequate way of sharing their thinking or finding a way out of the inevitable confusion that they are bound to meet in an abstract subject. Few children hear much discussion of a mathematical type in their homes; most parents lack confidence and interest in the subject, few think aloud when using numbers or doing simple calculations, and opportunities for developing pre-school children's concepts in mathematics are usually overlooked. Even during their years at primary school, many children, despite the relatively relaxed atmosphere in their classrooms, have not developed mathematical talking beyond the very basic level. They spend so long searching for words to express their ideas that either they have forgotten what they want to say before they find the words or they use the wrong words and fail to communicate their thinking.

How has this state of affairs arisen?

In the 1940s and 1950s most mathematics lessons in primary and secondary schools followed a fairly standard pattern:

1   The lesson started with 'mental' questions or a quick skills test (e.g. tables). This was marked immediately.

2   It continued with teacher input with worked standard examples on the board.

3   Exercise(s) were then set for pupils (possibly differentiated) which were done in silence or not, according to the dragon-like qualities of the teacher.

4   A few interjections were given and perhaps a bit more instruction from the teacher when difficulties were seen to arise and were clearly shared by several pupils. During this phase of the lesson those with difficulties queued for help.

5   Towards the end of the lesson a résumé of the ideas was given and, if the children were lucky, an opportunity to comment was provided.

In this system of organisation of mathematics teaching:

- The lessons were, ideally, quiet with the teacher doing most (all?) of the talking.
- There was no encouragement for pupils to share ideas and it was considered cheating if you asked your neighbour when you were stuck.
- Being 'stuck' was something about which to feel ashamed so children did their best to cover it up to the teacher, their peers and even themselves.
- Children did not have the chance to learn to express their mathematical ideas to one another or to themselves.
- It was assumed that there was a 'best' method for tackling any question which often involved applying a standard algorithm.

In the 1960s and 1970s we thought we had learned better:

- In primary schools the teacher (often thankfully) abandoned the didactic teaching part of the maths lesson.
- Children sat cosily in groups and the maths scheme did the teaching.
- The pupils worked through page after page at their own pace and were unlikely to be working on the same topic as their neighbour.

This was, if anything, even more catastrophic in terms of the development of a mathematical language than the previous system when at least the children listened to the teacher talking mathematics. Many children never heard mathematical words spoken and were left to decide for themselves how to pronounce words like 'percentage' in their heads. This word is difficult to recognise and sounds very odd when it is spoken with the emphasis on the first syllable and the c hard rather than soft. Worse than this, there was no chance to learn from the inflexion in a teacher's voice – a book is not very good at emphasising some words and tends only to explain an idea one way and say it only once.

Although there was often quite a lot of talking in maths sessions, little of it related to mathematics. Many maths schemes did not even require the child to write any mathematical words. The children each had a work book in which they recorded their answers. These books often provided little boxes or left spaces in statements ready for the one-word, or, more frequently, one-number answer to the question.

Much of the teacher's time was spent in managing the classroom, checking that necessary apparatus and other resources were available, attending to those who appeared to lack concentration, etc. It was an administrative rather than a teaching role. This system did not give children any chance to experiment with explaining their own ideas and communicating their mathematical thoughts.

As a slight diversion from the main argument of this chapter it seems necessary at this point to consider briefly the current criticism which faces teachers of mathematics in primary schools. From the results of an inquiry, it is estimated that pupils at the age of eleven years are, on average, two years behind the expected standard for their age in mathematics. Clearly many questions have to be asked before accepting the findings of the study, in particular about how the 'expected standard' is arrived at, but, however we teachers justify ourselves and blame other factors, we have to face some hard truths. Mistakes have been made and this is a good time to reappraise our teaching methods. The danger in a situation like this is that we throw the baby out with the bath water. Fuelled by the media, educationalists and others – including many who have never tried teaching in a primary school but who assume that, because they were once at school themselves, they must know how teachers should do their job – have tried to put their oar in to provide THE SOLUTION to the question of the best way to teach young children. It is tempting, especially it seems for politicians, to fantasise about the golden age of yesteryear when they were at their selective grammar schools or independent schools and all their peers were able to 'do' maths. They were taught in the way described earlier in this chapter (the 1940s and 1950s) and there seemed to be no problems. This was not the case. Most adults who were educated in the middle years of the twentieth century have grown up with a distaste for mathematics. Many say they never understood it; many were frightened of the teacher and expected to be punished if they were unable to perform a required calculation; and many suffered shame in front of their friends when they could not remember how to do a certain kind of sum. Do you recall the rule, *turn upside down and multiply*? What was it for? Why did it work? Have you ever used it since you left school? I was once presented with a book called *Why Do We Do Maths?* written by a class of nine-year-olds. One child answered: 'So we can be teachers when we grow up'! We must find a more effective way of teaching mathematics in primary schools. However, merely returning to methods used 40 years ago, when children were being brought up in a different world with vastly different technologies and totally different lifestyles and expectations of employment, will not be an effective solution. We have to combine the best of the old with the knowledge we have gained from recent research, the advantages of the methods used during the last 30 years, the available technological support and, above all, our own experience of living in the 1990s.

Sadly there are still many schools which have adopted the *laissez-faire* attitude of assuming that the maths scheme is an adequate teacher, and the often poor results of children 'taught' in this way have affected the national picture.

Parents and grandparents of the present cohort of primary children were educated in one or other of the systems described earlier in which the only role model for talking maths was the teacher, so they have seldom used spoken mathematical language at all. They have only written it down: this is not a normal method of interpersonal communication between people in the same room. We usually speak! This could offer an explanation for the current state of affairs in which, for the majority of children, discussions at home are mathematically arid. Since, of necessity, whatever method of organising the mathematics classroom, the child will be sharing talking time at school with up to (and sometimes beyond) 35 other children, it is important that there are opportunities for developing and practising mathematical talking outside the classroom.

In this chapter we consider various aspects of the development of children's mathematical language. In each section we proceed from particular examples to generalisations and then pose questions that arise. The conclusion of the chapter will revisit these questions, making some practical suggestions for ways of solving them in school.

We have reached the first of our questions: *How can we encourage more mathematical talking in the home?*

Mathematical English

We start with three examples.

Anna at three and a half enjoys watching eighteen-year-old Susie doing her A-level maths homework. Anna likes the unusual layout, the mixture of letters and symbols, the pictures which Susie draws on her graphical calculator, and she seems to have realised how much concentration is needed for the task and likes sharing that. She also realises that she is not allowed to interrupt with frequent chatter. (A good first lesson demonstrating the importance of persistence?) Recently Susie was tabulating data in a statistics problem:

A: What are you doing, Susie?
S: I'm drawing a table.

There was a slight pause.

A: Susie, tables usually have legs.
S: This one is a mathematical table – it's special.
A: Oh.

A little later Susie realised the columns in her table were not long enough so she extended them. This seemed to satisfy Anna, who said, 'Are those the legs of the table, Susie?'

She was grappling with the idea that an ordinary word like *table* could be used in a completely different and special context.

The word *long* can cause some interesting and amusing answers to questions. Eleanor was two and happily playing in the sand pit while her six-month-old sister was tottering around the garden on a walking frame. Their mother went inside the house very briefly and, on returning to the garden, discovered the baby howling, upside-down in a rose bush. 'How long has she been there?' she asked

117

Eleanor. 'Oh, 'bout a fortnight' came the reply. Anna's mother asked her how long she thought she had been in the bath. The answer: '10 centimetres.' Both these answers were perfectly reasonable as answers to the question 'How long?' Neither child had answered 'Thursday' or '5 kilograms' or even '6'; however, neither answer was reasonable in the circumstances. The fault was, of course, in the parent's expecting a young child to have developed the difficult and advanced concepts of time necessary to give a meaningful reply.

In 1956 Alison sat the entrance examination for Oxford University. At that time candidates had to take a general English paper which tested old-fashioned skills like précis. She can still recall the increasing sense of horror when she first read the passage; it was about *nemesis*, a word she had never met before and which appeared in every sentence. However, without understanding the meaning of the word she was able to complete the précis (probably badly – though she was successful in obtaining a place) using the same unfamiliar word whenever it seemed necessary. This 'cheating', or reading the surface of the text, would be almost impossible in mathematics. You have to understand every word in order to be able to solve a problem.

Children, student teachers and even qualified teachers can experience difficulty in taking in a whole question in mathematics when they meet a single unfamiliar word or term in the middle of the sentence, even though this word may be of no importance at all in understanding the idea. The gist of the whole argument can be lost because the reader is stuck on one word. Many years ago a group of 16-year-olds came out of a physics O-level examination and told their teacher that they didn't understand a particular question. The physics involved seemed very straightforward and the teacher was fairly confident the girls could cope easily with the calculation so she was both surprised and disappointed. It turned out that the problem was the examiner's use of the word *mallet* instead of the more familiar *hammer*. Similarly, the use of the Greek letter θ (theta) instead of the usual x for an unknown angle often causes problems when first introduced. Much practice in writing and saying the letter is needed before an effective explanation can be given in which the symbol is used.

Shuard and Rothery quote from Kane (1967):

> Mathematical English is a hybrid language. It is composed of ordinary English commingled with various brands of highly stylised formal symbol systems.
>
> (Shuard and Rothery 1984: 2)

To understand the language of mathematics involves not only learning specific mathematical words like *cosine*, *logarithm* and *parallelogram* but also interpreting words used in general non-mathematical contexts in particular and precise ways, for example *product*, *difference*, *power*. To make things even more difficult for children they will have heard mathematical words used incorrectly in conversation; for example 'Give me the bigger half of the chocolate bar.'[1] To develop a vocabulary in mathematical English and to appreciate that familiar words can have specific meanings in a mathematical context, children need to have considerable and prolonged experience not only of hearing others use the words but also of using the words themselves. The importance of precise use of language to express and interpret mathematical ideas cannot be overemphasised. Whereas the gist of what someone is saying is normally sufficient in general conversation and our spoken and written language usually contains superfluous words, this is not so in mathematics. A very simple example of this would be mishearing, or not fully concentrating on, the answer to a question 'How much does it cost?' The difference between the actual reply '£80' and the perceived reply '£18' is highly significant.

In the 1950s some well known work by Jean Piaget included questioning children about their understanding of the concept of subsets and intersection of sets. The findings of this research were later partly discredited because it was considered that Piaget had used terms in mathematical English in his questioning of the children which they might have misinterpreted. McGarrigle, exploring the same concepts 20 years later, rephrased some of Piaget's original questions and came to rather different conclusions. In her book *Children's Minds* Margaret Donaldson describes one particular example in detail. Piaget's original test involved the use of toy cows, three black and one white. Piaget asked the child 'Are there more black cows or more cows?' (Donaldson 1978: 44) Many six-year-old children gave the incorrect answer 'More black cows' because they compared the number of black ones to the number of white ones rather than to all four cows. McGarrigle, still using four cows, laid them all on their sides and explained to the child that the cows were asleep. He then asked 'Are there more black cows or more sleeping cows?' Although only 25 per cent had answered correctly when using Piaget's question, 48 per cent of the six-year-olds replied correctly to McGarrigle's question. Donaldson notes: 'It is essential to notice that we may not conclude that the children were, in some general way, not bothering to attend to the language – for [as in the example given] we must recall the dramatic effect of the inclusion or omission of a single adjective (Donaldson 1978: 50). She concludes: 'It looks as though he [the child] first makes sense of situations and then uses this kind of understanding to help him to make sense of what is said to him' (Donaldson 1978: 58).

We pose the second of our general questions: *How can we help children to develop mathematical English?*

Confidence in expressing yourself in maths

Confidence, or the lack of it, can be a significant factor in mathematical understanding. However, even very young children can sometimes handle complex ideas. The concept of negative numbers might seem fairly advanced for pre-school children but, with the encouragement of adults and the confidence to try to express ideas using the language they have already learned, children can cope with this fairly abstract idea of number, as shown in the following two examples.

Alison was with her mother at a bus stop outside a school. She was too young to go to school herself but was fascinated by watching and listening to the children who were on their way home. A child aged about seven joined the queue. She started talking to Alison:

'I bet you can't do sums. What is six take away two?'

[*The answer came immediately.*] 'Four.'

'What's seven take away five?'

'Two.'

'What's six take away eight?'

[*This needed a bit of thought.*] 'Two less than nothing.'

Alison's mother, herself a physics graduate, was surprised and interested both in the assumption made by her daughter that negative numbers were acceptable and that she had enough mathematical confidence to answer the question. Alison clearly lacked the mathematical English description *negative* (or *minus*) *2* but nevertheless had a concept of a continuum of numbers across the zero. The child asking the question was apparently unable to cope with this answer and the conversation came to an abrupt end.

Jeannie was four; her older sister Lizzie, aged eight, was teaching her to count. Jeannie was a good counter. She could cope with two-digit numbers and was beginning to get a feel for place value. Lizzie tried a new line of questioning previously unfamiliar to Jeannie:

'Start at five and count up' [*ordered Lizzie*].

'Five, six, seven, eight, nine, ten . . . when shall I stop?'

'That's enough, now start at five and count down.'

'Five, four, three, two, one, none, none-one, none-two, none-three . . . when shall I stop?'

I'd like to know what became of Jeannie, who must by now be over fifty! I'm willing to bet Lizzie became a teacher.

Perhaps mathematicians are essentially lazy or have a sophisticated view of the inadequacies of elaborate oral forms of language, preferring the written and symbolic. Children need to see the power of this shorthand and to appreciate the precision and satisfaction a mathematician experiences when, by careful choice of words and symbols, a lengthy expression can be reduced to a compact statement or formula.

This can be illustrated with more examples.

At the age of three Alison had already realised that her mother knew mathematical facts which could give answers quickly. One morning when her mother came into Alison's bedroom the little girl said:

> 'There are eight little windows along the top and four little windows down the side. How many is that altogether?'

'Thirty-two.'

'Thank you.'

Michela, whom we met at the start of the chapter with the milk bottles, had developed a fascination with big numbers by the age of four. 'Estimate the number of prickles on the Christmas tree' she demanded one evening. The subsequent discussion in which she suggested a way of tackling the problem by counting the number of prickles on one branch and *doing a sum* seemed to show that she had developed a respect for the power of mathematics and an appreciation of multiplication as a method for solving a problem. Incidentally, have you any idea how many prickles there are on a Christmas tree about the same height as a four-year-old? 1,000? 100,000? A million?

Michela's desire to get a concept of what a million looked like prompted the mathematical lodger we met previously to find a way of showing her a million. She obtained a quantity of pre-1972 graph paper which was calibrated in inches and tenths of an inch. Sufficient sheets of this graph paper were stuck on one wall in Michela's bedroom to give her a million little (tenth-inch by tenth-inch) squares. Unfortunately, as a trend in interior decoration this idea did not catch on but, for a few weeks at least, the pre-school North Oxford set of children had the chance of seeing a million squares. It is interesting to speculate whether any of them remember it now and what, if any, difference it made to their understanding and appreciation of number.

In his book *The Language Instinct* Steven Pinker gives some examples of 'near misses' in children's speech, a particularly appealing one being 'The ants are my friends, they're blowing in the wind' (Pinker 1994: 267). We can understand this; we know what the line should be, 'The answer my friend is blowing in the wind', although the child didn't and could clearly not have understood what the song was about. However, what if a child reciting the ten times table chants 'Seventeens are seventy'? This is the same sort of speech error but the implication of this particular near miss is somewhat different. It is hard to see why we should be teaching tables to a child whose understanding is clearly not yet ready for the concept of multiplication. It matters in maths:

How can we encourage children to experiment with expressing mathematical ideas using their own words?

This question links the first two, which related to early experience and precise use of mathematical English. Children can be unkind to one another and, in defence against this, very early in their school careers they may develop armour to shield them against the taunts of peers or the disfavour of their teachers. We all like to be right or well regarded. In particular, children do not want to say things that are wrong or perceived to be silly by the other children in the class. A possible result of this fear of showing yourself up as 'wrong' or not being fully understood is to inhibit the making of informed guesses or expressing hunches which often prove to have a sensible basis. This fear of peer pressure extends beyond the school classroom; arts graduates arrive at initial teacher training courses and serving teachers arrive on inservice courses with this same lack of confidence that they might be right in their assumptions and have to be gently coaxed to express their mathematical suggestions verbally in front of their colleagues.

The three questions revisited

The rest of this chapter addresses some possible answers to the three questions posed. All the suggestions have been tested in a classroom and are illustrated with practical activities and ideas.

How can we encourage more mathematical talking in the home?

One of the effects of the recent government proposals to make baseline assessments of children as they enter school is to raise concerns in parents about numeracy and literacy skills. Private nurseries offering structured curricula are multiplying and the Pre-school Playgroups Association has changed its name to the Pre-school Learning Alliance. Many parents, confusing assessment with testing, are worried that their children may 'fail' on entry to school. Learning for the under-fives is seen by many in a very narrow context and one only has to look at a magazine stand to see how publishers are enjoying a boom in the sales of material aimed at the parents of pre-school children, and designed for *learning in the home*.

Sadly, many three- and four-year-olds are spending time with pencils in their hands, ploughing through workbook pages, colouring meaningless letters and numbers, while parents feel that they are helping their children's academic progress. There is an urgent need for a national education programme for parents which would demonstrate the sterility of this type of activity for such young children. The vast amount of published material available is eroding parents' confidence in themselves as educators of their children. They no longer believe in the value of the conversations which take place as water is tipped from the cup in the bath, or as the weekly shopping is unpacked. The importance of these hands-on experiences, and the language accompanying them, needs to be reinforced through as many routes as possible, including use of the full range of the communications media.

One school recently responded to a request from anxious parents of infant children for more homework. The school maths co-ordinator arranged for groups of parents to attend workshops at which packs of instructions for mathematical activities which she had devised were assembled and numbered. These were then presented in the classroom as a library, available to both parents and children. Many parents were surprised, on receiving the homework, however, that it did not consist of pages of repetitive sums, but was a list of opportunities for mathematical play and conversation. Examples included 'When you drive or walk to school see how many different shapes of road signs you can spot. Talk about the names of the shapes', and 'Make a collection of leaves. How many shapes and colours can you see?' Despite initial reservations, as parents saw their children gain both real pleasure and a mathematical confidence from the activities, the library became a permanent fixture and extended to other classrooms in the school.

How can we help children to develop mathematical English?

When very young children first come to school, they are at an age when acquiring and using new vocabulary is a major part of life. New words are attractive. They present pleasures of articulation and experimentation, with long words a particular treat. New vocabulary is relished and used at every opportunity. As adults we are constantly feeding into this mental word bank, through our conversations with children, intentionally and incidentally.

Much of the development of mathematical language will be encouraged through the planned mathematical activities of the class, but there are rich opportunities throughout the young child's day. Educators working with young children will be more than familiar with those provided by modelling with recycled materials:

What could we draw around to help us to make a card wheel?

How could we join this cylinder to this flat surface?

What sort of shape do you need to make the roof of your house?

All of these activities offer opportunities for adults to model mathematical talk.

Role play corners provide opportunities for children to explore mathematical language and incorporate it into their personal vocabularies. An illustration of this was provided by a Year 1 class which was involved in a project about clothes. The role play area was set up as a fashion store. By looking at shapes, clothes were sorted into types and hung on rails. Similar patterns were then picked out and put together. Children talked about the sorts of things which might be written on labels and made their own tags with sizes and prices. Visitors to the shop were measured and orders could be taken with suitable negotiations over the costings of the garments. Although provision for mathematical activities had not been a priority in constructing the role play area, observing children in it revealed that a great deal of the conversation involved mathematical concepts:

The trousers are too short – haven't you got any longer ones?

The sleeves of this shirt are too tight. It's because I've still got my jumper on.

This label has a 10 on it but I'm sure I take size 4–6.

How can we encourage children to experiment with expressing mathematical ideas using their own words?

Many adults will remember with discomfort the mathematics of the 1950s classroom described earlier – the knowledge that a wrong answer would result in humiliation at best, punishment at worst. This is one area in which classroom practice has improved beyond measure. We now understand that a wrong answer can tell us a great deal about the thought processes of children, provided that we allow children time and opportunity to explain their thinking. In order to give children the confidence to do this we need to create an atmosphere of enjoyment in mathematics, and an understanding that all contributions are of value. This can be done through regular use of mathematics as the basis of classroom games and challenges. However, it is important to avoid the assumption that those children who remain silent are not taking part in the activity. These children are using the opportunity to listen to mathematical language, absorbing both the words and the ways in which they are used, before having the confidence to join in the conversation.

One popular classroom game is *I'm thinking of a number* . . . The children are told that a certain mystery number is between one and a hundred, but in their efforts to identify it, they may only ask questions to which the answers are yes or no. A limit of ten questions is allowed.

Initially hands go up with wild guesses.

'Twenty-four.'

'No.'

'Fifty-six.'

'No – only eight guesses left.'

As the number of remaining guesses is seen to diminish rapidly, some fairly intensive team talking begins to take place. Are guesses the way to approach this? How can the questions be made more effective? As a result of some more careful thinking, questions with structure and purpose begin:

'Is the number more than 50?'

'Is it an even number?'

Alex, aged seven, explained how he chose his questions:

> I try to imagine all the numbers in my head. If you guess a number it only
> gets rid of one number. If you ask something like 'Is it less than 50?' you
> can get rid of lots of numbers and you think about what's left.

Such activities not only encourage children to verbalise mathematical thinking,
but also require them to listen carefully to each other, considering the implications of the responses to each question before thinking about what to ask next.
The situation is not threatening. The spotlight is not on individual children who
become tongue-tied as they search for correct words. Rather, children are being
actively encouraged to engage in mathematical reasoning and debate.

Each morning a book arrives from the school office to record the number of
children having a cooked school meal, and the number who have brought a
packed lunch. This gives rise to an obvious opportunity for a little relevant maths
challenge:

> If there are 27 people here, and 13 of them are having a school meal,
> how many have brought a lunchbox?

Several hands shoot up and a correct answer is given, but it is the next step which
is by far the more revealing:

> You are quite right, the answer is 14. Can you tell us how you worked
> that out?

At first young children are unable to describe their thinking. They will say that
they *guessed* the answer or that they *just knew it*. The ability to retrace the
thinking and describe it to others develops with maturity and practice. The
responses to this same question, from an experienced Year 2 class, on a recent
morning included:

> 'I took away the set of 10 and then the four units.'

> 'Well, I know the sum was 28 take away 14 yesterday, and the answer
> was 14, so if each number in the sum is one less, then the answer
> must be the same.'

> 'I saw the sum in my head. I did 7 – 3 and then 2 – 1.'

> 'I know 3 + 4 makes 7 so the answer had to be 14.'

The insight into the often surprising number of ways in which children calculate
is extraordinary. All these methods are perfectly valid and demonstrate a degree
of mathematical sophistication which would never have been revealed by a mere

acceptance of the correct answer. However, the final strategy offered was as telling as any: 'I didn't really do the sum. I counted how many people said "sandwiches" because I knew you would ask.' That child had the confidence to explain an effective way of working with number in a class where all of the children have the opportunity to talk mathematics.

Note

1 In this chapter we are concentrating on verbal communication. For those readers who wish to learn more about the research into effective written communication of mathematical ideas, Shuard and Rothery (1984) gives an excellent analysis and overview.

References

Donaldson, M. (1978) *Children's Minds*, London: Fontana.

Kane, R.B. (1967) 'The Readability of Mathematical English', in *Journal of Research in Science Teaching* 5: 269–78.

McGarrigle, J. and Donaldson, M. (1974) 'Conservation Accidents', in *Cognition* 3: 341–50.

Pinker, S. (1994) *The Language Instinct*, Harmondsworth: Penguin.

Shuard, H.B. and Rothery, A. (eds) (1984) *Children Reading Mathematics*, London: John Murray.

8

LANGUAGE FOR SCIENCE

Rachel Sparks Linfield and Paul Warwick

> In both learning science and doing science the aim is to understand,
> meaning to have an explanation for what is known from which
> predictions are made fitting the available evidence.
>
> (Harlen 1993: 9)

At any level of scientific enquiry, developing this understanding relies upon
carrying out work that stresses the interdependence of the acquisition of science
concepts and science process skills. At primary level this involves children
engaging in a range of practical science activities, developing increasingly
complex ways of working and encountering increasingly complex concepts as
they move towards greater scientific understanding.

The ultimate aim of these activities is that children should become independent learners capable of identifying problems to investigate and capable of
applying their scientific knowledge to these problems. They therefore need be
taught about scientific procedures: how to turn problems into questions and to
plan investigations in which they predict, choose equipment, control variables,
decide which results to collect, make records and communicate conclusions.
They need to be given opportunities to acquire new knowledge and to use
existing knowledge by the application of these process skills. In this quest for
independence as scientific learners, language plays an indispensable role:

> At every stage in the science process, language skills can be developed
> to assist the learning of science and vice versa. Language is integral to
> the science cycle and having a context in which to use language is
> essential to improving language skills.
>
> (Sherrington 1993: 206)

This chapter considers the importance for children at Key Stages 1 and 2 not only
to acquire a scientific vocabulary but also to use language to clarify conceptual
and procedural understanding. In summarising these ideas, there are suggestions
for ways in which teachers can create the opportunities for using language for
these purposes.

A scientific vocabulary for conceptual understanding

The National Curriculum document for science requires that children at Key Stage 1 'use scientific vocabulary to name and describe living things, materials, phenomena and processes' (DfE 1995: 2) and at Key Stage 2 'use appropriate scientific vocabulary to describe and explain the behaviour of living things, materials and processes' (DfE 1995: 7). At Key Stage 2, therefore, children are expected to move from merely naming and describing to explaining. But why do children require a scientific vocabulary and what might be deemed *appropriate*?

Children will often ask questions which even research scientists might have problems in answering: 'How it get up there?' (Alice, aged two and a half, pointing to an aeroplane); 'Why do I float in the swimming pool but my daddy sinks?' (Jonathan, aged four years); 'Why is it easier to cycle on a bike with big wheels? William's bike's bigger and he always gets there first. And it's not 'cos he's stronger 'cos I can beat him up' (Roger, aged seven years); 'What is an atom?' (Kerstyn, aged eleven years). Frequently adults can be heard trying to answer these types of questions, avoiding technical vocabulary and in doing so causing confusion.

Whilst it can be argued that everyday words might offer the simplest explanations there are times when a single scientific word can have a particular meaning. Adults will sometimes feel that young children cannot cope with 'big words', an assumption not often borne out in practice. Indeed, specifically scientific uses of language do need to be introduced to children and, where relevant, the differences between their everyday and scientific meanings made explicit. Where children are able to use such words, sentences may be less cluttered and children are then able to develop more accurate scientific concepts. Figures 8.1 and 8.2 show extracts from stories written by Year 2 children, demonstrating the enjoyment of using scientific vocabulary.

The rainbow was lick my chromatography paper and it had lots of difrent colours lick my black did in chromatography and the princess climed it and livd happly ever after.

Lucy

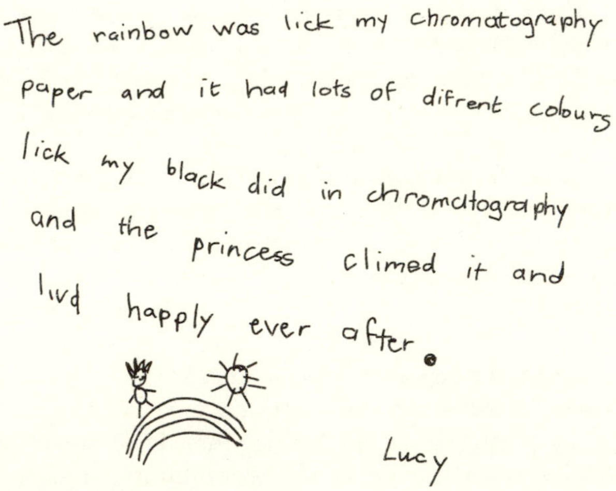

Figure 8.1 Extract from Lucy's story

Lucy's class had done simple chromatography experiments using felt pens and filter paper. Clearly the experiment was memorable since she used the results to describe the rainbow in the story that she was writing. Her teacher later commented that whilst Lucy often made basic spelling errors *chromatography* caused no problems! Alan's class had spent time dissecting owl pellets. After dissection the bones had been identified and sorted into sets. A term later he wrote in a fairy tale:

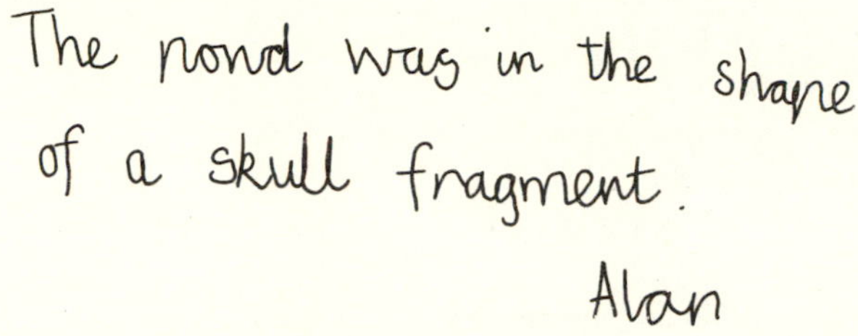

> The pond was in the shape of a skull fragment.
>
> Alan

Figure 8.2 Extract from Alan's fairy tale

As with Lucy, Alan had clearly remembered the term and was proud to use it. These illustrations demonstrate, not only that young children are capable of and enjoy acquiring and using technical vocabulary, but also that such words can enrich learning beyond science.

The use of technical language can enable children to have more coherent discussions to clarify ideas and to communicate. A simple example of this was observed recently in a Year 4 class carrying out electrical activities. Elizabeth and Edmund who were working together shared a basic technical vocabulary. They had been given a circuit diagram and were trying to set up a parallel circuit to light up two bulbs:

ELIZABETH: This bulb won't work.
EDMUND: Is the switch on?
ELIZABETH: Course it is! You know we need a complete circuit.
EDMUND: The bulb might be loose?
ELIZABETH: No I've checked that. Perhaps it's the batteries?
EDMUND: No because they lit the other bulb. Let's do it all again.

They proceeded to undo the circuit and methodically checked each component. The fault was found to be due to the two batteries being connected incorrectly.

ELIZABETH: Oh look, we are silly. This should have been the other way round. See positive to negative, not positive to positive.

It was particularly noticeable that Edmund and Elizabeth, who were said by the class teacher to be of average ability for the class, could discuss electricity so fluently. The correct terms were used, both children clearly understood the electrical concepts and the discussion was unhampered, unlike that of the second couple observed. Bethan and Donald were also judged by the teacher to be of average ability but did not fare so well when they had problems with a similar electrical circuit. The children did not have a basic vocabulary related to electricity and their discussion was hesitant and punctuated by the need to hand-wave.

BETHAN: It won't work.
DONALD: What won't?
BETHAN: This, you know. It goes all the way round.
DONALD: It must be broken.
BETHAN: No look. It's going all the way round. [*Bethan points to a jumble of connected leads.*]
DONALD: Perhaps it's this? [*Donald points to the batteries.*]
BETHAN: Or this? [*Bethan points to the switch.*]

Bethan and Donald then proceeded to dismantle the circuit, examine each component and then appeal to their teacher for help. Unlike Elizabeth and Edmund they did not share a basic science vocabulary relating to electricity. Whilst both children's written work indicated knowledge of words such as *bulb* and *circuit* their lack of confidence or readiness to use such words made their discussion less fruitful than that of the first pair of children. The practical activity was undoubtedly hampered as a result, and their abandoning of the task was clear evidence of a lack of conceptual understanding.

The key question is whether having the linguistic tools with which to approach the task would have helped Bethan and Donald. Certainly the view expressed by Vygotsky (1962), amongst others, that speech actually enhances conscious understanding and helps in overcoming conceptual difficulties, suggests that those adept at expressing ideas fluently may have a distinct advantage in their progress towards conceptual understanding in science. The ability to integrate correct terminology into explanations would clearly also be of considerable value to the learner.

Complexities do arise in science, where many technical words also have meanings different to those in everyday usage. For example, *force* within science is a push or a pull. Yet in everyday life we speak of *the airforce* as well as *being forced to do something*. Similarly in science *weight* is a force exerted due to the pull of gravity measured in newtons. Yet daily in mathematics children are asked to *weigh in kilograms*. The same words are used in a variety of situations and, unfortunately, sometimes result in confusion over scientific concepts because of inaccurate use of scientific terms. What is probably most important is that children come to understand the different contexts in which words take on a particular meaning. If this is understood then the same words can be used for different purposes within these contexts without confusion.

Technical words can, indeed, enable children to build clear concepts. For example, concepts of *floating* and *sinking* will start to develop through water play. A clear scientific understanding will not come, however, unless children have a basic knowledge of *density* or the fact that something will float if it is light for its size but sink if it is heavy for its size. In other words a ferry will float but a ball-bearing will sink. *Heavy*, *light* and *weight* tend to have multiple meanings when used in different contexts. By Year 6, however, children are able to replace these words with the more technical word *density*. These everyday examples reflect Sylvester Bradley's opinion that:

> In learning science we have not only to learn the specialised vocabulary of science but we also have to build up a language that is rich and wide ranging so that we can use it to conceptualise and to communicate . . . we need to be aware of the difference between the common and scientific meanings of words so that we do not inadvertently cause misunderstandings.
>
> (Sylvester Bradley 1996: 10)

A scientific vocabulary for procedural understanding

We are concerned not only with language to develop concepts and knowledge, however, but also with language to develop and express procedural understanding. This is complementary to conceptual understanding. It is the understanding of scientific procedures, both practical and intellectual, that is required to put science into practice. In the words of Gott and Duggan it is the 'thinking behind the doing' (Gott and Duggan 1995: 26) and it is vital if children are to develop into questioning scientists with the ability to address a range of increasingly complex problems.

Throughout this chapter the concern is with the ways in which language enables children both to understand scientific ideas and procedures and to express that understanding. Recent research at Homerton College (Warwick et al., unpublished) focused on the expression of procedural understanding by comparing children's spoken and written accounts of science investigations. The concern was with the ways in which Year 6 children used language in spoken and written accounts to express their understanding of various *concepts of evidence* (Gott and Duggan 1995: 31). These relate to the various stages of practical investigative science and might be expressed as follows:

- the planning stage – understanding variables and fair testing;
- planning and carrying out – understanding aspects of measurement;
- recording and communicating – understanding and interpreting different recording methods.

131

Two examples from each area give a flavour of the research findings and reveal how children use language to express understanding in relation to these broad areas. There are interesting differences between using written and spoken language to express procedural understanding. In an investigation on paper strength, Will writes:

> We put strips of paper in between two tables. We were going to hold the paper against the table with our hands and put weight in the middle to see what kind of paper holds the most weight before it snaps. The sugar paper was the strongest . . .

When asked to talk about the investigation, Will clearly has an understanding of fair testing and variable control that is not expressed in his simple written methodology. Thus, when asked what was changed in the investigation, he tells us:

> the amount of weight that the paper could hold changed, and the piece of paper changed. We had sugar paper, watercolour paper, plain paper, crêpe paper, newspaper and sandpaper.

When asked what was kept the same and why, he replied:

> we held them all in the same places, they were all the same length, the tables didn't move, so the gap stayed the same. We put the weights in the middle. If we had put them on one side it would have been an unfair test, there would have been less paper on one side to hold it.

The idea that the essence of simple fair testing is that one thing is changed whilst others are kept constant is clearly expressed verbally, whilst in the written account little of this richness appears. Similarly, in speaking about an insulation experiment Tamsin demonstrates a good grasp of variable control:

> The materials changed. All the containers needed the same amount of hot water at the same temperature, and we tested them at the same time. If you had more water it would stay hot longer. They all started at the same temperature . . . They had to start the same because if one was cooler than the other it would cool down quicker.

This contrasts with the written account of the activity, which makes no mention at all of appropriate aspects of fair testing. It is a contrast that appears time and again in the Homerton research. How do we explain this tendency for children to reveal greater understanding of variables when speaking about written accounts of their investigations than is revealed in the accounts themselves? Is it because children in some way feel more constrained when writing than when responding to spoken questions? Does the focus of teacher questioning during practical activity get lost in the production requirements of the written account of the investigation? Do children simply not know how to express this important investigational aspect of practical work in a written record? A key issue here relates to the purpose of the writing. One reason for these features not appearing in the writing may be that they have been adequately dealt with during class discussion, or that they were not a priority focus for that session. These points will be returned to later in the chapter.

Some consideration is now needed of how children express understanding of measurement and ways of recording results. In practice, the inclusion of graphs or tables in a written account is often taken as adequate evidence of children's understanding of the information contained in them. Whether this does provide genuine evidence of understanding, however, may be open to question. In the Homerton research the following questions were used to see whether children expressed significantly greater understanding of this aspect of investigative science than was expressed in the written accounts.

First set of questions:

- What units did you use for your measurements and why?
- What did you use to take your measurement? Was there anything else you would have liked to have used but didn't?
- What was the point of doing the test [n] times?

Second set of questions:

- Why did you/didn't you design the table before you did the experiment?
- Why did you use this type of graph for your work?
- On your graph, why did you make the [x] axis go from [n] to [p]?
- What does this graph tell us about your results?

Responses to the first set of questions suggest these Year 6 children saw little value in analysing the presentation of the data – conclusions in this area seemed obvious. Responses included 'We measured in seconds. Nothing else would do' (David); 'Seconds were best because there was nothing over a minute' (Rory); 'We used a ruler to measure the height' (Amy); 'We were quite accurate. More than one person timed each one' (Martin). The line of questioning adopted clearly did not encourage the children to think more deeply about this aspect of the work.

The language used in talking about graphs (the second set of questions) revealed rather more. David, for example, in discussing a burning candle investigation, reveals that he 'designed the table after the test, because we didn't know what the results were going to be'. He then suggests that 'you could write large, medium and small at the bottom and seconds at the top in tenths, and then do a bar line graph. That would have been a good way to show the results.'

Similarly, Amy gives her analysis of appropriate results in her presentation of her cress seed investigation:

> Results were recorded as a set of daily observations. I could have done a chart with two columns, one for the light and one for the dark. The dates are down the side. Observe on each date how high each one was, and what colour. Measure the height in centimetres. Could use millimetres, but the numbers would be higher. I don't think any other type of graph would be suitable for these results.

In being asked to justify graph choice the children were having to use spoken language to demonstrate their understanding of the most appropriate way of communicating their findings. With the majority of the written work analysed as part of the Homerton research the children had been provided with a table format into which to put results. They were rarely required to interrogate the data beyond demonstrating the important ability to draw broad conclusions and generally showed comparable levels of understanding in their written and spoken responses. For example, Figure 8.3 shows Martin's table of results and conclusion about the burning times of candles under different jars.

Large	40·17 secs	43·12 secs	49·47 secs
Medium	24·0 secs	25·65 secs	26·39 secs
small	12·24 secs	8·04 secs	10·53 secs

My conclusion is the bigger jar has more oxygen so that is why the flame lasted longer

Figure 8.3 Martin's table and conclusion

When asked what the table revealed about the results he was able to say that 'you can see which jar lasts the longest' but didn't feel able to add anything about the individual results. Similarly, Will's investigation into paper strength yielded the table presented in Figure 8.4, about which he felt there was little more to be said than that it showed 'which is the strongest paper'.

From our observations we have found that it is not until tables and graphs are being prepared that the teacher is able to assess understanding. What is often accepted as evidence of understanding is the product and this assumption may be false. Ways of interrogating the data, perhaps through written accounts, need

Sugar paper	1 kg 210
water colour	900g
plain paper	600g
crape paper	380 g
Newspaper	300g
sand paper	520g

We found out that the plain paper was stronger than we thought it would be.

Figure 8.4 Will's table and conclusion

to be considered so that a clearer view of procedural understanding can be developed.

Conclusions

The ways in which teachers help to develop children's conceptual and procedural understanding in science are many and varied. It is important to get children to express their ideas through spoken or written language. Indeed, oral articulation of ideas in particular is now widely held to aid the process of concept formation, rather than just being a means of expressing existing established ideas (Vygotsky 1962; Bruner et al. 1966). In addition to this, teachers require evidence of understanding to be able to assess children and to devise the next steps in their learning. With this in mind, the following broad points seem particularly pertinent:

- Clear conceptual and procedural objectives need to be decided upon for any session.
- These objectives need to be conveyed to the children.
- An appropriate means of developing understanding needs to be considered for each objective. Whether this is best achieved through carrying out a practical task, through discussion or through attempting to answer specific points as part of a written record will depend upon the nature of the objective.
- Whilst ideas can be reinforced and refined through repetition, it is not always necessary to consider the same aspects of a practical science activity in discussion *and* in written accounts. They can be used for different purposes.
- Children's responses should be valued as their best attempt to convey understanding.

Classroom suggestions

Below are some suggested ways in which teachers can encourage spoken and written language development in science, and thus hopefully promote both conceptual and procedural understanding:

Introduce technical words at appropriate times and within contexts that allow children to grasp the distinction between scientific and everyday usage. Young children gain great satisfaction from using 'big words', but these should be introduced where they are likely to aid understanding. Make large class dictionaries of scientific words. Encourage children to find the words and to write the definitions.

Think carefully about the procedural aspects of the science activity that are to be given particular stress. Devise questions that will encourage the children to focus on these aspects and that will require them to explain why they have done things in a particular way. Consider sometimes asking children to answer these specific procedural questions within their written accounts.

Be inventive and flexible when asking children to write up experiments. It is not always necessary to get children to record the whole investigation. Collaborative records, pictures, spoken reports, word-processed reports and many other ways are all useful. Consider the reason for recording the experiment, who is going to read it and why, and ensure the method of recording matches these.

So much writing is done purely for the teacher to check that the child has completed an activity, where a more purposeful approach may be to keep in mind why scientists make records – to be able to communicate and justify relevant aspects of their work. A simple account of what has happened in an activity is perfectly justified, provided that other information about the children's level of understanding is acquired through observation, questioning and discussion.

Allow time for children to discuss, both with peers and adults. This is sometimes understandably missing in the structure of a busy science session.

A science area set out within the classroom will encourage children to take an interest in science beyond their normal classroom work. Put out magnifying glasses, simple experiments, paper on clipboards, and pencils. Allow the children to *be* scientists and to report their findings back to the class.

Encourage children to ask the teacher questions. What, as a result of the investigation, does the child still want to know? With this in mind, the recording format for investigations suggested in Figure 8.5 may be helpful as a way of getting children to record their findings for some practical science activities. The boxes can be any size, perhaps even used as pages of a concertina book, and can be completed using drawings, diagrams, notes, sentences, or any combination of these as appropriate.

The task →	I think → (prediction related to task)	Other things to ↓ think about (consideration of variables/fair testing)
If I did this again I would . . . (suggestions for ways to modify the activity) I'd now like to ask . . . (question for the teacher)	My investigation to _____ _____	I need (resources)
↑ What I found out ← (conclusions from the results)	What happened ← (results)	What I did (method)

Figure 8.5 Investigation recording format

Acknowledgements

Thanks are given to Jenny Docherty for her work in interviewing children for the Homerton College research.

References

Bruner, J.S., Goodnow, J.J. and Austin, G.A. (1966) A Study of Thinking, New York: Wiley.
Department for Education (1995) Science in the National Curriculum, London: HMSO.
Gott, R. and Duggan, S. (1995) Investigative Work in the Science Curriculum, Buckingham: Open University Press.
Harlen, W. (1993) Teaching and Learning Primary Science, 2nd edition, London: Paul Chapman.

Sherrington, R. (1993) 'Science and Language', in R. Sherrington (ed.) *ASE Primary Science Teachers' Handbook*, Hemel Hempstead: Simon and Schuster Education, pp. 196–206.

Sylvester Bradley, L. (1996) *Children Learning Science*, Oxford: Nash Pollock Publishing.

Vygotsky, L.S. (1962) *Thought and Language*, Cambridge, MA: MIT Press.

Warwick, P.T., Sparks Linfield, R., Stephenson S. and Docherty, J. Unpublished research into procedural understanding in science, Homerton College, Cambridge.

9

LANGUAGE AND MUSIC

Jane Edden

Music and language sit comfortably together. They always have. Historically, we can think of storytelling and song being used as an exchange, as entertainment, even as a work aid. In our society, we are surrounded by examples of how the one influences and interacts with the other to heighten our whole experience. An obvious example is opera with its well-known interdependence of music and language, but there are other ways, perhaps more accessible to a wider public, in which we can see the one supporting the other just as meaningfully. Take any song. A short musical introduction will alert the listener to the intended mood, and set the scene for the message of the words. Musical language will be selected to marry with the text and the success of the whole will be dependent on a carefully chosen blend of descriptive sounds which echo the meaning and weight of the language. Film and television scores operate in a similar but broader way: sometimes music is used to describe the visual image, but very often it is heard in endorsement of the spoken word. It could be argued that not enough attention is paid to understanding the subtleties of the way the affective process works. Why should it be necessary? What benefits are there to be derived? Obviously it is deemed important enough in the secondary classroom to be used as a focus of exploration, for time is often given through project work to look at how the one can influence the other. In the primary school, however, scant consideration is given to what we all in some way make use of and enjoy. With younger children there are some largely unexplored and underestimated opportunities for teachers to develop language through musical activities. To what ends? By opening up a line of thought that encompasses the two in tandem, teachers can fulfil and enrich the requirements for the National Curriculum in both English and music, as well as providing imaginative and exciting learning experiences for children – and indeed for the teachers themselves. How can this be achieved?

First of all this becomes possible if we adopt the premise that exploration of sound needs to go hand in hand with exploration of language. This seems quite obvious if we accept that in order to help children make sense of their auditory experiences they need to verbalise their thoughts. Perhaps it is easily overlooked, however, that by encouraging children to search and find the 'right' word (in their eyes) to describe any given sound or sound experiences, we are opening up

139

the possibilities not only of increasing their vocabulary but of helping them find ways of expressing themselves in an imaginative and unrestricted way. From the earliest beginnings in the infant school, children can embark on a journey of discovery into the world of sound. How might this work in practice? For the purposes of this chapter I shall look in turn at composing, performing and listening activities, remembering that in a classroom situation it is desirable that there should be an integrated and holistic approach to music teaching.

Words and music

Take composition as a starting point. How can we facilitate the act of inventing in a classroom setting? Examining the word itself it is clear that there are immediate links with language. In the days before 'creative writing' children often had to write numerous 'compositions' both in English lessons and for homework. The use of the same name implies that there is a parallel process for the creator, namely the freedom to combine words – or sounds – of one's choice into a cohesive and satisfying whole. Teachers find little difficulty in helping children say what they want to say on the written page, but often feel very threatened when having to help them in the musical compositional process. Why should this be? The reason may well come from insecurity on the part of teachers, thinking themselves to be 'unmusical' or perhaps having had uninspired or even negative musical histories. However, if teachers start to think of themselves as *facilitators* in a similar kind of way to when helping children write stories, then the emphasis is shifted from what they feel unable to do to what they do very well. The key to this change in thinking is through the use of language.

By using a series of questions devised as pre-compositional games, children can develop the skills needed in order to compose. The first of these is an ability to listen attentively. This is not so easy for young children who have been born into a world which is bombarded with sound to which they do not necessarily need to pay attention. By asking the first question – *What sound?* – the teacher helps to engage the children's concentration. A simple game to start the process is to ask the children to shut their eyes and to listen to any sound they can hear within the room. They find this fun and will be enthusiastic to respond to the question 'What did you hear?' It might be they 'heard John sniff' or 'the heating click on'. Maybe they will choose an unusual descriptive word which the teacher can then explore. Whatever they reply, they will be focusing their attention in a very intensive way. The next stage of the game is to shut their eyes again and listen to any sound beyond the classroom but inside the building. In most school situations extraneous sound will be in evidence and will act as useful material on which children can practise concentration skills. Again discussion follows as the sounds heard need to be verbalised. The last part of the game entails asking the children to turn their attention to the sounds outside the school building. Whether the school is in the heart of the countryside or in an inner-city area there are always sounds to listen to and subsequently discuss. In using three areas as a focus – inside the classroom, inside the school, outside the school – the teacher is encouraging deepening concentration, and ultimately discrimination, necessary tools with which to compose. It has been the language used to describe the sounds that has been the enabling factor. The foundation stone for compositional work has been laid.

Developing the language of music

The next question to ask is *What kind of sound?* The implication here is that in moving on to the next question, the children know *how* to listen in an active sense, and can therefore proceed to the next stage. (Any kind of similar intensive listening activity/ game will consolidate their ability to concentrate.) Still in the role of facilitator, the teacher encourages the children to dig a little deeper in order to describe any given sound. If, for example, the child describes the sound heard outside the window as a *loud* sound, the teacher would want to go into the accustomed role of drawing out further information from the child. On probing, the children might provide words such as *booming* or *thundering*; and through the teacher's positive feedback on this striving to find a more exact description for the sound, the children come to learn that it was worthwhile and fun to try and find the right word to describe the sound. This serves them well not only in a musical sense, in that they are beginning to think about sound in a serious and committed way, but also as a very real way of increasing their vocabulary.

There are two other benefits. The first of these is the gradual acquisition of a musical language. Through a comprehensive search for the appropriate descriptive word, the children can gradually be introduced to the idea of musical elements. Sounds which can be played on a tuned instrument might be *higher* or *lower*, but collectively they can be subsumed under the heading of *pitch*. One sound on its own or many sounds played together, provide a different *texture*. Different instruments produce different qualities of sound. Children can be introduced to the new concept of *timbre*. The list of elements set out in the National Curriculum document may look fairly threatening as it stands, but through combined investigation of sound and language, through direct experience, this musical terminology can come to be understood as the vocabulary children use in order to compose.

The other advantage of such an exploration is the possibility of accessing the imagination and the whole world of feelings. The power of sound and its many memories and associations can be a potent catalyst for unleashing previously untapped creativity and emotions. By encouraging children to respond in a way which is personal to them, the teacher begins to acknowledge the child in a very special kind of way. The questions *How did it make you feel?* or *What did that remind you of?* can be the basis of a different kind of relationship between teacher and pupil and one in which the teacher may well be able to learn about and from the child. Individual opinions can be valued in a way that not only respects the child's unique imaginative and creative thinking, but as a result contributes to a sense of that child's self-worth and autonomy. Articulating a personal response to any given sound can thus be an experience which can be valued on many different levels, one which is transmitted through the spoken word.

As children come to care more about finding the right word to describe a sound, so attention will be given to finding the right soundmaker to produce any desired sound. So the question emerges: *what soundmaker?* Imagination takes a sideways step to embark on a search beyond traditional sound sources (perhaps of classroom instruments) to satisfy the need for a particular required sound. Opening up children's thinking to the huge range of vocal possibilities and body percussion can lead on to collections of soundmakers from the environment. Having only a few instruments in school does not have to be a disadvantage – unwanted packaging, old flowerpots and even kitchen utensils may serve as interesting soundmakers. It is the discussion that takes place around such a search that is worth encouraging. As the imagination is excited, so descriptive language is stimulated, and compositional possibilities are extended. In one particular class where the teacher was new to this way of working, she was astounded to observe one small group of composers spend five minutes discussing what for them was to be the 'right' sound for grass. Not only did the attention to detail and the ensuing discussion excite her, but the children's involvement and commitment to the process confirmed her belief in the work. This is a good example of how music and language can be inextricably linked.

A framework for composing

There comes a time to provide an opportunity for the children to combine sounds – in other words, to compose. Once the children have had adequate exposure to playing with, exploring and discussing sound, then it is time to introduce a framework in which they can put into practice some of their newly acquired skills. Interestingly enough, the most satisfying way of doing this is through a simple picture book or a poem. Language is used as an inspiration. As such, it is worth noting that not only are sounds combined to produce a composition, but language and sound are combined to enable this process to take place. One successful way of working is to choose a particular picture book and introduce it as a class activity. Picture books with a few words on the page, for example *Rosie's Walk* by Pat Hutchins, are ideal. The book may be introduced in story time, but may be given a higher profile if for example it is used as a stimulus for a class topic. Whatever the chosen form of presentation, however, the children will gain knowledge and understanding not only of the storyline and characterisation, but of any nuances that may occur in the pictures. The way is thus prepared for the sound script to emerge.

This is best begun as a class activity, perhaps using a Big Book, then developed as part of a rolling programme of group activities with groups of five or six children. With the children seated in a large circle with a selection of sound sources available in the centre, discussion of the story starts the process off.

Having established who the main characters are in the story, this might proceed along the following lines: 'What do we know about Rosie? What kind of hen is she? What kind of sound/s might we use to portray her? Would we want to use our voices? A wooden instrument? Tuned or untuned instruments? Why? Would we use one sound or more than one sound? Why?' With children brimming over with ideas, the teacher steps into a facilitating role, enabling individual experimentation with the sound sources, while the rest of the class engage their concentration skills. These initial experiments can be followed by group discussion in which ideas can be shared, accepted, rejected and justified. By the time children take over the work in their small groups their imaginations are fired and they are committed to the group process of telling the story in sound (a narrator can be used in the early stages of the work) by means of exploration, discrimination and discussion.

In coming back together as a whole class, either to share the whole story or various parts of the story, the teacher is ready to make a tape recording of each group's contribution. This serves a number of purposes, not least of which being that it can be a source of motivation (and fun!) for the children to know that their efforts are going to be made permanently accessible. It also gives them the opportunity to return to their piece at a later date, in order to make refinements after they and others have appraised their efforts. This process of appraisal following any composition is of both linguistic and musical value, not to mention the accompanying sense of personal achievement. When children hear the results of their work there is a tendency to focus on the negative aspects. However, finding a way to help them value their efforts can have repercussions in terms of work in other subject areas, not to mention self-esteem. In playing back the piece, the teacher would first invite the group in question to comment on what they *liked* about their piece. 'What worked? What are you particularly pleased with? At which points does it truly sound as you intended it to sound?'

Not until they have given themselves the credit for that which they believe to have been a success (they may need gentle help at this point) need the teacher turn to the questions 'What didn't work so well for you? Which part would you like to change? Why?' At first children may find more to say about what they didn't value, rather than what they did, but with practice this is replaced with their confidence and pleasure in being able to talk about the positive aspects. After the composers have appraised their work it is then opened up to the rest of the class to give positive feedback. Surprise is often shown at this point by the makers, for they cannot quite believe that what they are hearing is about their piece. In this way, confidence and self-esteem are built. The discussion gives the process of appraisal its impetus and helps children gain an increased musical and linguistic vocabulary as a result of this close scrutiny. Through the use of language comes understanding which can then be reinvested in a deeper and more satisfying musical end. The entire compositional process is dependent on a thorough exploration of language.

The skills of active listening and appraising can be practised not only as an integral part of the compositional process, but also in a much broader context. Recorded music can be used in a variety of ways in the classroom, all of which involve either discussion or the written word. How do children respond to and make sense of what they've listened to? How can we give children meaningful experiences of music which may be beyond their culture, or their time? In what ways can we satisfy the requirements of the National Curriculum without repeating some of those deadly experiences some of us had in our own schooling when we were made to sit at length listening to sizeable chunks of 'good' music which appeared at the time to have little relevance to us? Indeed, it may seem daunting to have to teach something about which we feel very insecure ourselves. However, as before, adopting a facilitating role is invaluable in terms of helping children explore and express their responses to any piece of music. Language is the enabling vehicle.

Writing about music

It is helpful to look at one or two practicalities before taking a closer look at starting points. As children often have a short concentration span, it is worth remembering that two minutes' playing time is probably the maximum. It is better to play the same excerpt several times over than an extended version at any one time. Repertoire should be drawn from a wide range of sources. In order to give the children the richest possible listening experience from which they can then form their own judgements, they need to be exposed to music from a broad spectrum of historical periods and cultures (this can neatly enhance the history and geography National Curriculum). This should include music played on a variety of instruments as well as the human voice.

Encouraging the children to keep a listening diary can fulfil a number of needs. By asking them to record (a) what they heard; (b) a few facts about the piece; and (c) what they thought about it, gives a seriousness to the act of listening to music, as well as allowing them to take ownership of their own responses to any one piece. This is important and far removed from the indoctrination already described. Permitting children to say *I don't like this because* . . . is encouraging them to make their own judgements without prejudice. When children record in their diaries their own responses to a piece of music, their opinions may well be as a result of two different ways of listening to the music. A **cognitive** response will describe what they know – for example, if they have been played 'The Elephant' from *The Carnival of the Animals* as part of a topic based around David McKee's storybook *Elmer*, they would perhaps describe the instrument and the quality of the sound it makes: 'I could hear the double bass, making really low sounds.' This is what they heard and this is what they know. It is quite possible, however, that they find themselves responding in a more imaginative or emotional way – for example: 'I could imagine Elmer walking through the jungle feeling really sad, because he was different from the other animals.' This is an

affective response, when there is a move away from factual knowledge to imaginative experience. Sometimes listening involves an inextricable blend of the cognitive and the affective. Both forms are valuable and have their own place not only in developing musical understanding but in opening up the world of the imagination and the feelings. The way to access this holistic approach is to help children continually focus their listening and then discuss the outcomes.

In what ways can this be done? Music can be played as an integral part of a topic and as such becomes relevant for the children – they have an in-depth understanding of the topic material and are therefore better equipped to engage in discussion about the piece. A specific example shows some of the options there might be for listening activities. If the topic were 'Journeys', a particularly appropriate listening piece might be the delightful *Little Train of the Caipira* by Villa-Lobos. The first decision to be made would be whether or not to tell the class the title of the piece. Although there is no one right way to proceed, if the children are not informed in advance the way is wider open for an affective response without any preconceptions. Whatever the desired outcome, however – artwork, imaginative writing, poetry or even a combination of these – the first task is to discuss the piece to establish both what they imagined was happening in the music and how the effect might have been achieved.

Brainstormed ideas, recorded by the teacher on the board, could start with the children's affective responses. These could be elicited from questions like 'What could you imagine happening? Where were you? How were you feeling? What kind of train were you on? What kind of countryside can you see?' Children are thus encouraged to explore their imaginings/ feelings in depth. Their answers can easily be linked up with a more cognitive approach. For example, a simple question like 'What made you think you were on a train?' might lead children to describe certain percussion instruments which *sound like a train*, or they might tell you that the music gradually gets faster – *just like a train* – or maybe, if you have explored the concept of repeated pattern (ostinato), that they can even hear an ostinato which sounds like the wheels – a wonderful insight into how a composer might achieve a particular effect. After enough time, the music can be played again and further thoughts explored.

The ground is now prepared for the children to translate their ideas and thoughts into a story, a poem or perhaps a piece of art work, gaining and reinforcing musical understanding while at the same time giving full rein to their imaginations. There are other advantages, too: playing one piece like this can also access other areas of the curriculum – the history of the steam train, for example.

There are other ways of helping children focus their skills in a meaningful way. One of these is to play a related piece of music as a follow-up to their own compositions. If the class have composed 'Storm' pieces it would then be appropriate to play a piece by a professional composer on the same theme. For example, the storm from Britten's *Peter Grimes* or from Beethoven's 'Pastoral' Symphony could be explored in terms of 'Are there any similarities between your piece and what you've just heard? How do you think they "made" their thunder?' In discovering that there are indeed likenesses, perhaps the use of dynamic contrast, children come to understand that although professional composers have access to more sophisticated instruments they nevertheless use the same raw materials (the elements discussed earlier) to manipulate and organise sound. This not only gives a further credibility to the act of composition, but also deepens musical understanding, particularly if there is opportunity to engage in discussion about technique. How for example does a drum roll work?

Story and song

Perhaps one of the most obvious but maybe unexplored ways of linking music and language is to take as a focus a piece of programme music – music designed to tell a story. Well known examples include *The Sorcerer's Apprentice*, *Peter and the Wolf* and *Vltava*. The story could feature in story time and be interwoven with extracts from the music. The children can be asked to identify certain key points in the story by putting their hands up at the relevant moment. They might listen out for an intended idea, as in the first appearance of the broomstick or the spell coming into the boy's head (*Sorcerer's Apprentice*), or for a particular instrument – the sleigh bells in the sleigh ride from *Lieutenant Kijé*, for example. Or they might be asked 'What instrument can you hear that we have on the music trolley?' There are possibilities for further extension activities – puppet making and storyboard writing are just two ideas which could develop from this way of working. A dramatised performance might even evolve from a story which really inspires the children.

In such a performance, as in any other area of performing, language plays a crucial part. We know that the essence of any successful performance depends on a communication with an audience. In the case of a song, the way in which the words are delivered alerts us to whether or not the message is being felt from the inside rather than just being mechanically or technically offered up. As teachers, we need to help children understand what they are singing and furthermore feel what it is the songmaker wanted us to feel. It is a sense of caring about what they are communicating that is important. The way to arrive at this outcome is of course through discussion. This time, however, it is the text which is examined alongside the accompanying melody. An initial exchange of ideas can look at how the words convey the mood and message of the song, as well as familiarising the children with any difficult or little-known words. They might like to ponder why the songwriter chose one particular word or phrase rather than another. This can be followed by questioning about how the songwriter might have used the music to reinforce the idea of the words. This can be achieved even at a very simple level: for example, in a lively cowboy song the rhythm may remind the children of the horse's hoofs. Questions like 'How does the composer make us think of riding through the prairie?' begin to open up children's thinking. There are direct links of course with their own compositions.

An understanding of this kind leads on to how the children will perform the song. Questions might be about the use of dynamic contrast: 'Should the chorus be louder than the verse? Why? Why not? Maybe one line could do with being sung quieter/slower . . . possibly one word needs particular emphasis.' It could equally involve a discussion on texture: 'Should we add any instruments?', or timbre: 'Wood or metal?' It is now the manipulation of the musical elements which forms the basis of decision making for the children. The teacher is again in the role of facilitator, assisting children to produce the best possible performance which is true both to the song itself and also to their interpretation of it.

It can be seen that for children to arrive at a point at which they are pleased with their presentation they have come to learn about the true nature of performance from its many different facets. From gaining an understanding of the songwriter's intentions, both textually and musically, they have been involved in discussion and negotiation to present that song in a committed way which demonstrates involvement of a very personal kind. If they are feeling it from the inside there is every chance that they will then be able to communicate to any audience.

Understanding the relationship between language and music highlights the interconnectedness of all musical activity. Whichever aspect is being explored, the others are hovering on the sidelines. Composition ends in performance, which is then listened to and appraised. Performance can evolve from a listening experience, and understanding the compositional process can make for an improved performance. It is the act of listening, however, which is the thread that is central to all musicmaking. The act of listening is also an integral part of the teacher's facilitating role in being able to explore music and language in tandem. It begins with encouraging and listening to children's ideas arising from a focus of sound. Through discussion and subsequent musical and related activity, the teacher enables the child to develop musically, linguistically, emotionally and imaginatively.

References

Hutchins, Pat (1970) Rosie's Walk, London: The Bodley Head.
McKee, David (1988) Elmer, London: Red Fox.

Part 4

NARRATIVE ACROSS THE CURRICULUM

The child's experience of story is not, of course, restricted to what is read aloud from written texts. From a very early age all of us engage in 'storying', creating fictions in which we replay and recombine actual experiences and construct imaginary extensions and alternatives to them. In young children's imaginative play, alone or with other children, we can see this storying in action and we can note how here, as in the world of story presented through books, it is language that creates the context against which the action takes place.

(Wells 1985: 252)

Many educational writers have pointed out the centrality of narrative to learning. It is a way of ordering experience, answering both to emotional and cognitive aspects of social and cultural existence. At its most everyday and ordinary, narrative exists in anecdote, gossip and what is often called social chat. But even these forms presuppose a certain ordering and selection of experience to fulfil specific intentions: for example, when we have to 'own up' to something, we are likely to tell a story selecting and highlighting events in order to minimise the parts which show just how much we were at fault. When we tell anecdotes about any incident we don't just re-run events like an unedited tape or video recording, we necessarily select. In these selections we begin to categorise experience, a cognitive operation which sets mental frameworks for later, more complex forms of categorising, selecting and generalising experience or facts. In our thought patterns, then, narrative is pervasive, helping us to develop ways of ordering ideas which in the future will be the basis for constructing more formal kinds of learning.

Narrative also plays a part in our emotional development. We do not just organise ideas, we also organise our feelings through narrative. Aspirations, disappointments, joys and fears are rehearsed and replayed in the stories we tell ourselves and in the stories we tell others. Inside our own heads and in telling our

149

friends about happy or tragic moments, we use narrative to give shape to our feelings, sometimes to help us cope with our emotions, at other times to note – and learn from – experience. Gordon Wells suggests that 'Making sense of an experience is to a very great extent being able to construct a plausible story about it' (Wells 1986: 196). However, stories do not simply offer a personal interpretation of experience:

> Because they occur in the context of social interaction and are produced in conversation, they, like all other conversational meanings, are jointly constructed and require collaboration and negotiation for their achievement. In this way, members of a culture create a shared inter-pretation of experience, each confirming, modifying, and elaborating on the story of the other.
>
> (Wells 1986: 195)

Narrative begins, then, in our social experience of language. It is shaped and formed by the ways in which the social and cultural groups which we inhabit make sense of everyday experience to fit the expectations of the culture. Someone who lives in a non-literate culture will have different ways of taking and using narrative experience from another person whose culture depends heavily on print. Shirley Brice Heath's (1983) work with three different communities in the Piedmont Carolinas in America shows that any one culture's ways of making sense of the world through narrative may not be shared or even understood in the classroom. In the three different communities she studied, expectations of literacy and the place of narrative varied. In families in the middle-class community the print environment, story reading and literacy practices in general were very similar to those that the children would encounter in school. In the other two communities there were significant contrasts between what home and school saw as valid ways to use narrative. In the poorer white community, reading the Bible was a major literary event. To this community Bible truth was literal – what is written is fact – so that the kinds of practices encouraged in school – seeing stories as imaginary, making them up or changing them – were unfamiliar and often unacceptable ways of treating narrative. In the black community reading was very much a public affair so that solitary reading was seen as 'odd' and stories, orally told, were used to explain cause and effect, to explore moral issues and to be elaborated on. In school, the kinds of reading practices related to stories – asking children to answer questions about characters or events and concentrating on verbal content rather than meaning – were very familiar practices to the children from the middle-class community but very alien to the children from the two other communities. This dislocation between school expectations and home experience was to have serious consequences for the children's learning. This is not to suggest that the poorer homes were less rich environments for literacy; on the contrary – the potential for successful literacy was there all right but their varied ways of using narrative were not recognised in the classroom. From her study, Shirley Brice Heath argues that there should be greater awareness of the literacy practices of the home. Gordon Wells argues equally forcibly, and from equally rich research material, about the need to acknowledge home experience of language as contrasted with school uses (Wells 1985, 1986).

More recently, Hilary Minns, working in Coventry, studied pre-school children and their literacy experience. One example very powerfully suggests the importance for teachers of getting to know about ways of taking and making stories at home:

> Gurdeep's parents want him to succeed at school, so the mainstream school culture is important to them. They also want him to become literate in Punjabi, and to understand his own Sikh traditions so that his cultural heritage is preserved both for himself and his own children in future years. He listens to his mother as she reads to him from the holy book and tells him stories she heard as a girl in India . . . he listens to the priest reading from the Guru Granth Saheb at the temple; he listens to his father reading a bedtime story in English.
>
> (Minns 1993: 27)

Every child brings significant experience of story into school with them. From these everyday forms and functions of narrative spring the more formalised and consciously shaped stories, accounts and explanations which we recognise in printed books, demonstrations of how to do or make something, films, lectures, newspapers, oral storytelling. The structures of narratives give children an experience of the essential characteristics of written language.

Since narrative is such a demonstrably powerful means of learning – about things, about ourselves, about others and about our emotional worlds – it is important to look carefully at how narrative enters the educational process. This involves looking at the models available in books, pictures, technology, as well as thinking about the processes involved in moving between spoken and written narratives and the relationships between them. However, narratives do not come innocently into the classroom – or anywhere else, for that matter. They carry with them the expectations and preoccupations of the cultures from which they spring. The ways in which our cultural worlds operate will influence the texts which we use as models; developed practices in relation to gender or class will be reflected in the texts – spoken, visual and written – which are available in the predominant culture. And the available forms are often those which have permeated the expectations of a school curriculum, suggesting that some kinds of narrative forms are valuable and others less valuable. There is not scope here to follow that particular aspect of learning through narrative, but it is certainly worth discovering just how powerfully young people understand, use and subvert both the popular and accepted forms and the ways in which these are constructed.

Questions about valuable narratives and how best to use texts (written and spoken) in the classroom lead inevitably to questions about genre. Recently, there has been a great deal of criticism of narrative practices in classrooms, particularly those termed *recount* genres. There is undoubtedly a tendency towards a ritual of following every activity with a written account which permeates (and stultifies) much that goes on in primary classrooms. Linguists who have gathered evidence of recount/narrative as the most common from of writing experienced in primary classrooms argue that children should be taught to write in other forms or genres – for example explanation, instruction, argument. There is no controversy about the importance of introducing developing writers to a wider repertoire of possible forms of writing. The current debate about genre largely hinges on the categorisation of *narrative* as something opposite to argumentative, explanatory and persuasive forms of writing. However, the opposition of narrative and non-narrative can be a distraction. What is genuinely and importantly worth pursuing is the relationship between chronological ordering of events, narrative and other forms of writing. What are the salient differences? Which texts are genuinely non-chronological? The next consideration is how children can come to learn to use different forms of writing to fulfil their own intentions. These issues can be effectively dealt with in all areas of the curriculum.

Making explicit what children know

Increasing attention is being paid to text construction, and initiatives like the National Literacy Strategy see teaching about texts as a key to progress in literacy. Much of this knowledge can, of course, be founded on what children already know about texts. As Hilary Minns, Gordon Wells, Shirley Brice Heath and others have shown through their research and many teachers have found through sensitive practice, children come to school with a great deal of explicit knowledge about texts. The opening move is to recognise children's reservoir of knowledge. From there, it is a short step to planning activities that help children to develop ways of talking and writing about texts which can bring these hidden understandings to the surface – to make their implicit knowledge of language and text structures explicit. Looking at or listening to children's narratives can help in deciding just what kinds of intervention will enable children to develop their explicit knowledge about language.

Harold Rosen has described the ability to tell stories as 'an explicit resource in all intellectual activity' (Rosen 1987: 15). He argues that scientific, geographical, palaeontological and archaeological accounts depend on narrative. He puts forward two, now well-known, propositions:

(a) inside every non-narrative kind of discourse there stalk the ghosts of narrative and

(b) inside every narrative there stalk the ghosts of non-narrative discourse.

There are always stories crying to be let out and meanings crying to be let in.

(Rosen 1987: 12)

The chapters in this part deal with narratives of different kinds and their relationship to non-narrative forms. Helen Bromley argues that storytelling offers a range of possibilities for learning – cognitive, affective, experiential and textual. She has designed boxes containing different objects specifically to encourage children to tell stories which draw on their knowledge of mathematics, science, geography and technology. By listening attentively to stories constructed by children from the very early years through to age eleven, she argues that teachers can witness powerful transformations of knowledge through the opportunities narrative offers for reshaping and reconstituting experience. Storytelling offers open access to learning for all children; it allows them to show what they know and what they can do with language. It is the perfect medium for entitlement. From Helen Bromley's observations, children will learn best when they are able to make links between all the different aspects of knowledge which they accumulate as they grow older. As Rebecca says at the end of Chapter 10, through storytelling you learn how to overcome problems in making your meanings clear. Storytelling allows links to be made across all areas, so that children are not just given knowledge but produce knowledge and transform it into understanding through their own language use. Helen Bromley argues that children who are allowed to do this through narrative are 'surfing the sea of knowledge, not being pulled down and drowned by the currents of curriculum delivery'.

The verbal and the visual

Where Helen Bromley works from objects and the children's experience to build stories, Bob Seberry began with a story to build a technology project. He is a lecturer in technology at a college of education; Jane, his wife, has a Year 4 class in a nearby school. The puppet-making project which they undertook together allowed him to cover a wide range of technology objectives whilst also developing the children's reading, writing, speaking and listening. One of the most interesting features of the project was the clear evidence that the process of design is very like the process of text construction, beginning from early drafts (oral, designed or written) and following through to final evaluation of the effectiveness of the product. They also helped the children to see the interconnectedness of visual and verbal modes of representation.

In *Before Writing*, Gunther Kress distinguishes between the narrative and visual modes. Where two-dimensional visual representation takes place in the spatial mode:

Narratives are not spatial; their natural medium is speech – what happens in time, as one thing, one action, after another. Therefore the order of the narrative – events happening in time – runs parallel to the order of the medium of representation – things said in time. From that point of view writing is also a temporally ordered medium: we read one thing after another. So there seems to be a 'natural' coming together of the medium of space, with (spatial) analysis and classification; and the medium of time, with actions, and the succession of events unfolding in time.

(Kress 1997: 136)

He poses the questions:

If the spatial lends itself 'naturally' to processes of analysis and classification, does it do so more effectively than the verbal does? If the verbal lends itself more readily to the representation of action and of dynamic events, to representation in the narrative form, does it do so more effectively than drawing does?

(Kress 1997: 137)

and goes on to suggest that it might be best to use each medium – the visual and the verbal – to the fullest of its potential in education.

Ian Eyres works with young bilingual learners. In Chapter 12 he describes work undertaken with John Ayton and his class of Year 4/5 children. The class contained three children from ethnic minority groups with varying experience of English, one of whom had joined the school quite recently as a virtual beginner in English. As a Section 11 funded teacher, Ian Eyres's job is to promote the achievement of black and bilingual pupils within the mainstream, which means that he works collaboratively with class teachers to develop teaching approaches that will benefit both minority and majority pupils. This chapter focuses on the progress of one child in particular as he worked within the whole class project. The planning for progress in language was built into a history project which began with a story leading to a visit to a local archaeological site. Since about half the class were identified as having special educational needs, particularly in respect of reading, the aim overall was to build more confident literacy as well as developing spoken English. Narrative seemed the ideal way to start.

The children were to become archaeologists themselves, working with artefacts found on the site and making a video film of the day's work. Ian Eyres took pains to explain to the children that the video was for more than just making a record of 'the day out', as in a family holiday. It was to 'provide a medium for individuals or groups to make a deliberate record of their under-standing of what they had found'. In practice, it provided much more than that; the initial West Stow video work became the starting point for the children themselves to produce video programmes about their 'finds'. The children were able to reflect not only on the archaeological knowledge they had gained, but also on their use of different forms of language according to audience and purpose.

At the end of Chapter 12 Ian Eyres refers to the apparent complexity of the project which the class undertook, pointing out, however, that language is complex and teachers have to be sensitive to the complexities as well as to the diversity of the language users who work in the community of the classroom. The children did not see the project as too complicated; to them it was a purposeful activity where they could use their own experience of language and television, combining verbal and visual narratives to make sense of what they had learned.

References

Brice Heath, S. (1983) *Ways with Words: Language, Life and Work in Communities and Classrooms*, Cambridge: Cambridge University Press.

Kress, G. (1997) *Before Writing: Rethinking the Paths to Literacy*, London: Routledge.

Minns, H. (1993) '"Don't Tell Them Daddy Taught You": the Place of Parents or Putting Parents in their Place?', in M. Styles and M.J. Drummond (eds) *The Politics of Reading*, Cambridge: Cambridge University Press.

Rosen, H. (1987) *Stories and Meanings*, Sheffield: National Association for the Teaching of English.

Wells, G. (1985) 'Pre-school Literacy-related Activities and Success in School', in D. Olson (ed.) *The Cognitive Consequences of Literacy*, Cambridge: Cambridge University Press.

Wells, G. (1986) *The Meaning Makers: Children Learning Language and Using Language to Learn*, Portsmouth, NH: Heinemann.

10

IN WHICH WE ARE INTRODUCED TO THE BOXES AND SOME CHILDREN, AND THE STORIES BEGIN

Helen Bromley

I will put in the box
the swish of a silk sari on a summer night,
fire from the nostrils of a Chinese dragon
the tip of a tongue touching a tooth.
                                   Kit Wright[1]

The notion of boxes being containers for stories is not new. As a young child I can clearly remember the anticipation that I felt on hearing the following lines:

Here is a box, a musical box, wound up and ready to play,
But this box can hide a secret inside, can you guess what is in it today?

These were the opening lines to the BBC children's programme *Camberwick Green*. Each week a story would be woven around the character that arose from inside the box, and as the figure started to appear I can remember trying to make guesses about the possible content of the stories. Little did I realise that many years later I would be watching the children that I taught create stories from boxes in a very similar way. This chapter describes my experiences with children, stories and boxes.

The arrival of a set of toy woodland animals had caused great excitement in my class of four- and five-year-olds. They had been introduced as part of some work developing from a picture book entitled *The Happy Hedgehog Band* by Martin Waddell. Looking across the classroom on one particular occasion, I noticed that, for the fourth day in a row, Paul, James and Rees were playing with these toys. They were very involved with their play, showing signs of concentration and involvement that were not typical of their behaviour in class. It was obvious that this play was a source of great excitement to them. They were working

156

collaboratively and remained on task for long periods of time, often for the whole afternoon. It was interesting, too, to watch their behaviour when it came time to pack away the day's activities. They would carefully hide the creatures in various parts of the classroom so that they could continue their story the following day, without fear of other members of the class interrupting their 'serial' by taking the animals for themselves. Any activity which was engaging the children at such a high level deserved further investigation on my part.

I decided to spend some time observing their play more closely. I made several important discoveries. Not only were the children making up wonderfully exciting stories; it was obvious that they also knew a great deal about the natural history of the animals that they used, far more than I would have thought. This play deserved to be given high status, and so a regular routine developed in class. At the end of each day, children who had worked with the small animals would be invited to retell their story. Often they would be holding the animals as they retold the stories and it was interesting to see how these props aided retelling and also gave confidence to children who would not normally have had the courage to speak in front of the whole group. The rest of the class would listen attentively while the tales were told and retold, often being embellished or altered in the process. These sessions were much enjoyed by the class, and did indeed serve to give the activity extremely high status, with many children wanting to have a turn at telling their story. After the stories had been told, there was always an opportunity to reflect on them, and it was through this activity that I came to realise the potential of story for looking at children's own knowledge of a wide variety of subjects.

This knowledge was made explicit though discussion and questioning. Questioning the children about their experiences was very interesting. On one occasion, I asked them which parts of their brain they thought they had been using to make their stories. Paul replied, 'We've been using our imaginations, Miss.' Another member of the class, on hearing this discussion, said 'I think that they've been doing scientific thinking.' It was this last comment that really made me think. If, through structured play, I could make children's prior knowledge explicit, then I would be able to teach them more effectively. My ability to motivate the children would greatly increase, because I would have a greater understanding of where their interests lay. James, for example, was a very reserved boy, and it was only through the medium of storytelling that I came to be aware of just how good his general knowledge was. Paul, who found the secretarial skills of writing difficult, was able to demonstrate, through storytelling, that he could structure, draft and edit a story of some considerable length. The same was true of all the children who played with the small figures. Not one child who participated in this activity failed to make a story. This was undoubtedly because the activity built on what children do naturally – make stories through play.

I decided to capitalise on the success of this and introduced a variety of similar activities into the classroom. Miniature worlds were set up in the sandpit and the water tray, for example. Pirate figures and rocks were added to the water, as were mermaids. Dinosaurs and fossils were put in the sand, with a set of tools including a soft-bristled brush and a magnifying glass. On each occasion, the results were the same – a wonderful selection of stories combined with children's knowledge about a whole range of topics being made explicit to me. It was becoming apparent that certain situations showed how children (including those as young as four) are aware, not just of scientific facts, but also of the culture associated with being a scientist, historian, or whatever. Watching children carefully examine the fossils, and discussing the rights and wrongs of removing the fossils from the 'site', was enough to convince me of this. Analysing children's stories to look at where they had gained this knowledge was also revealing. Obviously books provide some information, but interests of particular families were reflected, as were TV, films and video material.

It occurred to me that there must be other ways to promote the use of children's storytelling across the whole curriculum. It had always been the norm in my school to use story books to teach across the whole curriculum, but we had not looked at the information that could be provided by listening to children's own stories, for anything other than English. How to do this effectively? I had heard of something called storyboxes, from a colleague. These were boxes which contained a small number of objects, for children to make stories with. This seemed a good way forward, for all sorts of practical reasons. Children would easily be able to find space to work with the contents of a box, whatever the size of classroom, and whatever else was going on at the time. It also occurred to me that perhaps it would be possible to alter the boxes in some way, so that they too could be part of the story. I set out to put together some storyboxes of my own.

Initially, I set up a geography box, a music box, a history box, a maths box, a science box and an RE box. As I have continued to work with children, the nature and contents of the boxes have changed from those I used initially; the insides of the box have been used to form dragons' caves, villages and even a polar landscape. Two examples of these are:

The geography box: The lid of the box is covered with wrapping paper which has an old-fashioned map of the world on it. Inside are some sheets of material, blue and green, a couple of passports and a toy aeroplane.

The Egyptian box: The lid of the box is covered with wrapping paper depicting Egyptian figures. The box itself is lined with sandpaper and cut so that it folds flat when the lid is taken off. It also contains two toy palm trees and several small Egyptian figures (the sort available from museum shops).

Using storyboxes in the early years

I will put in the box
three violet wishes spoken in Gujerati
the last joke of an ancient uncle
and the first smile of a baby.

There were several types of history box and I decided to try out one in particular with four-year-olds and then again with ten- and eleven-year-olds. The results were fascinating.

I was invited to work in the Early Years classroom of a colleague, where approximately 25 children attended school on a part-time basis. I took in a shoe box that was constructed so that when you took off the lid it folded down flat. It was covered in green velvet to resemble grass, or carpet, or whatever the children decided it should be. Also in the box was a set of Playmobil toys. These were little figures, dressed to look as if they came from the Victorian era. There was a grandpa, some children, other male and female figures and a pennyfarthing bicycle.

I worked with four children who were told that they could make up a story with the figures. They were to decide when the story was finished and then tell it into the tape recorder for me. This was enormously motivating for the children. They were all excited by the prospect of making the story, particularly as it involved playing with the toys and being able to *have a go with a box*. I was known in this particular class as the shoe box lady, as I had visited them on a variety of occasions before, each time with a different box. I was working with Gavin, Rosie and Daniel. These children were very different in personality. Gavin ordinarily found it difficult to stay on task and had shown no particular interest in storying prior to this visit. Daniel was an articulate child with a vivid imagination who really enjoyed listening to stories and poems. Rosie, the only girl, was a very talkative child and obviously highly motivated.

Anyone who has had the opportunity to observe young children at play will not be surprised to hear that their involvement with the toys was total. They quickly divided the people and props up amongst themselves and began to make their stories. The whole process was fascinating to watch. This is partly because the composing process is made visible through the use of the small toys. Inevitably children first characterise the objects from the box and decide names and personalities for them. Then there is a period of experimentation when lots of ideas are tried out, just like in the drafting process. Editorial decisions are also made, through the removal or setting aside of some of the toys. These are valuable skills for writers to develop, and in this context children are not hampered by problems with secretarial skills; they are using language to experiment, take risks and explore possibilities. The availability of the small toys helps to make all this explicit, as the children give what amounts to a running commentary on the actions of the toys. The presence of the adult and the tape recorder are not insignificant either; here is an interested audience, and a way of making the stories permanent.

Here are the finished stories, as told into the tape recorder:

Gavin

> Once upon a time there was a little girl who had no baby and one day she had a baby and she saw a man riding a bike. She wanted to jump on it, so on she jumped. She dropped her baby and she dropped her flowers and they went in the grass, they did and they suddenly were lifted up and they were lifted up into the boats and they splashed in water and they bumped into a chair, they bumped into a chair, they bumped into a computer, they bumped into a whole house, they bumped into a teddy bear, they bumped into rabbitses, and they bumped into boxes and they bumped into loads of people and they bumped into a pub, and they bumped into, they did, bricks and chairs and boats and they bumped into the whole wide world.
> The End

Rosie

> Once there was a man. He was a Grandpa. He was a helicopter man and he had a spinning thing on his hat. He flew up into the air. Up, up, up into the sky. Then he landed back down. He fell down and broke his head.
> The End

Daniel

> The Old Man and the Naughty Bicycle.

> Once upon a time there was a man who had a bike and he bumped into someone else's bike. Bam! He went past a girl, who jumped on the back and they fell over. There was a lady with a pushchair and they bumped into that. The baby flew out. BRRRmmm. She hopped onto someone else's bike while they were in the shops. They came out and had a shock. Their bike was stealen [stolen]. AAAH! She came riding back with it. They didn't come back again.

The children had spent some considerable time on perfecting these stories, particularly Gavin, who returned to his story after a break at playtime, determined to get it right. The class teacher said that she had never seen him so involved in an activity before. The storybox had provided him with an opportunity to demonstrate what he could achieve.

It is important to look at the knowledge that the children have that becomes apparent through their stories. None of the stories (except perhaps Rosie's, with her identification of the grandfather figure) reflects the historical potential of the toys, although, when questioned, it was apparent that the children did know that they were not supposed to represent modern-day people. When asked how they knew this, they referred to both the clothes and the bicycle. In this instance, the opportunity for children to show this historical awareness was made explicit through the context of discussion after the story had taken place. However, I would argue that the children's stories themselves made other types of knowledge explicit, and that this is equally valuable.

Looking at Rosie's story first, it is fascinating to think about the thought processes that have gone on in order for her to decide that the grandfather figure can be a *helicopter man*. This particular figure is dressed in a quilted smoking jacket and cap – with a tassel on the top. Because the toys are made of moulded plastic, the tassel does not move, but is moulded to the hat itself. Consider, then, the way Rosie has used past experience and prior knowledge to decide that he can fly. We can only guess, because sadly I did not ask her how she had arrived at such an editorial decision. Perhaps something about the tassel on the toy reminded her of the blades on the helicopter and of how they turn to lift that type of aircraft. She uses that knowledge to predict the possibility of flight for Grandpa. I find all this remarkable. I am not arguing that she knows precisely how a helicopter works, but she has clearly demonstrated that she understands something about the process. During her play with the toys she was to be seen 'winding' the tassel with her finger, before lifting Grandpa up in the air, for that fatal flight! This whole story seems to be an example of a child being so secure in reality that she can subvert it and make it into nonsense for her own and others' pleasure.

All the stories show the children's developing knowledge of story language and story structure. They have used devices such as repetition and a series of events culminating in a climax, familiar to all of us. Gavin's story particularly reminds me of *Angry Arthur* by Satoshi Kitamura, with its emphasis on increasing amounts of destruction. What all the children were doing involved daring to take risks, negotiating, problem solving, initiating, anticipating and having the opportunity to reflect on and consolidate their knowledge and understanding.

Looking across the curriculum at Key Stage 2

I will put in the box
a fifth season and a black sun
a cowboy on a broomstick
and a witch on a white horse.

Still searching for a way to use the storyboxes as a means of providing opportunities for cross-curricular use of language, I took the same storybox and one or two others into a class of Year 5 children. The children had been studying the Victorians for a term when I went in to work with them and had recently been on a trip to a museum where they had experienced 'Life in a Victorian classroom'. Most of the boxes contained assortments of Victorian-style Playmobil people, but one box was specifically Victorian:

The Victorian storybox: This contained an old key, a fan, and black-and-white and sepia postcards of people from the Victorian era, some in antique-looking photo frames. (These photographs were in fact postcards from the National Gallery, but the children were unaware of this.) The lid of the box was covered with wrapping paper depicting famous Victorians.

The children were working with the boxes in pairs, in friendship groups. I gave them the same task as I gave the four-year-olds – to work with the contents of the box until they had a story that they were satisfied with. I said that they could either use all the objects in the box for their story or select some. When they felt happy with their story they could tell it into a tape recorder. Despite all being ten and over, the children were thrilled to open the boxes and find toys inside. One girl said, 'Are we really allowed to have these, Miss?' After the initial excitement of such an unusual opportunity had worn off, the children's methods were remarkably similar to those of the nursery children. In fact all the groups that I have worked with go through a broadly similar process:

- checking the contents of the box, finding out the potential of each object – e.g. whether it moves, comes apart . . . ;
- discarding the items in the box that they do not want to use;
- labelling the characters (this also involves making decisions about which characters the children involved are going to be responsible for);
- exploring a whole range of possibilities;
- getting down to composing the story;
- drafting;
- scene setting;
- editing;
- arriving at the final version.

The stories were produced over a period of an entire morning and into the afternoon. The children were so absorbed in the activity that they did not want to go out to play, preferring instead to stay and carry on with their story. All of the stories were of a high standard – well structured and entertaining. Three in particular bear closer examination.

Brian and Ross were given the box containing the photographs, key and fan. They quickly discarded all the objects in the box except for the key and one of the photographs depicting three late Victorian/early Edwardian footsoldiers posing together outside an ammunitions room, cigarettes in hand. Their story ran to eight chapters. Although too long to be reprinted in full here, I have included the chapter headings in order to show what the boys achieved:

Brian Tate and Ross McGuire

Essentially the story involves the boys exploring an old house and finding a key. The key opens an old chest containing the photograph, into which the boys fall. They get involved with the soldiers, who turn out to be a bad lot. In order to return to the present, they have to formulate a plan and escape from the police. What amazed me about their story was their in-depth knowledge about law and order in Victorian times. Reading their story would have left you in no doubt as to the fate likely to befall anyone caught stealing.

As with the younger children, their use of language during the process of making the story was as revealing as the completed versions of the stories themselves. It was remarkable to see how the children manipulated the toys in front of them, acting the story out as they composed it. The use of objects in storytelling offers an authentic opportunity to clearly observe the writing process in action. Lizzy and Jane were particularly fascinating to watch. They had a set of figures that included the grandfather and a family. They decided, quite rightly, that the family were well-to-do and set about telling the story of their subsequent downfall. At each significant point in the story the figures were set up in a way that reminded me of a still from a film. For example, when news of Grandfather's death from typhoid reached the family, the girls painstakingly arranged the toys so that the children were clutching at the mother's skirts. It became even more like a filming process when the girls came to a part of the story that they found difficult, or became unsure of where to go next. In effect, what they did was to rewind the story, by moving the toys backwards to the beginning and going over the story discussing possibilities and exploring new ideas as the story progressed.

One particular discussion stood out. When the family heard of Grandfather's death, the mother and father and eldest daughter decided to leave immediately by horse-drawn carriage to go and make the funeral arrangements, leaving the younger children with a friendly next door neighbour. However, they never made it to Grandfather's house – the horse took fright in the woods and all the family were killed in the subsequent accident! What Lizzy and Jane needed to do now was to decide how the children back at home heard the news. There was a great deal of debate about what methods of communication would have been possible – particularly as to whether or not telephones would have been available. Both the girls knew that it was a Victorian invention – but would it have been as widely in use as it is now? It was Jane who eventually solved the problem. 'I know,' she said. 'They could read about it in the paper, like in *Brookside*.' It was the perfect solution. They made a miniature version of the front page of the newspaper for the toys to hold. I felt that this particular piece of plot fitted well with the whole tenor of the story. It is interesting to note that of the two girls involved, Jane would have been described by the teacher as the less able. Not in this situation.

The third pair, Beth and Stacey, produced a play, called *The Victorian Sunday*. They had a set of figures that were not so well-to-do as those mentioned above. When asked how they knew that their family was poor, clothing was the key. These toys are dressed mainly in brown and cream, with cloth caps and headscarves. The girls' use of language extended beyond the spoken word here. They made notes for themselves and produced a script. In their final telling of the story they used the toys like puppets, giving each of them a particular voice. Like a play, the story is told mostly through speech, with some narration. What became very obvious was the girls' knowledge of life in Victorian times. A brief extract illustrates this point:

> The children got the job of going under the machinery and picking up dirt and fluff. After a month or two, Ellen got really concerned about the children working at the workhouse. So Ellen decided to rescue the children herself. Ellen set off to the workhouse and pretended that she worked there.
>
> Ellen saw them picking out fluff from under the machines and whispered 'Hannah, Joshua . . . '
>
> Hannah and Joshua started talking and the overlooker caught them.
>
> 'There is no talking, only working!'
>
> Ellen crept up to the children and took them quietly out of the workhouse.
>
> 'Thank you very much for rescuing us, Ellen.'

This section of the story clearly demonstrates the girls' knowledge – of the jobs that children were likely to be given, the dangerous nature of these jobs, and of conditions inside the workhouse. The notion of links between fiction and non-fiction are not new, but I have found it fascinating that children consistently draw on their knowledge of the facts to create their own fictions. There are implications for assessment here. When I showed Beth and Stacey's story to the class teacher, she said, 'But we wouldn't have known that Beth knew anything.' After reading the girls' work she admitted that she would never look at them in quite the same way again. Her expectations had been raised. All children should be entitled to such opportunities to show what they can do.

Children as makers of boxes

My box is fashioned from ice and gold and steel
with stars on the lid and secrets in the corners.
Its hinges are toe joints
of dinosaurs.

By now, thoroughly convinced of the success of the storyboxes as a means of promoting the use of language across the curriculum, I decided to investigate what would happen if children were invited to make their own. So far, I had made all the boxes, determining their appearance and their contents. I wanted the answers to two questions in particular: would opportunities for the use of language across the curriculum be further enhanced if children were involved in the production of the boxes themselves? Would the nature of language use differ in any way?

For this project I worked with a Year 5 girl, who was already familiar with storyboxes. She was told that she could design any sort of storybox that she wanted, and then make her story. What I hadn't foreseen was the way that the making of the box and the composing of the story would become embedded in one another.

Rebecca approached the task with great enthusiasm. Initially she found it difficult to choose between three themes for her storybox: journeys, Africa and animals. Eventually she decided on creating a box that would help her make a traditional African story, to explain something, as she said, 'like Rudyard Kipling'. She did manage to incorporate all three themes in her final story. At this point I asked her to draw a concept map of what she thought making a storybox would involve (Figure 10.1). This was a revelation in itself, particularly her acknowledgement of play, fantasy and research and the links made between various strands of opportunities for learning. Although she did put a few African artefacts in the box, it was apparent all the way through that the most valued objects in the box were those she had made herself. These included tortoises, a jaguar and the wise woman and her hut.

Here is her story:

How the tortoise got his shell

The tortoises had had enough. Every day they went out for a walk down by the water hole, and every day one of them was eaten. King Tortoise had to do something about it, his people were getting worried. He went to Mother Quimbande, for advice. 'Mother Quimbande, Mother Quimbande,' he said, 'What can I do? My population is getting eaten. Do you have any magic potions or anything you could recommend to me?' 'Well, here are three magic potions you could try. Take them back to your people and rub them on twice each day. Try each one on a different tortoise.'

The tortoises tried them. First of all they tried the little potion, which was called Mahaha. They rubbed it on, twice a day, on an unfortunate orange tortoise. The tortoises skin did not become thicker or harder it only became yellow. They tried the next one. They rubbed it on a blue legged tortoise. They rubbed it on and it had the same effect, so did the last one.

King Tortoise took the potions back to Mother Quimbande and asked 'Did you have anything else?' She said 'No, no that was the last of my potions. You will have to go out and look for a cure yourself.'

So, by and by, the tortoises set out across the desert. It was hot work, but it was to help them in the end. They all split up and went towards different places. One to the North, one to the west, and so on. One tortoise was a particularly lazy tortoise. It was the brother of the one whose skin had turned yellow. He said to himself 'This looking is not worth anything. I shall have a rest down under this tree.'

As it was Autumn, the leaves began to fall. He slept for a few hours and when he woke up, he found it was almost impossible for him to move. He tried to move his joints and then suddenly he heard a ripping noise. Then he succeeded. He looked round towards his back to see what had caused the problem. It was leaves. Loads and loads of dry leaves. Stuck to his back. 'That was it!' he thought to himself. He'd found the cure at last. He ran off to tell the others and stopped on the way back for a drink at the water hole. He didn't notice a jaguar perching silently in the bushes. Just as the tortoise bent down for a drink the jaguar leapt out onto him. They had a tough fight, but overall the tortoise won, because his hard shell now covered with leaves, protected him. He put on more speed than usual, just to get back to the camp.

He waited for the others. When the others came back, King Tortoise said 'What have you got on your back, my dear boy?' He said 'The cure to all our problems!' They all went off to where the tortoise had been sleeping and rolled in the leaves. When they had done this, they went back to Mother Quimbande to show her what had happened. She congratulated them and said 'I must write that down in one of my special potion books.'

From that day to this, the tortoises have been protected by that wonderful discovery a few hundred years ago.

And that is the story of how the tortoise got its shell.

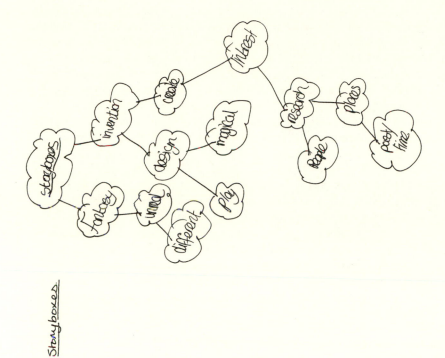

Storyboxes

Concept map.

1. play
2. Invention.
3. Unreal.
4. past/time
5. different
6. people.
7. places.
8. Unreal.
9. design
10. Interest.
11. research
12. Fantasy.
13. magical.

Figure 10.1 Concept map for storyboxes

I found the whole project a revelation. There were a huge number of cross-curricular links, not just in the final story, but throughout the whole production process. I observed mathematics, science, geography and technology, as well as a considerable amount of English. I was particularly impressed with the amount of mathematical and technological knowledge that was used during the making of the box – the calculations for the angles on the roof of the hut, the decisions that had to be made about appropriate materials to be used and the constant experimentation and reflection that accompanied the whole process. The making of the storybox seemed to provide the ideal context for these different areas of knowledge to become less disparate, for them to be used for a purpose that was meaningful for the child.

It is worth looking at this from the child's point of view. Having asked Rebecca if she had enjoyed the project, I then asked her why she thought it was such a good thing to do. Here is her reply:

> I think a storybox project is good because it gives you a chance to do what you want to do for once, because the work's not all set for you, it's not all been planned. You can do the story about whatever you want. It's up to you how it finishes . . . and it gives you a chance to make things, it gives you a chance to use all different things to make it. It's quite good because you can take a lot of time over it. It's not something you have to finish in ten seconds flat. Which is most things we have to do, because Mrs X always expects us to finish like a piece of work and a picture in a morning.

I also asked her what she felt she had learned by making her own storybox, rather than using one that had been put together first. Her answer was very revealing:

> When you work with people and the storybox is all made out for you, you learn about the person . . . because you learn about the person, and how they like stories and stuff. But with that kind of storybox, when you make everything yourself, you learn about making things, you learn how to overcome problems, like if you've got a sun and it's too low, you learn how to cope with problems like that.

Storyboxes across the curriculum

> I shall surf in my box
> on the great high rolling breakers of the wild Atlantic
> then wash ashore on a yellow beach
> the colour of the sun.

All my observations indicate that storyboxes can provide children with authentic opportunities for using language across the curriculum, whether they use a box put together by the teacher, or a box they make themselves. All the children that I have worked with have been highly motivated to use the boxes and all have experienced success. Subject knowledge is made explicit, providing the teacher with valuable information. For these reasons alone I would recommend the use of storyboxes in all classrooms.

However, I think there is more to it than that. The use of language promoted by these boxes crosses the curriculum in ways that are extremely powerful for children as learners. Whatever the subject being studied, it has been shown that it is important to plan to meet the learner's social needs as well as their cognitive needs. These social aspects of learning include:

- contribution of prior knowledge to the task;
- personal investment;
- matching tasks with learners' interests;
- making sure that the medium of curriculum delivery does not mask the child's ability.

Storyboxes provide the perfect context for all these concerns to be addressed. This is because they build on and extend the natural ability children have to create stories through imaginative play. Risk taking can be encouraged within a framework that is safe. In all my work with storyboxes so far, I have never seen a child 'fail'. Success is integral to the project.

Looking back on all the children that I have worked with, I feel that it is important to emphasise the equality of access to the learning process which storyboxes provide. All the children were able to make the boxes work for them, whatever their age, gender, perceived ability or level of fluency in English. Each time I have used the storyboxes with children I have been impressed with their ingenuity, imagination and originality. These are qualities which we would want to encourage across all areas of the curriculum. The boxes have supported children who do not always have the opportunity to make their implicit skills and knowledge explicit in the context of school. The use of storyboxes also promotes independence and confidence, reflectiveness and increased knowledge and understanding. These skills are not bound within specific subject areas.

This work clearly shows that exciting opportunities exist for supporting children in their use of language across the whole curriculum through the medium of story. The youngest children are able to use language that is appropriate to a subject, be it music, history or science. As teachers we have a great opportunity here, to support children in acquiring not just the body of knowledge associated with a particular subject but also to be part of that subject's culture. Children naturally take on the role of historian, scientist or mathematician, during the process of making the story. They work extremely hard to make sense of what is presented to them, all the time constructing new meanings, building on prior knowledge and making connections, as Jane did in using a soap opera plot to solve a problem in her Victorian story. This is what learning should be about. In addition, much of the success of the storyboxes is that they are the servants of the children. The learner is central to the process, in control, yet being supported and enabled by the context that has been prepared for the learning to take place. The children's work from storyboxes always shows qualities of openness and immediacy. There is a vitality to all their work which is infectious and invaluable, reflecting the uniqueness of individual children. The storytelling process endorses the fact that knowledge is part of the culture in which it is developed and gives children an authentic opportunity to evaluate these cultures for themselves.

As educators we can get bogged down trying to fit learning into boxes of one kind or another – the boxes on our record sheets, or the 'boxes' of curriculum areas: English, maths, music, etc. It can be only too easy for us to open the box that contains the children's knowledge, slip some more knowledge inside and then keep it firmly shut. Every now and again we lift the lid and slip in a little more knowledge. But what tends to happen is that the information stays in one place, separated from what children already know from their experiences outside school. Effective learning allows for free association between all the different aspects of knowledge which children accumulate as they develop. It allows links to be made across all areas, for knowledge not just to be given, but to be *produced*, through the children's language use. This mirrors children's experiences in the world outside school, experiences which are not put into separate curricular compartments but which are seen more holistically. Storyboxes provide a means of offering children the chance to develop the use of language with eagerness and curiosity in an enjoyable context, while teachers can observe the process of learning as well as the product.

Children use language in order to learn from us and from each other. Their need to deal with aspirations, dilemmas and hopes might be difficult to measure but it undoubtedly feeds success in all curricular areas. Life outside school is inevitably 'cross-curricular'. As teachers, we need to allow children to use language to live it to the full. Ultimately it is not so much what we put in the box which matters but what children choose to conjure from it. Then they are surfing the sea of knowledge, not being pulled under and drowned by the currents of curriculum delivery.

Acknowledgements

I should like to acknowledge the help and support of Janet Towlson and her class at Sunnymede Infants' School, Billericay, Essex, and Mrs Hardwick and her class at Collingwood Primary School, South Woodham Ferrers, Essex.

Note

1 All verse extracts are from Kit Wright, *Cat Among the Pigeons*, Harmondsworth: Puffin Books, 1989.

References

Kitamura, S. and Oram, H. (1982) *Angry Arthur*, London: Andersen Press.
Waddell, M. (1993) *The Happy Hedgehog Band*, London: Walker Books.

11

'MY PRIORITY IS LANGUAGE'

A design technology project

Bob and Jane Seberry

Our title quotes the response of one primary school headteacher when I asked if I could carry out a design technology project in the school. As the project developed, it became very clear that design technology and language can enhance each other. Although I had completed this work before the publication of the document *Design & Technology and the Use of Language* (SCAA 1997) I fully endorse the following statement:

> D & T provides a wide range of opportunities for the development of language. Designing and making requires children to move between abstract thinking and concrete actions. Evaluating existing products requires them to articulate their ideas and to compare and contrast their own views with those of other people. Such activities provide a rich educational environment for the development of language which questions and investigates, expresses thoughts and ideas, plans, refines and communicates intentions, and evaluates the activity and the product.
>
> (SCAA 1997: 1)

The work went further than these somewhat pragmatic points, however. My own [Bob's] interest in storytelling and a previous link with Japan led me to decide that I would use a traditional Japanese folk tale as the basis for a project with Jane's Year 4 class. The whole project was planned to take place over four weeks. There was a Japanese girl in the class and the children were studying Japan in their geography lessons, so that the story had relevance for the children as well as being a familiar vehicle for me. I wanted to explore, via a specific project, how the skills and knowledge of both D & T and language can be developed. In particular, I wanted to identify just where the two areas of the curriculum interrelate. I decided to do this by getting the children to produce a puppet show based on the story of *The Peach Boy*. I had done a similar project before but had not paid attention to the language implications. For me this was an opportunity for some explicit attention to the use of language.

172

We began the work by showing the class some Japanese artefacts – puppets, a kimono and some pictures – which prompted an informal discussion about Japanese customs and way of life. I then read them the story of Momotaro, the Peach Boy, explaining that this was a traditional Japanese folk tale approximately 300 years old. I tried to make the reading lively and interesting. I then showed them a video I had produced of a puppet play of the story, and they interviewed me about the video. This provided the initial stimulus, and the children became very excited about the prospect of being involved in the project and of being filmed themselves.

We asked the children to rewrite the story using a set of six cartoons with brief captions. This provided the thread through their work. They arranged the cartoons on paper in the correct order and then wrote a paragraph underneath each one. Some children chose to write their paragraphs in rough first and then to redraft them; others felt confident enough to begin writing their final drafts straight away. Their reaction to this first activity was very pleasing. At least half of the class wanted to continue writing through their break. They felt that they had good reason to put pen to paper; they were encouraged to write creatively and imaginatively, and to sequence and to organise their ideas. Some children developed the writing into an IT task by producing a word-processed version of the story. The work was revised and redrafted independently, and some children read out their stories to the rest of the class. Figure 11.1 shows Jessica's version, with the cartoons interspersed.

Once the children had a secure grasp of the story it was time to turn it into a play script. Using their own texts they highlighted the words spoken by the narrator. By doing this the pupils were learning the use and value of direct speech and the difference between the narrator's role and the characters' parts. They found that it involved using a different style of writing from their stories as well as writing for a different audience. Whilst their Peach Boy stories had been written for themselves and the teacher to read, the script was likely to be heard by people outside their immediate classroom circle. Some children chose to use a word processor to make the script easier for others to read. When the work was completed, the children worked in pairs discussing their writing. Writing play scripts is a difficult task; the extract from Jessica's script (Figure 11.2) shows how she has adapted and extended her story into entertaining dialogue which echoes the language of the original tale. The children then took turns to read out their scripts to the class, with a friend as the narrator. This stimulated much discussion. The children were asked to listen carefully before commenting on each other's work. Finally, two scripts were chosen to be used in the final performance. Throughout this process the children had gained not just a greater awareness of language and the range of ways it can be used; they had learned to work in a group, collaborating with and supporting one another. They had come to understand the need to be tolerant, to listen, to communicate courteously, and finally to reach a resolution.

The Peach Boy Story

Cartoons courtesy of Georgina Amos

The old woman finds an enormous peach.

Once upon a time in Japan an old woman and an old man lived on a hill in the country. One day the man went into the forest to cut wood and the woman went down to the river to wash the clothes. Suddenly an enormous peach came floating down the river, the old woman was astonished - She decided to take it home for her husbands supper.

Why look! There's a baby boy inside the peach.

Figure 11.1(i) *The Peach Boy* story (cartoons courtesy of Georgina Amos)

her husband was very pleased lets cut it in half right away, but just as they started to cut a small voice said don't cut me! Suddenly the peach popped open! "Don't be afraid," said the small boy who was inside "the god of heaven saw how lonley you were without a son so he sent me to be your son. Years later when momotaro (which means peach boy) was 15 he said to his father," You have looked after me for all my life so now I want to help you, you have told me stories about ogre island and how they have done bad things and now I am going to conquer them". So his father agreed and he set off with some millet dumplings

Peach Boy makes friends with the Dog, the Monkey and the Pheasant.

On the way he met a spotty dog it growled at him but when he gave it a millet dumpling it calmed down and went with him. Soon he met a monkey the monkey and the dog started to fight but Momotaro said no and gave the monkey a dumpling and he went with them. Next they met a pheasant Momotaro gave the pheasant a dumpling and he went too!

Figure 11.1(ii) *The Peach Boy story* (cartoons courtesy of Georgina Amos)

Peach Boy and his friends go on an adventure to Ogre Island.

When they got to the seas edge Momataro announced "we must build a boat to get across to Ogre Island". So that is what they had to do. They built a boat out of logs and trees and set off across the sea to Ogre Island. It was a long way and the sea was quite rough. Whenever the night came they pushed logs in the seabed all around the boat so it wouldn't float away and go to sleep

Peach Boy celebrates victory over the Ogres.

Figure 11.1(iii) *The Peach Boy* story (cartoons courtesy of Georgina Amos)

As they came doser they could see the Ogres
fort it was a large one and the walls were extremly
high. How are we going to get in asked the animals don't worry
Momotaro said I have a plan. First he orderd the pheasant
to go and peck the Ogres then the rest of them, the monkey
the dog and Momotaro attacked. They got in the gate
when the ogres weren't looking and started a proper fight.
If was terrible but finnally Momotaro and his friends
won and they celibrated their victory before getting the
Ogres to hand over the treasure.

The friends bring the treasure home to Peach Boy's parents.

Momotaro and his friends packed their treasure into
the boat and set off across the sea back to shore
They finnally get back and using the wood from
the boat they made a cart. Then they loaded the
treasure in and trundled it to the boys
parents. The boy's parents were very happy and
the all lived happily and kept the freinds for
pets

Figure 11.1(iv) The Peach Boy story (cartoons courtesy of Georgina Amos)

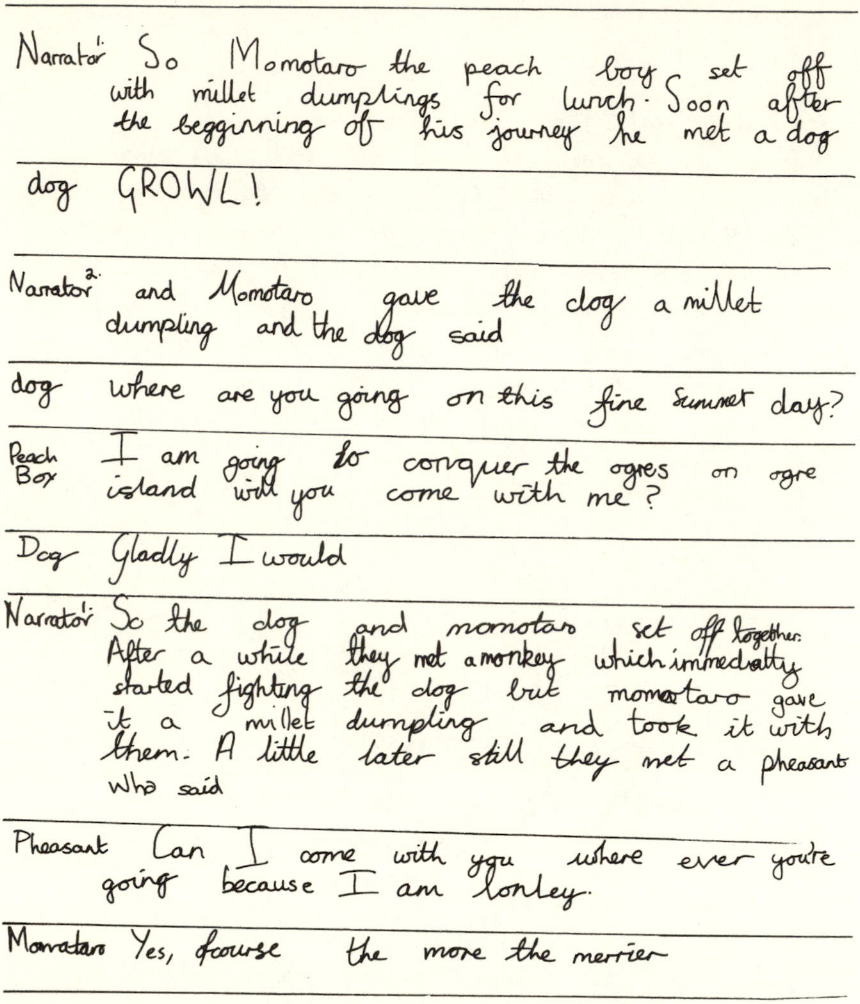

Narrator¹ So Momotaro the peach boy set off with millet dumplings for lunch. Soon after the beggining of his journey he met a dog

dog GROWL!

Narrator² and Momotaro gave the dog a millet dumpling and the dog said

dog where are you going on this fine summer day?

Peach Boy I am going to conquer the ogres on ogre island will you come with me?

Dog Gladly I would

Narrator³ So the dog and momotaro set off together. After a while they met a monkey which immediatly started fighting the dog but momotaro gave it a millet dumpling and took it with them. A little later still they met a pheasant who said

Pheasant Can I come with you where ever you're going because I am lonley.

Momotaro Yes, foourse the more the merrier

Figure 11.2 Extract from Jessica's play script

Getting ready for the play

Each pupil was given a worksheet requesting them to list the steps involved and the tools and materials needed in order to design, make and evaluate a puppet for the play. This could be a character or a prop. I demonstrated various techniques of puppet making to help the children make their own decisions. They were asked to make a drawing first and then to list the tools and materials that they would need (Figure 11.3). This was followed by a list of the steps involved in the making of the puppet. Collectively they had to ensure that they made one of the characters and props needed for the play. This stage of the process generated another form of writing which had a different style and purpose – one where sequencing, clarity and precision of language were very important. When the puppets were designed, the children were asked to write notes on how they could improve their puppet if asked to make it again.

Once the puppets were made, the scripts were given out to the children, who learnt their parts and then rehearsed the play. The children worked in groups learning the script and harmonising the spoken word with the movement of puppets, for example deciding sides from which the puppets would make their

List the materials and tools you will need for making the puppet.

1 copper wire 2 cloth 3. wood 4. saw 5. Axe 6. Scissors
7. String 8. Drill 9. pens 10. ruler 11. Pencil
12. Glue 13. Nuts 14. metal pole

Write out the steps you will take in making the puppet

1. Look at my design for the puppet.
2. Collect all the materials and tools needed for making the puppet.
3. Cut the wood to the right size and shape.
4. Cut the cloth to size
5. pin right sized planks together to make panel
6. pin the mask on the right place.
7. Drill holes in mast thread string through and tie sail on
8. pen; nail heads on wood to look like the ship is nailed together. glue on bolts and screw pole into place

When you have made the puppet please answer the following questions.

What did you like about designing and making the puppet?

Most I liked making the sail and drawing the picture of my boat.

How could you improve your puppet if you were making it again?

I could improve my puppet by using a slightly different glue

Figure 11.3 Materials and tools needed for making a puppet

entrances. They chose, designed and made appropriate props to enhance the performance, for example millet dumplings, the ship and treasure, and then they made the scenery. In terms of language development this shifted the focus from mostly writing to speaking and listening. They had, of course, used their ability to talk as they discussed their writing and their puppet design but this was speech of a different kind – a more performative kind which is not so usual in everyday classroom work. It was different, too, from their experience of drama, where they were used to improvised dialogue. Here they were being asked to interpret the words of others in a rather more formal way.

This was a very exciting part of the project. The children designed posters to advertise the play, paying attention to the ways in which posters capture people's attention; they had to decide on layout and colour as well as shape and size of letters – all good visual learning for D & T as well as introducing them explicitly to the language and presentation of persuasive texts. This had become a project which developed social understanding and collaboration. So in line with that area of learning, therefore, two different performances of the play were given in class, so that all the pupils could take part. This also acted as practice in preparation for the performance in front of the video camera, with the head-teacher present.

When the puppet play was filmed the children showed themselves ready and able to perform for the camera. They were aware of the need to speak clearly and succinctly and were proud of their polished performance. The video was then shown to the class both for pleasure and also for discussion and evaluation (see Figure 11.4). The pupils showed that throughout the project they had developed their critical faculties; they were clearer about what was good and what had worked well. They were keen to point out how things could have been slightly changed or improved. Jessica's example shows not only that she has developed a good sense of dramatic emphasis but that she has learned a vocabulary to talk about using language: 'The individual voices could be slightly raised in certain parts' (see Figure 11.4). The evaluative element of this project showed some impressive analytical judgements.

Finally, the children were asked to write a letter about the puppet play to a friend or sibling who had not been able to see the performance. This provided another real audience, and an opportunity to practise more formal writing skills. It was drafted, revised and rewritten to ensure that it conveyed the best impression to its recipient (Figure 11.5). The children kept copies of their letters so that they could include them in the final presentation – a folder which contained all of their work bound together with a title page, a contents page and a personal photograph. The children took particular pride in the presentation of this folder.

Conclusions

Learning through story brought the project alive. The children loved having a definite goal to work towards. On the way, they developed language skills, social

Peachboy Video

1. **What was good about doing the play?**
   What was good about doing our play was making the puppets it was interesting to see everybody else's puppets, Some people had to improvise.

2. **What did you enjoy most?** I enjoyed having the play filmed and making the puppets

3. **How could the performance be improved.**
   a) **Narrator** The performance of the Narrators could be improved by the Narrators reading ahead of what they are saying

   b) **Individual voices** The Individual voices could be slightly raised in certian parts like Dog, you can have as many bones as you want Dog will be louder.

   c) **Movement of puppets** Some of the puppets could move more naturally

Figure 11.4 Evaluation of the video activity

and interactive skills and design techniques, and gained an introduction to Japanese culture.

In terms of design and technology outcomes the children had been given opportunities to:

- work with a range of materials and components;
- work independently and in teams.

181

Dear Louise and Robert,

I thought you would like to know (especially Robert) about a play we did at school it is based on a Japanese story called the Peach Boy this is what it is like. There is an old man and an old woman and one day the woman went down to the river to wash the old man's clothes, when suddenly she saw an enormouse peach floating down the river towards her. She took it home for her supper but when the were about to have supper a baby boy came from the peach and told them the lord had sent him to be your son. When he was fifteen he went to fight the ogres on ogre island with 3 friends, a monkey, a spotty dog and a pheasant. When the got to the shore they built a boat and sailed to ogre island. They defeated the ogres and brought the treasures back to the old man and the old woman and they lived happily ever after After hearing the storey we cut up some cartoon pictures and put them in the right order. Then We stuck the cartoons on to a piece of paper and wrote the relevant paragraph underneath. When we had finished writing the story we wrote the story as a script, for the whole play (not just one puppet). In our Christmas holidays we made puppets for whatever character we were going to be I made a boat it was flat a bit like a shadow

Puppet (but it wasn't one) and some people made hand puppets. I had to improvise because we didn't have what we needed, for example when we moved house one of our tool boxes was taken by mistake it had gluegun sticks in and we were going to use glue gun to stick the boat puppet I was making together, most of the other glues were paper glues and the boat was mostly wooden. Then we learnt our lines there were not many people who had to learn lines so it didn't take very long.

After that we rehearsed the script it was fun but it was more interesting in some bits than in others - When we performed in class it was really really fun first we practised behind Mrs Seberry's desk then we practised in a proper theatre, finally one friday a man came to video the plays it was wonderful the also took photos of each of us individually with our puppets last of all we saw and discussed the video the video was great and the discussion was very interesting I would like to do something like it again. I hope you enjoyed reading this letter

Figure 11.5 Jessica's letter about the puppet play

They had developed their designing and making skills by being able to:

- draw on personal experience to help generate ideas;
- clarify ideas through discussion;
- develop criteria for designs and suggest ways forward;
- evaluate their design ideas bearing in mind the users and the purposes;
- speculate on the effects of different approaches to a practical problem;
- evaluate their products as they are developed, identifying strengths and weaknesses;
- develop their design and technology capability through focused practical tasks, e.g. reading for information about techniques in worksheets;
- explore, develop and communicate aspects of design proposals, and evaluate design ideas and products.

It is noticeable that many of these skills depend on language for their development. The children had also extended their knowledge and understanding in design and technology, particularly in the areas of control, products and applications, quality and vocabulary (Department for Education 1995: 4–5).

The language products (written and spoken texts) had been:

- a series of six paragraphs, one for each of the cartoon series above, relating the Peach Boy story in the children's own words;
- a script (handwritten or word-processed) for presenting the tale in a puppet drama;
- stage directions for the presentation;
- creation of posters and advertising material;
- performance of the show;
- letter to a friend/member of the family about the play;
- evaluation of the performance (oral and written) using a video;
- evaluation of the puppets used in the show (oral and written).

This represents a wide variety of texts for varied audiences but alongside these experiences were the processes of discussion, analysis, choice, reasoning and justification. The children learned to collaborate on spoken and written texts and developed noticeably in self-esteem and confidence. These social experiences derived from working in groups were bonuses. After we had completed the project we felt that we could certainly reassure anyone whose priority was language that, as the SCAA document points out, 'D & T provides a wide range of opportunities for the development of language' (SCAA 1997: 1).

Acknowledgements

With thanks to the children at St John's College School, Cambridge for their willing co-operation in this project. We should like to thank Kevin Jones, Headmaster of St John's College School, and Marilyn Taylor, Head of the Junior Department, for their help and support and Georgie Amos for the drawings.

References

Department for Education (1995) *Design and Technology in the National Curriculum*, London: HMSO.
School Curriculum and Assessment Authority (1997) *Design Technology and the Use of Language*, London: HMSO.

12

'DON'T LOOK OUT OF THE WINDOW, YOU'LL ONLY HAVE TO WRITE ABOUT IT!'

Developing texts from first-hand experiences

Ian Eyres

From my earliest days as a teacher I have always believed in the value of 'real experience' in children's learning. I soon came to realise, however, that experience is no more than the raw material of learning and that in order to make sense of their experience, learners need to find ways of organising it, both for the sake of clarifying its inner logic and also to be able to relate the experience to their existing knowledge. As a Key Stage 2 class teacher, the medium through which I would most commonly ask young learners to reorder and explore their experience was that of writing. Working, as I now do, with young bilingual learners has taught me to look for additional systems of representation (e.g. drawing) which allow children to express and manipulate what they know without necessarily having mastered the full range of a less familiar language and its writing system. In this chapter I describe how I worked in partnership with John Ayton, the teacher of a vertically grouped Year 4/5 class at Priory Junior School, to develop approaches to teaching history which begin in first-hand experience and then offer stimulating ways of organising and expressing that experience.

The context

Priory Junior is a large school on the eastern edge of the city of Cambridge. Most of the children come from surrounding estates of local authority housing. Class 7 is one of five vertically grouped Year 4/5 classes. Around half of the children in the class had been identified as having special educational needs, mainly because of low attainment in reading. The class contained three ethnic minority children: Wei Ha, a Cantonese-speaking girl who had joined the school as a virtual beginner in English the previous January and who, with bilingual support,

185

had made excellent progress; Cui Bo, a girl from mainland China, who is a confident user of English; and Dominic, a Year 5 boy whose family originates in Jamaica. Dominic is confident, articulate and often insightful in situations where he can contribute orally. He is, however, a reluctant reader and writer and appears to experience particular difficulty in this area. At the time of the project the school was awaiting a psychologist's assessment of his special educational needs. As a Section 11 funded support teacher my job is to promote the development of children's language throughout the curriculum. I decided that my time in the class (two mornings per week) would be most usefully spent supporting the class topic work on the theme of *Invaders and Settlers*. In this age of long and medium term planning it would be vain to claim that we chose the topic, but in fact it was one which suited us well – John is a history specialist while I was keen to explore ways of helping children use language to evaluate, analyse and present historical information.

The aim of the project was to give support to the lowest-achieving children in the class, through a programme of work which would stimulate, engage and challenge the whole class. For me, Dominic was of necessity a specific focus of the project, but we expected that all members of the class would benefit from activities which would increase competence and confidence in reading, writing, speaking and listening. At the outset our stated goals were:

- to give children opportunities for using various sources to find information;
- to give children opportunities for presenting information and opportunities to encounter primary sources of evidence through a site visit and through handling artefacts.

They would have access to reference books, pictures and replica artefacts as secondary sources. Their work would be presented in writing and drawing and through the media of a conventional topic book and of video, so that by the end of the project not only would they have an understanding of the Roman and Anglo-Saxon periods of English history, but they would also be more skilled in identifying, evaluating, selecting and presenting relevant information and *en route* have had many opportunities for practising such basic skills as planning, negotiating, collaborating and questioning. Much reading and writing would be done within this purposeful context.

When planning with Dominic particularly in mind, I was concerned that conventional topic work, structured (as it often is) around reading and writing activities (even, or perhaps especially, the limited reading and writing required by worksheets), would not allow him to express his understanding of a subject, or to develop it further. During the previous term I had worked with Dominic on a one-to-one basis and had seen some progress in his writing. Over the course of the term he had managed to write a number of quite lengthy pieces of fiction and autobiography. Although these were emphatically 'all his own work', they could not have been written without unbroken individual attention and a reader's response at least once a sentence. This I felt was largely due to the fact that he found spelling individual words such hard work. Although Dominic had proved himself capable of composing a substantial text, in one important feature his work differed from conventional pieces of writing. Dominic was never alone with his thoughts. One essential respect in which writing differs from conversation is that in the former the author has to construct a complete argument without the prompts and encouragements of a conversational partner. Dominic's writing, on the other hand, rather than being the product of a dialogue with the text itself, represented one side of a conversation with me. Despite this difficulty with committing his ideas to paper, Dominic had shown himself time and time again, in the context of small-group and whole-class discussion, to be capable of grasping quite complex ideas and offering original observations. The fact that the biggest bar to Dominic's development appeared to be spelling difficulties reminded me of some of the older bilingual pupils I have taught. Often they have many sophisticated skills at their disposal and are capable of constructing elaborate texts in their first language, but restrict themselves to offering simple sentences in English, often simply because of limits to their English vocabulary. Dominic's many compositional skills were evident from his spoken utterances. We had decided that video would be an exciting and practical medium for all the class to present some of their learning; an additional benefit of the medium, it seemed to me, was that it could offer Dominic the freedom to assemble an elaborated text with some degree of fluency and independence.

Starting with stories

Early in the project (the Roman period) we were determined to establish ourselves, in the eyes of the children, as a teaching partnership, so we began with some whole-class work which involved both teachers in distinct but equally active roles. During the first half of term the class made a study of archaeological remains of Roman forts in the north of England, including those on Hadrian's Wall. The partnership's contribution to this work was in the form of two creative writing themes. John began by reading an account of the finding of two skeletons under the floor of a stone building near Hadrian's Wall. The skeletons were apparently those of two murder victims. He told the children about all the evidence which archaeologists had found and asked them to reconstruct what they thought might have happened, in the form of a murder story. I divided my time between supporting individual writers (including Dominic, of course) and writing the beginning of my own version of the story, a text which I shared with the class at the end of the first of two writing sessions. Although in recent years (thanks to the numerous demands on teachers' time) the practice seems to have become less widespread, the idea of teachers modelling reading is well established in many classrooms. The modelling of writing, however, happens less frequently. Personally I find the practice useful for three reasons. First, it is a way of suggesting themes and structures without imposing them (and thereby opening the door to potential failure). Second, it is the most reliable motivator I know; children want to do what they see their teacher (or another important adult) doing. Third, it offers a basis on which teacher and pupil can discuss every aspect of their writing – they are fellow writers.

Following this activity John and I exchanged roles and I took the lead in two sessions in which children, in role as Roman legionaries, were asked to write letters home from a new posting on Hadrian's Wall. They were able to use information they had gained from their study of the Roman army, together with new information taken from reference books. It is worth noting that this research was not the contextless *see what you can find out about* . . . form of research. The children already knew a great deal about the subject before they approached the books. Scanning for information is so much easier when the majority of what you are looking at makes some sense to you, even if it only means that you understand a subject well enough to reject it. The letter-writing task also gave the research a purpose and the final drafts of the letters were used to make a display in the classroom. They also provided very useful material for the assessment of the children's understanding of the period.

Working on-site

Cambridge is within 25 miles of the reconstructed Anglo-Saxon village at West Stow and this seemed an obvious starting point for work on the next set of invaders. I had taken classes to West Stow before and had always done so with children more or less in role as resident Angles – complete with costumes and storytelling round the fire in the hall. This time John and I decided to take a different approach, encouraging children to take the part of archaeologists, making detailed observations and interpreting their findings.

The morning was spent with the centre staff. The children first learnt about the ways in which archaeologists work on a site like West Stow, and then went on to examine and discuss a set of Anglo-Saxon artefacts. This session laid the foundations for further similar examination in the classroom. In the afternoon the class explored the village in groups. Each group had a task to perform which involved looking for clues to determine the function of the different buildings and each was accompanied by a teacher, a learning support assistant or parent. My group included Dominic, Wei Ha and Cui Bo.

Before the trip I had arranged to borrow a camcorder. I felt that a video record would be a good way of bringing children's observations back into the classroom in a form which would be easily accessible to the whole class. It also enabled the children to concentrate on making their observations, secure in the knowledge that they could be fully recorded without the need to make detailed notes – an important consideration given the extent of many of the children's basic literacy skills. It would give them the opportunity to present and preserve the full flow of their thoughts at the same time as gathering a visual image of the subject in hand. In other words, the camcorder could record both more fully and more easily. I also had a suspicion that the children, as experienced viewers, would be comfortable with the medium and possibly be familiar with some of its techniques.

Before the trip I explained to the class that the camera was not there simply to record the events of the day, as it would be in, say, a family holiday video. The purpose of it was to provide a medium for individuals or groups to make a deliberate record of their understanding of what they found. I told the whole class that if they had something they wanted to say *to* the camera then they would be able to do so. Although the offer was genuinely open to all the class – it is a small site – looking back at the tape more than half of the contributions are from the three bilingual children. At this stage I think my conception of the role of the camcorder was that it would be analogous to a combined notebook and sketchbook.

Creating video texts – in context

Dominic's first contribution runs:

> This thing here's called a pole lathe and they used this, like, if they had something there stretching like this to that long piece of branch, put a piece of wood there, put a chisel against it and and it . . . shave off the wood to make it round. And I'd like to remind you again, this is called a pole lathe.

The first thing you notice about this text is that it is clearly an example of Dominic's speech. It contains a number of specifically oral locutions (*This thing here . . . like*) and a false start. As is the case in many conversations, it is linked to its physical context (the image on screen includes much pointing). It differs from conversational speech, however, both in that it does not seek support from a fellow speaker/listener and in the fact that it has a distinct shape. It begins with an introductory sentence, continues with a main section which expands on the introduction and then is brought to a neat conclusion. I cannot say whether Dominic's ability to construct such a well formed piece is the result of his exposure to written language through the medium of books read aloud or of his exposure to examples of exposition on TV. Whichever the reason, his description represents something of a bridge between spoken and written texts. Just as his supported writing demonstrated that he was capable of handling the low-level mechanics of writing, this recording shows his ability to work with higher-level linguistic (or literary) structures.

Dominic's second effort is in a similar vein, but this time it includes reference to an audience.

> As you can see, over here, there is a pot where they used to hang on here and they put it on there and they put food in and they cook it and they light the fire down there.
> That's it.

The difference in tone of the final *That's it*, addressed to the camera operator, shows clearly that the opening *As you can see* refers to an audience separated from the speaker by both time and place. Again we are offered an assessment opportunity which none of his written texts had afforded.

In the Anglo-Saxon hall Dominic reported the speculative views of his group.

> We're not really sure how the fire, how the smoke come out. But we said that it possibly did come out there, but we're not really sure about where the smoke goes.

All the texts so far contain the kinds of broken sentences, with their false starts and inconsistencies, that are characteristic of speech, a medium which does not allow for revision. Speech on video is, however, capable of revision. Dominic's next shot began:

> These patterns we found on the outside of the door . . .

Despite this apparently good start (complete with very professional gestures), Dominic indicated a wish to start again. His second attempt ran:

> This is the pattern what we found on the oldest house and it goes around the door framing. And we think they used to make it, we think they used a . . . chisel.

The first sentence gives us more detail than 'take 1' and uses a more precise word, 'door framing'. The second (unrehearsed) sentence reverts to speech's customary imperfect fluency.

Dominic's use of video recording, then, reveals several aspects of his knowledge of text construction for which his teachers had previously had no clear evidence.

Wei Ha's contributions were revealing in a different way. At this stage, although long past the so-called 'silent phase' which beginner bilinguals often go through, she was still a fairly reserved member of the class and her contributions, both oral and written, tended to be careful and 'safe'. The camcorder gave her licence to speculate:

> This case is a um cupboard for clothes because it got the lid on it and maybe you can put secret things for it because it's got a lock on it.

and

> I think that people who have eaten the hens left their eggs down here so then they can cook their eggs for dinner. Or just get more chicken with it.

and

I think this is for putting clothes when it's not washed yet. So they just leave it here and then later on they wash it somewhere.

Cui Bo showed a similar willingness to speculate:

This is for a bath. Long time ago. They went in there and while they were in their bath the clothes that they had to take off they hanged on this bit.

Investigating and interpreting artefacts

At West Stow the children had been introduced to the work of archaeologists and had looked at houses reconstructed on the site of a real Anglo-Saxon village. They had also had a brief opportunity to examine one or two objects. We wanted to extend this experience of real artefacts further, but the availability of real medieval objects is limited. In the past I had used artefact collections from the *Suitcase of History* range produced by Sue Perry, a former Cambridgeshire curriculum adviser. I thought it might be worth contacting Sue, even though to my knowledge her collections did not go back further than the Victorian era. As luck would have it she had just begun putting together sets of replica objects from earlier periods and was able to supply us with quite a dramatic collection which ranged from small knives and drinking vessels to pleasingly large objects such as an adze and a yoke.

As well as being on display in the classroom, for children to look at, touch and talk about, the artefacts were to prove useful props (in both the theatrical and coalmining senses!) for the video sequences. They were also central to a number of directed activities aimed at encouraging on the one hand close observation and recording and on the other purposeful speculation.

On the day the objects arrived we tried a brainstorming activity. I introduced the technique by producing the adze and explaining brainstorming as a technique in which you say everything you can think of about a subject with the appointed scribe recording all without question. When contributions began to flag, I encouraged the class to think about what it was made of, where it would have been made, its purpose and who would have made it. The class then worked in pairs on an object of their own, brainstorming for five minutes, using a prepared sheet (Figure 12.1). Next, the pairs were given an organiser sheet (Figure 12.2) which gave them a framework for sorting their thoughts and presenting them in an organised way through answering questions. In this way a link was made between the artefacts and the geography and social and economic structure of the village. Throughout this activity children had the opportunity to discuss their thoughts with their partners, with other children and with the teachers.

After this exercise the children were asked to imagine they were archaeologists recording a find as accurately as possible with detailed drawings, measurements and verbal descriptions (Figure 12.3). In the course of discussing this, the

Brainstorm Sheet

Use this sheet to write **any** ideas you have about your object. Work as quickly as you can. Don't stop to wonder if your ideas are good or not. (You can do that later.) Write down any questions you have, too.

You have exactly five minutes.

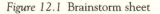

Figure 12.1 Brainstorm sheet

inevitable question came – are these objects 'real'? John and I agreed that this question was best left for the class to investigate and we devised a worksheet on which each pair would have to list reasons for and against believing in the authenticity of a given artefact before deciding on their own opinion (Figure 12.4).

Most were able to check their object's appearance against pictures in reference books (again we were glad of the opportunity to send children to reference books with a purpose), to remember what they had seen at West Stow and to consider the effects of ageing on different materials (something which the staff at West Stow had talked about). It was not long before almost everybody was satisfied that the objects were not genuine. We were then able to discuss their value as a source of historical information: were they simply worthless fakes or could they still teach us something? Did the fact that they had been provided by someone I described as 'a history teacher' make them reliable? We had begun by treating the artifacts as a primary source. Now they had been revealed to be a secondary source the class had to decide just how reliable they felt they were. While these activities were taking place the children were also preparing and shooting their next video sequences.

Organiser Sheet				
Use this sheet to organise the ideas from your brainstorm. Add any other ideas you think of. *Questions and uncertain ideas should have a question mark after them.*				
What is it **made of**?	**Where** did the materials come **from**?	**Where** in the village **was it made**? (A special building?)	What **tools** were used to make it?	What **special skills** were needed to make it?

Figure 12.2 Organiser sheet

Creating video texts – in the classroom

After the trip John and I wanted the children to reflect upon what they had learned at West Stow, we wanted them to extend their knowledge and we wanted them to make links between their various discoveries. Finally we wanted them to present their learning for others to see. The medium would again be video, though this time they would have the opportunity to prepare and rehearse, and thus develop their work beyond the spontaneous footage gathered in the field. The material to be interpreted and presented included the video recording, children's own memories and notes, booklets from West Stow, reference books, picture sets and a collection of replica artefacts. In creating a more crafted text, the children would need to decide what information should be included and select or make the objects and images which would support their dialogues and voiceovers. While not all groups ended up working to a written script, all used writing in planning their piece.

The first thing we did, of course, was show the footage which had been shot at West Stow. This caused considerable excitement and a useful discussion followed, much of it dedicated to reflection on what worked well and what didn't. It was obvious that most of the time the speakers were thinking on their feet and

---

Recording a find

You have just found an Anglo Saxon object. In case it gets lost, stolen or destroyed you need to record exactly what you have found.

Draw
Draw the object as carefully as you can. You may need several drawings to show everything.

Measure
Make a rough diagram to show the main measurements.

Describe
Write an exact and detailed description of the object. Don't leave anything out!

Continue on another sheet if you need to.

Figure 12.3 Recording a find

that the stumbles and mumbles which sometimes resulted did not make good television. I explained to the class that we wanted them to work in groups to produce a planned and scripted sequence on some aspect of West Stow. (We deliberately made the theme as wide as possible and were prepared to accept any reasonable interpretation.) Visual support could include children's own pictures, pictures found in books and the artefacts. The children also had the option of appearing on screen themselves.

Names: _____   _____

Real or Fake?

Give three (or more) reasons for thinking this object is genuine

Give three (or more) reasons for thinking this object is a fake

Do you think it is real or a fake?

If it is a fake, can we still learn anything from it? Is it reliable evidence?

Figure 12.4 Worksheet: real or fake?

The children set to work (in friendship groups) with visible energy and absorption. We noticed that quite a high proportion of the groups were engaged in writing lengthy scripts on large sheets of paper. Further enquiries revealed that all of these were expecting to shoot these texts as part of their programme. Rather than explaining (individually or *en masse*) that this would not make for exciting viewing we decided to bring forward the production of the first group's programme to the second half of this first lesson. We promised the girls concerned that they

195

would have a chance to remake their programme when they were happier with its content and they agreed to present what they had prepared so far. The result of this first attempt was a short scripted talk delivered by two 'talking heads'. The programme ended with some relevant (but soundless) drawings.

Our second session we began by showing the girls' programme and I introduced the idea of planning a sequence by using a simple storyboard – a sheet of paper folded into eight boxes – to be used alongside their scripts. As well as helping children decide how their material was to be organised and presented, the storyboards were an aid in the selection of relevant material. Those scripts which had already been written in poster form were put to use as low-tech autocues. Recording took place over a period of four weeks, with later programmes incorporating later classroom learning – another example of video as an assessment tool. The *News Report* (see below), for example, is evidence that the boys had made links between the kinds of workshop found at West Stow and the manufactured objects they were examining.

The programmes themselves took a variety of forms. The most impressive mixed the makers' own large, colourful pictures and maps with voiceovers. (One even had an opening credits sequence with a recording of (authentic?) Anglo-Saxon music.) Other groups followed a similar pattern but included 'talking heads' where they had no visual support. Programmes like this represented a style of presentation, disembedded from a material context in a way which is characteristic of written texts, and many of the children found it difficult to work in this way. Some, therefore, chose to make use of the textual support offered by a question-and-answer format or of the contextual support of the artefact collection. Dominic's group used both.

ANDREW: This is Andrew on *News Report* about the Anglo-Saxon tools. Over to Alan.

ALAN [*with an adze*]: This is a thing where you just carve the top of of the wood off and then you can make tables or something and that and this was made from a blacksmith and this was made from a carpenter.

CARL [*with a sheepskin*]: Well this is the sheepskin, and . . . when they get meat they don't waste the skin, thy use it for covers or clothes or something. You could put it on the ground for a rug or something like that . . . over to Mark.

MARK [*with a spindle*]: Er, this is a spindle, for making wool . . . and it's made out of wood and probably made I don't really know how they made this round but they might have chiselled this bit with a sharp thing to cut this off.

DOMINIC [*with a yoke*]: I think this is for . . . well they used this, instead of just carrying it with your hand, your hands gets worn out, they used this like to carry buckets of water or milk from the cattle or from the river and um this is how they carried it. They carried it like this. They didn't bring it like this because they need some support on here and here so they carried it like this. They didn't bother carrying it like this because water [would come?] out here, but they carried it like this.

ANDREW: How did they make the hook?

DOMINIC: The hooks? Well I think it was made . . . this was made from a blacksmith and this was made from a woodworker's shop. And the hooks were kind of bent. First they got a long metal and then they bended it, but they had to make it hot, so they couldn't use their hands. Over to Andrew.

ANDREW [*with a scythe*]: This is a scythe what they used for harvesting the wheat and they probably put a flame on it and to get this round bit really sharp and chop the wheat well and probably span wool around that and probably made it by a carpenter or somebody who lives by a blacksmith. It's all rusty now.

ALL: Bye!

Although they were working to a written storyboard it is clear that the boys' speeches are not scripted. One advantage of this is that we can be sure that they understand what they are telling us – from this example we see that they share a vision of the village as a more or less self-sufficient community in which members must make the things they need for themselves and their neighbours.

Some groups mixed scripted questions with spontaneous answers, as in this sequence:

JANE [*voiceover – screen shows a boy holding a large woodworking tool*]: Mark Prior is going to tell us about an object that the Anglo-Saxons used to use.

MARK: It is an adze. It's made of steel and wood.

JANE: Where was it made?

MARK: It was made in a blacksmith's and a wood shop.

JANE: What kind of people used to use it?

Some of the groups used a mixture of presentational techniques as well as a range of resources to present their piece. In this sequence the presenters managed to find effective published pictures to illustrate their own discoveries:

KELLY [*to camera*]: Hello and welcome to West Stow. We are reporting on a trip about Anglo-Saxons.

SAMANTHA [*children's picture of pot*]: This is a cooking pot from West Stow Anglo-Saxon village, and the pot was made of metal.

KATIE [*photograph chosen from a picture pack of hall*]: This is the hall. The pot was in the hall when we went on our trip. The hall was used for meetings and feasts.

SAMANTHA [*photograph of inside the hall*]: This is a picture of inside the hall. As you can see, the cooking pot is hanging on a chain where they cooked their food.

KELLY [*three girls to camera*]: This is the end of our report on West Stow Anglo-Saxon village.

ALL: Bye.

This final example combines scripted commentary with an improvised interview. The pictures had been carefully drawn to illustrate the points being made:

ALISON [*to camera*]: Welcome to our programme about an Anglo-Saxon workshop.

BECKIE [*drawn picture*]: Anglo-Saxons had a workshop to make all the things they needed. [*drawn picture*] They made little weapons and knives. They made tools and jewellery and probably shields. [*back to picture 1*] The Anglo-Saxons used the things around them to make the things they needed. [*zoom in to centre of picture*] This is a picture of an Anglo-Saxon workshop.

ALISON [*shot of interviewer*]: What if they needed a knife and they didn't make them?

BECKIE [*shot of interviewee*]: They could not go out and buy them so they swapped things instead. For example, if you made clay pots you would swap one for a knife.

ALISON [*both in shot*]: Where did they get the iron from?

BECKIE: They got the iron from the mines.

ALISON [*to camera*]: Now you know about the Anglo-Saxons. That's all for today, folks.

BOTH: Bye!

Concluding the project

The last few sessions consisted of the usual scramble to get everything finished. All the children had a good deal of work (much of it a by-product of their research for the video sequences) which needed to be collected into their topic book. The last few groups needed to get their sequence recorded and then we were able to show the completed video to the whole Year 4/5 unit. The children were proud of their work and received positive feedback from peers and teachers alike. John and I certainly felt that it had been a successful unit of work. Anything which left the children so enthusiastic at the end of term must have something to say for it, but what could be our reasons for claiming success in terms of learning?

First of all, enthusiasm is not something to be discounted as a frivolous extra. The topic was interesting enough to keep the class thinking right to the end, and since nobody stays enthusiastic for long about things they don't understand (except maybe X *Files* viewers) we had an indicator that the class had a continuing grasp of the main concepts of the topic.

Discussion with the children, their written work and the video all demonstrated an appropriate understanding of the needs and motivations of the communities studied and of the workings of their economic and social systems. They had been able to derive and be critical of information from primary and secondary sources and the more able could articulate the principles by which they were working.

What distinguished the Anglo-Saxon part of the project was the way in which the children were very actively involved in their learning. Much of the work meant dealing with concrete objects or pictures and most was collaborative. (Even the relationship between myself as camera operator and the video presenters was a collaborative one – though the level of support I offered did vary according to need.) The organisational talk involved in the activities was not only valuable for its own sake, but often ensured that all group members had a common understanding of the subject in hand.

The children were deliberately given a good deal of choice in how they approached the work, partly because responsibility implies ownership and understanding, but also because such choice allowed each group to use its existing skills to best effect. The open-ended nature of the video making (and other research tasks) meant that the children felt secure in taking risks and therefore in using their abilities to the full.

Members of Dominic's video group, working without a script, were able fully to demonstrate their familiarity with some of the artefacts and to explain their place in the life of the village. It was clear that they were also drawing on their knowledge of TV conventions and their ability to handle the larger organ-isational structures of texts. If they had been restricted to saying the things they could write down in the available time their contribution would have been far less satisfying. On the other hand, some of the other groups were able to show a much greater level of sophistication in their understanding of village life, in their use of sources and in their choice of modes of presentation. Allowing the work to be differentiated by choice in this way meant that every group's task was challenging and everybody produced a result to be proud of. Inclusiveness and differentiation sometimes appear to be at odds with one another. This project offers an example of a way of teaching which sets out to benefit particular individuals, not by withdrawing them or giving them specially differentiated tasks but by taking their needs into account when planning for the whole class. Planning in this way tends to give rise to a curriculum which is interactive and collaborative and in whose activities children have a clear sense of purpose – qualities which are valuable for all learners. Every learner is a full member of the intellectual and social community of the classroom.

Working with a number of media allowed us to revisit the same information several times. Although there are undeniable virtues in simple repetition, revisiting ideas also allows for their refinement. This was made explicit in some of the artefacts tasks, while revision and redrafting played a big role in the planning of the video sequences. All this was consonant with the pervasive theme that information needs first to be gathered and then shaped, before it can be presented to an audience.

So far as our original aims were concerned, John and I felt satisfied that children had had valuable experience of using and presenting historical information. The effect of exploiting the link between oracy and writing is more difficult to quantify in the short term. We were happy that there had been many opportunities for the exercise of oracy skills. The children had discussed and shared ideas and opinions relating both to subject matter and its manner of presentation. Negotiation was frequent, disputes rare. We knew that the children had all used writing in preparing their spoken presentations and that they had used speech in collaboratively drafting their writing. Many had shown in their (recorded) speech that they were familiar with the structural conventions of written language which they were rarely able to express in their writing. It seems likely that in the long term such active experience of a wide range of compositional skills can only be of benefit. What was incontrovertible was that children had been using reading and writing with a growing confidence. There is nothing like a real (and highly motivating) purpose, especially if it is being pursued in collaboration with others, for sweeping away inhibitions and other blocks to competence. Without explicit direction, children had been reading to identify, select and connect key information. They had taken notes and used them to produce progressively more crafted scripts. Some of their writing, in the form of titles and captions, was made suitable to appear on screen. Some was destined to be read aloud and some, in the form of questions and prompts, was used to support spoken language.

Looking back over the last few paragraphs I fear I may have left an impression of a vastly complex project. In fact, any use of language is complex and as teachers we need to be sensitive to as many elements of that complexity as we can be. I don't believe, however, that the children were groaning under the weight of the project's complexity. Their aims were relatively simple and in practice the complexity was mostly manifested as single-minded activity. In the course of a term the project had prompted many questions. In the final week the most commonly asked was *When can we do this again?*

Part 5

THE LANGUAGE OF
REFLECTION AND
EVALUATION

Reflection has a significant part to play in the learning process, if teachers are concerned with pupils accommodating new information into what they already know. Reflecting on what they have learned and the way in which they have handled the learning process will help pupils deepen their understanding of the product and the process of learning.

(Reid et al. 1991: 3)

The emphasis here on reflection as an integral part of the learning process is important. Often reflection is reserved until the end of a series of activities, where it may well become the starting point for a new cycle of learning. The SCAA document *Use of Language: a Common Approach*, for example, states that 'using language to reflect on what has been learnt is a vital part of confirming knowledge' (SCAA 1997: 6). Reflection and evaluation are increasingly becoming recognised as ways of supporting critical thinking at all stages of learning as well as helping children to make explicit to themselves and others what they know, understand and can do at the end of a series of activities.

Much of this reflection and continuing evaluation happens through talk. An interesting feature of much of the work in this book is the important role played by talk in shaping and communicating learning throughout the curriculum. Attention to language is not just focused on literacy but on speaking and listening, too. Another recurrent feature of many of the chapters is the social nature of language and learning and the importance of the teacher's role in structuring opportunities for genuine dialogue in constructing knowledge. Much current educational thinking about scaffolding learning and constructing knowledge owes a debt to Vygotsky's work on the interactive nature of language and thought. This is summed up by Bruner's commentary on Vygotsky's contribution to a theory of education:

His basic view was that conceptual learning was a collaborative enterprise involving an adult who enters into dialogue with the child in a fashion that provides the child with hints and props that allow him [sic] to begin a new climb, guiding the child in next steps before the child is capable of appreciating their significance on his own. It is the 'loan of consciousness' that gets the child through the zone of proximal development.

(Bruner 1986: 132)

The 'loan of consciousness' from adults to children is an essential element in learning, supporting learners as they get to grips with new conceptual demands. Once they have had some experience and practice they are then in a position to move out of the zone of proximal development – the area in which their potential is transformed into reality. It is language which mediates this; including, importantly, the language of reflection and evaluation. Bruner reiterates, however, that language is social and communal, as he reflects on his own process of educational theorising:

I have come increasingly to recognise that most learning in most settings is a communal activity, a sharing of the culture. It is not just that the child must make his knowledge his [sic] own, but that he must make it his own in a community of those who share his sense of belonging to a culture. It is this that leads me to emphasise not only discovery and invention but the importance of negotiating and sharing – in a word, of joint culture creating as an object of schooling and as an appropriate step en route to becoming a member of the adult society in which one lives out one's life.

(Bruner 1986: 127)

Since talk is necessarily social and cultural there is a clear link between language, learning and communities – at home or in the classroom. Bruner continues with what has become one of the most quoted extracts from *Actual Minds, Possible Worlds*; perhaps this is because it so succinctly expresses what teachers implicitly know:

Much of the process of education consists of being able to distance oneself in some way from what one knows by being able to reflect on one's own knowledge.

(Bruner 1986: 127)

The classroom and school, then, are sites for creating a community of learners, guided by teachers who can scaffold experiences. One more ingredient is needed, however – a sense of critical enquiry about what is to be learned:

> What is needed is a basis for discussing not simply the content of what is before one, but the possible stances one might take toward it . . . The language of education, if it is to be an invitation to reflection and culture creating, cannot be the so-called uncontaminated language of fact and 'objectivity'.
>
> (Bruner 1986: 129)

This returns to one of the points made in the introduction to this book: that the relationship of language and learning is more than simply getting children to 'use' language or 'express themselves correctly and appropriately' (SCAA 1997: 6). Language is more than communication, and its interaction with learning is more than a process of taking in facts. Language does not just provide evidence of learning, it contributes towards the construction of knowledge and under-standing; it helps learners place themselves in the world. This includes having a critical view of knowledge; critical reflection in Bruner's words is 'a metacognitive step of huge import' both for pupils and teachers. 'The language of education is the language of culture creating, not of knowledge consuming or knowledge acquisition alone' (Bruner 1986: 133).

Douglas Barnes, in considering the role of talk in constructing knowledge, emphasises the legacy of learning which grows from communal understanding:

> Learners must indeed 'construct' models of the world but the models they construct are not arbitrary; the experiences on which they are based do not come from nowhere. They are responses to activities and talk that they have shared with other, usually older, members of the community . . . Exploratory talk does not provide new information. When we talk of learners 'constructing' meanings, we refer to them manipulating what is already available to them from various sources (including first-hand experience), exploring its possibilities, and seeing what can and cannot be done with it . . . By participating in activities and talk we internalise both the categories and the ways of going about things that are essential to our social environment.
>
> (Barnes 1992: 127–8)

With this reminder about the communal nature of learning, Barnes at one and the same time underlines the importance of home communities whilst also drawing attention to the communities in schools and classrooms which offer special opportunities for learning. As Bruner points out, the learning is not simply of facts but the development of opinions, of preferences, of choices, based on analysis of evidence and critical engagement with texts of all kinds as well as of emotions and sensitivities worked out through everyday social – and textual – experience.

A critical educational theory

This suggests the development of an educational theory of language and learning which takes account of the view that it is more dangerous to prohibit than discuss, which can engage in interrogation of the content, presentation and stance of texts offered as sources of learning. This involves teachers in being confident – or courageous – enough to encourage children to develop their own opinions, think about them, question them, engage in debate and dialogue and, ultimately, emerge with clearly held views and enduring knowledge. This is often most effectively done through talk, as Tatiana Wilson's work in Chapter 13 shows. Her class were engaged in reflection and evaluation throughout their science and humanities work; critical analysis became second nature to them as they debated some very complex geographical, economic, political, social – and moral – issues. Once the critical edge had been honed by speaking and, importantly, by listening, and fed by reading, the children were then able to express complex, informed and sensitive opinions in writing. Aided by the processes of reflection and evaluation, critical oracy leads to critical literacy.

In his contribution to a wide-ranging and provocative book, *New Readings: Contributions to an Understanding of Literacy*, Alex MacLeod outlines the possibilities for critical literacy:

> Just imagine that the goal for education really was the nurturing of new generations, who can think and decide and act for themselves, who plan and behave democratically, who care about the society they live in as well as their own future.
>
> (MacLeod 1992: 116)

This is a timely and ironic warning about what education is supposed to be about. The links between language and learning are not simply to provide learners with competence or the ability to communicate effectively or to be able to handle the demands of reading and responding to a wide range of texts. The dynamic interaction of thought and language ought to encourage energetic interrogation of what is presented as the content of learning. If one of the strands of English is to develop discrimination and the ability to make informed and thoughtful choices about texts, then encouraging pupils to think for themselves is essential. Tatiana Wilson shows how this might be done.

Alex MacLeod sees *thinking for themselves* as a very social act. Whilst valuing home language and literacy experience, he sees schools as unique environments for critical and reflective learning:

> Schools may have many things wrong with them, but one thing they have, which is not found so ready-made in communities outside, is a forum where people whose lives and cultures are very different can be engaged in dialogue over long periods of time. The interaction is

continuously recharged by the events of the curriculum and by events in
the world, local and international.

(1992: 116)

One of the strengths of the classroom lies in the people who inhabit it. The
children and adults in any classroom represent an enormously rich and varied
resource of language – and other – experience and expertise. Jennifer Reynolds
found that her Year 4 class had a remarkable reservoir of group experience of
reading; they also had opinions about the books that they had read. In wanting to
develop their critical analysis of texts she teamed up with Sally Elding, who
knows about computers in the classroom, and collaboratively, with the class, they
developed a database on which they could record – and from which they could
access – information about the books they had read. Storysearch, as outlined in
Chapter 14, does not simply hold numerical information about titles, authors or
numbers of books read by any individual, it is a database developed to include the
results of discussion and individual reflective evaluation of the children's reading.
The process of analysis needed before being able to input the data means that the
reader has to get to grips with issues of genre, authorial stance, underlying themes
and subtleties of characterisation. This is rather different from the traditional
book review. One important feature of the work is that it developed through
discussion and negotiation between pupils and teacher, and between individuals
and groups of pupils, over a couple of years. And the developments and
amendments continue, as Sally Elding and Jennifer Reynolds explain.

Capturing language

Talk is a central feature of the chapters in this part of the book, although they
include strong elements of literacy. As other chapters have shown, there is great
variety in the kinds of talk texts which children can be encouraged to experience
and use. In terms of reflection and evaluation, talk has great value, but one of its
qualities is that it is ephemeral. It has been compared with writing on water.
How, then, do teachers capture talk texts and use them to feed back into the
process of reflection and evaluation? There are several ways, some already
mentioned earlier in the book – writing down what has been talked about, tape
recording talk, drawing – but one of the most fruitful ways of capturing talk,
which has become widely available only in the last decade or so, is the use of a
video recorder. The last chapter in this part looks at areas where talk makes
a great contribution and where literacy is not traditionally a part of the subject.

Patricia Maude looks at language in relation to physical education, pointing
out that although talk is one of the key language elements in PE (the other is, of
course, the language of movement) it is unusual to consider the role of the subject
in developing language. However, the PE curriculum is ideally set up to develop
reflective as well as communicative uses of language in its three attainment
targets: planning, performing and evaluating. Chapter 15 makes very clear the

breadth of opportunity for language development beginning from the child's very early life when adults support and encourage the development of walking, running and playing through language specific to movement, place and position – *pick up the ball, lift your arms up high*. Patricia Maude sees movement, physical education and language as necessarily interrelated. Children do not just learn how to move through the use of language, they learn the language of movement – physical and verbal – and learn about language through physical education. Since PE has a built-in evaluative element, the use of video and written reflections contribute to the further development of movement.

This chapter summarises the spirit of all the contributors to this book; it is guided by certain educational principles about the relationship between children, language and learning. The book as a whole is founded on a theory of teaching and learning which from the very earliest years:

- recognises children's existing experience and makes thoughtful plans to build on that experience;
- creates an environment where learners take an active part in negotiating and organising their own learning;
- acknowledges the importance of all partners in the learning process – families and teachers, adults and children;
- has high expectations of children's potential;
- offers challenges, but provides models, examples and scaffolds to help children tackle them;
- allows for some risk-taking;
- values critical enquiry;
- provides opportunities for collaboration, reflection and evaluation.

The cycle of planning, teaching and learning, and evaluating leads to the next set of plans for learning. The following chapters show how language plays its part throughout this process, critically contributing to reflection on what has been learned.

References

Barnes, D. (1992) 'The Role of Talk in Learning', in K. Norman (ed.) (1992) *Thinking Voices: the Work of the National Oracy Project*, London: Hodder and Stoughton.

Bruner, J. (1986) *Actual Minds, Possible Worlds*, Cambridge, MA: Harvard University Press.

McLeod, Alex (1992) 'Critical Literacy and Critical Imagination: Writing that Works for a Change', in K. Kimberley, M. Meek and J. Miller (eds) *New Readings: Contributions to an Understanding of Literacy*, London: A&C Black.

Reid, J., Forrestal, P. and Cook, J. (1991) *Small Group Learning in the Classroom*, London: The English and Media Centre.

SCAA (School Curriculum and Assessment Authority) (1997) *Use of Language: a Common Approach*, Hayes, Middlesex: SCAA.

13

GREAT DEBATE

Tatiana Wilson

One very effective way I have found of enhancing language development is by using debate. This has not only contributed to an issues-based approach to studying both science and the humanities, it has also been a useful tool in developing skills in English. Over the past few years I have organised and planned for many different debates, and their success means that I now try to include them in my planning for each term's work.

On a visit to Exeter Museum we came across stuffed animals in the natural history section which prompted a science debate where the children argued for and against keeping stuffed animals in museums. Figures 13.1 and 13.2 show examples of pro- and anti-stuffing views.

The children made a wide range of other points:

> All the animals they have in the museum have died of natural causes or if they were shot it would have been accidentally. Keeping animals in a zoo is much more cruel.

> In our history when there were no cameras or videos people couldn't bring back any evidence of new findings from other countries so they had to stuff animals. Now we've got videos and cameras we don't have to stuff them any more.

> We have had these stuffed animals for 100 years so it would be a waste of time to destroy them. We can use them to educate the children of today.

> Unlike the television in the museum you can get a close-up on an animal. Stuffed animals can also educate children and show the proper beauty in them.

> What example are you setting for future generations?

Not only have the children been able to gather a range of differing views about the issue, they show in their writing that they are taking on the language structures of reasoned argument.

I am Christina Suckley, the museum curator. I think that it is right to stuff animals because it will teach our childrens children about animals. If there is an animal that is endangered and it becomes exstinked, then it will be the only propper way to see them. They would beable to see them on the computers but it is not the same as seeing them property It does not hurt the animal and I'm sure that they would help today's children if they knew they could.

Figure 13.1 Argument in favour of stuffing animals

Hello, I am Harry Parry. I work for the B.B.C and I also work on computers.

I think that with the knowlege of computers and t.v we have no need to stuff animals.

From my experience on computers we have no need for stugged animals On a C.D.Rom you can see the animals run and hear them roar. What good is a still stugged animal in a glass cage?

I also work part time for the BB.C. I am a camera man and just last month I was working with Richard Attenborough who works with animals. When I got home after filming my family said what a lovely programme you filmed and with that I joined this group on stugging animals.

Figure 13.2 Argument against stuffing animals

Other classes have debated the pros and cons of the Aswan Dam in Egypt (Figures 13.3–13.6) and show the level of sophistication which one Year 6 class were able to reach about complex social, environmental, economic and historical issues through their experience of debate. They have been able to identify on the one hand the potential break-up of communities which such a project can cause and the loss of archaeological evidence, but also the possible advantages to the economy and the improvements in health care.

At the same time they have learned to express their ideas in the style of formal argument and persuasion. On other occasions I have looked with classes at the arguments for and against organic farming, the most useful thing you could have to help you survive on a desert island, and so on. Basically, where there is an issue I try to help the children debate it.

The reasoning behind this is clear. I cannot think of many activities that support so much both in terms of considering issues and in developing language which are so simple to do and as effective in extending children's skills. All children need to understand the power of words and the conventions of different genres in order to maximise the way they use language for their benefit in the

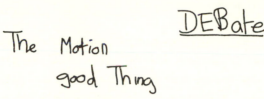

DEBate

The Motion

good Thing

C.   A farmer. Before the Aswan High Dam was built we used to struggle to survive. We worried about the wether all the time and wether the rains were going to be too small of too great. Now we know that we will have enough warter for our needs and that our corps will not fail or be wased away. I am a happier person for it. I know that each year I will be able to provied for my famliy. Now that we know we will not strave we do not need to sale what we do not need. We can sell and buy luxuries insted. our life is better becase of the Aswan dam.

Figure 13.3 The Aswan Dam: pros and cons

Debate The motion,

"This house believes that the Aswan High Dam is the best thing that could have happened to Egypt"

A home owner: I am speaking for many of the thousands of people who where forced to leave their homes and their communities because of the Aswan High Dam. My family had lived for many generations by the river Nile and had enjoyed a good life in a community we belonged to. Since the Aswan High Dam has been built we have been forced to live elsewhere further away from the banks of the river Nile, in an area of less fertile land. We are away from our friends and our family has been split up. We never wanted the Aswan High Dam to be built all it has brought is misery to ordinary people like me. The Aswan High Dam has meant that the rich have got richer while the poor are even poorer than before.

Figure 13.4 The Aswan Dam: pros and cons

A businessman. Since the Aswan High Dam we have been able to make our factories more efficient and we can use state-of-the-art machines which has meant that our profits have been greater and I am richer then ever. Machinery is better for business as we can keep our factories open all day long and produce much more than before. Machines don't get tired like people do and they make less mistakes. The Aswan High Dam is good news because it means that Egypt can go from strength to strength in the future.

Figure 13.5 The Aswan Dam: pros and cons

An archaeologist. It is difficult to astertain precisely what has been lost forever under the waters of Lake Nasser. There maybe many unknown treasures that will never be discovered — perhaps even finer finds then that of Tutankhamen which as you all now was only uncovered resetly. It was a godish decision to build the Aswan Highdam as many tourists come each year and now many precious sights have been damaged forever and others lost forever under the waters of lake Nasser.

Figure 13.6 The Aswan Dam: pros and cons

future. By making a point of view explicit in speech it is easier then to write it with greater authority and clarity. Recently I studied Benin with a Year 6 class, so we considered whether Benin artefacts should go back to Nigeria or not. We were fortunate, as Bernie Grant MP had sparked a brief media debate by expressing his belief that the artefacts should be returned. With information from books and media reports we began to put together our ideas for a debate.

The process of preparation

Usually our debate work happens towards the end of a topic as I use it as a tool for consolidating what the children have learned and applying that knowledge. Throughout the topic I try to raise the children's awareness of bias and the need to be able to justify any point of view they put forward. In the past I have been used to working with other adults in my classroom so that organising the groups was not a problem. More recently this has not been the case and I have found it easier to manage the class by working on two debates simultaneously, as I find smaller groups easier to support. For each debate there will be a *for* and an *against* group so that there are four groups working at any one time. I usually select the groups. I try to stretch the children appropriately. For example, if someone is already sure about one side of the argument I will encourage them to argue against their own opinion as that involves more learning. A shyer child might be given more choice about the group they are in.

When the groups are decided I usually then have a whole class session. I go through the main points of both sides of the arguments and ask the class to think of possible witnesses who would enhance their point of view. For our debate about whether the Benin artefacts should be returned to Nigeria the children suggested a teacher from Devon, a museum curator and a Nigerian immigrant all arguing for the artefacts to stay. On the other side we had a teacher from Nigeria, the Oba of Benin and a lawyer. When everyone is clear about the whole picture of the debate they split up into their groups to write their speeches. If it is possible, half the class remain in the classroom and the other half work outside so that opposing sides cannot hear what is being discussed. I give each side notes about the main points in their argument and the three ideas for witnesses who will strengthen their point of view. If they have not done this kind of activity before, I stress the need to be able to pretend that as individuals they are completely convinced by the strength of their views and to keep up the idea that the other side's arguments must be flawed.

At this point the two groups of children work secretly, writing their speeches in smaller groups, making props and collecting costumes. Some children decide to take on a new name – recent ones have been Jennifer Dandelion the animal rights activist or Professor D.L. Sausage, curator of Exeter Museum – and they may choose to wear what they feel are appropriate costumes. Others will make posters or draw charts that will enhance their argument (usually with a fair amount of poetic licence!). Because these are secret activities there is always a great deal of anticipation amongst the class and excitement about what is to come.

When I have gone through the speeches with each side and given a few tips on body language and other ways to enhance their delivery, I then suggest that they should consider what they think the opposition might be arguing, and any flaws in their own arguments. That is probably the hardest part of the whole activity as there is a fine balance between encouraging children to think through issues that you think should arise and spoon-feeding them with your own preconceptions. At this point the groups formulate a list of questions they may want to ask the opposing side. They may also jot down a few ideas related to sticky points or weaknesses in their own arguments.

On the day of the debate the classroom is cleared of desks and the children sit in two groups facing each other with a gap in the middle. The half of the class not involved in the debate form the audience. If possible, another adult videos the proceedings and I sit between the groups as the chair.

The children hear each of the speeches in turn – one for and one against the motion and so on. I try to call the witnesses so that they match, with the arguments juxtaposed as clearly as possible. The speakers are encouraged to perform in role, speaking from 'personal experience' and using props as much as possible. I emphasise the importance of encouraging each other and ban any booing (which can arise just from the children's enthusiasm and excitement) from the start. The audience applaud each speaker when they have finished. After the speeches I thank the speakers for their eloquent contributions and briefly recap the key points we have heard before we break to go into our two groups again.

In each of the groups the main aim is to think of good questions to ask the other side that will show flaws in their argument. Having done this the groups then think of ways of supporting their own 'beliefs' in the light of what they have just heard so that they are more prepared when the class join together again. This can take from two minutes to half an hour depending on the quality of what has gone before and whether I feel a particular group needs specific teacher input.

When the class is together again the discussion begins. I have a rule that none of the speakers can reply to a question. This is to ensure that a larger proportion of the class is able to formally contribute to the debate. Questions are intended to prompt further debate, for example:

> If the artefacts go back to Nigeria, how can you educate people about Benin?

> If there are Nigerian people living in England, how are they going to be able to learn their country's culture?

> Who would pay for the artefacts to be transported back to Nigeria?

You have had our artefacts for a long time. Do you still need them to learn?

Don't you have laws about stealing? Yes. So why can't we have them back?

Who made these artefacts that you stole from us?

The other important lesson learned by composing questions is that in complex social, geographical and historical issues there are no easy answers. After each question is asked, the group who are to provide a response have a few moments to work out their answer. Any children wanting to reply are given the opportunity to do so. The questioners are then given the chance to respond to answers they have just heard and so a dialogue develops. I usually allow three questions from the opposing side and three from the audience, although this is flexible, according to the context of the debate.

The audience are then encouraged to vote for the side they felt argued best. I used to allow the children who were involved in the debate to vote but found that almost invariably the votes were straight down the middle as they had convinced themselves that their group must be better. I have tried various lines of persuasion to encourage them to vote in a more detached way but with no success, which is why I have decided that it is better if they do not have the right to vote. As a class we then have an initial brainstorm, highlighting the bits that individual children thought were the best or most important points, then we leave the debate alone for a few days.

The cool light of reason

Later, when the class are less emotional about the debate, we watch the video of what we did. As each part comes on the screen we first focus on what is good about it and then discuss ways it could be better next time. We list these on a large poster and usually include things like body language, especially the way the children use their hands and eyes, voice control and how they emphasise the points several times. This session is one of the most important as it is here that the class really learn to reflect on the greater impact of some ways of using language and presenting it over others. It is here that some of the subtleties of spoken English can be examined with a degree of depth and rigour in a context that makes such careful analysis both understandable and relevant.

Sometimes in cross-curricular teaching certain activities lend themselves naturally to enhancing many different skills, and debate seems to be one of those. First, it helps children to get to grips with the different sides to an argument. Then it encourages them to think carefully about the type of people who might share a particular view and their reasoning which goes to support that view. As the children deliver their speeches in role they often take on mannerisms and body language that they have associated with their characters. Listening to either side and then forming questions for the opposition means that the children have to find holes in the other team's logic as well as ways of dealing with the flaws in their own arguments.

When a debate like this has finished and the class have watched themselves on video it is easier to look back and reflect on ways of improving speakers' performances next time, whilst also recognising technique that has proved successful. In addition the written work produced from debate and the oral understanding is much clearer and more eloquent than might otherwise be expected across the ability spectrum.

Figures 13.7 and 13.8 give two examples of opposing points of view. Other contributions cover even more aspects of the debate:

> I am a teacher at St Thomas High school. I think the artefacts from Benin should stay here in Britain so the children can learn about them and also investigate them because some schools don't have any resources and not very many books on Benin artefacts in schools so what we need is a lot more books on Benin artefacts if the artefacts go back to Benin.

> I can easily get a replica of it if you want. It won't be worth as much but will look the same and educate the same way.

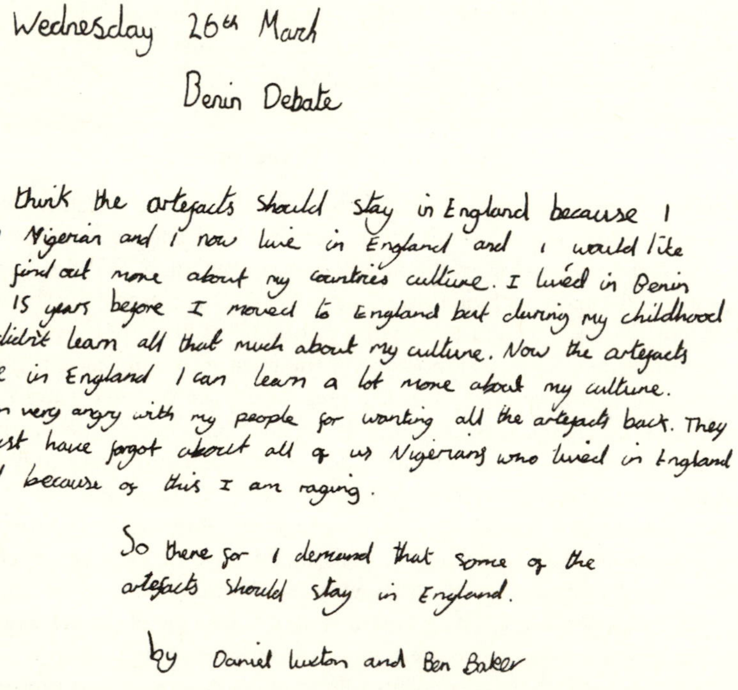

Wednesday 26th March

Benin Debate

I think the artefacts should stay in England because I am Nigerian and I now live in England and I would like to find out more about my countries culture. I lived in Benin for 15 years before I moved to England but during my childhood I didn't learn all that much about my culture. Now the artefacts are in England I can learn a lot more about my culture. I am very angry with my people for wanting all the artefacts back. They must have forgot about all of us Nigerians who lived in England and because of this I am raging.

So there for I demand that some of the artefacts should stay in England.

by Daniel Luxton and Ben Baker

Figure 13.7 Benin debate

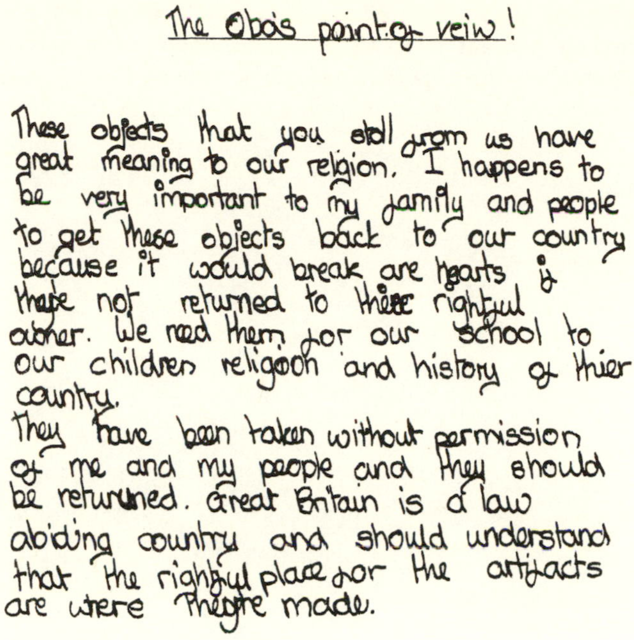

The Oba's point of veiw!

These objects that you stoll from us have great meaning to our religion. I happens to be very important to my family and people to get these objects back to our country because it would break are hearts if thaye not returned to thiee rightful owner. We need them for our school to our children religooh and history of thier country.
They have been taken without permission of me and my people and they should be returned. Great Britain is a law abiding country and should understand that the righful place for the artijacts are where theyre made.

Figure 13.8 The Oba's point of view

> I am a teacher in Nigeria and I would like to say you have done wrong in the past like having people for slavery from Nigeria . . . If you give our artefacts back we will take it as an apology for what you have done. As a teacher I know how important it is for the children to feel that you are sorry about the things you have done in the past.

I am convinced that as teachers it is imperative to make strong and clear links between oracy, reading and writing in our classroom practice. These different facets of language development support each other. In the children's work on Benin it is obvious to me that their experience of debating, asking and answering questions fed directly into their ability to write in persuasive and argumentative genres. It is an obvious point but one that I feel is in danger of being blurred by the way the National Curriculum for English is organised. It can appear that the complexity of language is not important and that it is therefore possible to compartmentalise language development into crude attainment target and level descriptors. The further compartmentalisation into subject areas and the formulaic approach of the Literacy Hour threaten to fragment children's learning experiences even more. In my experience, using debate can foster focused reading, thoughtful writing and engaged and assured oracy, besides developing subject knowledge gained from such activities. The combination of attention to language and opportunities to see the complexities of some of the issues covered in the curriculum means that the children gain a fuller and more engaged understanding of relevant concepts. Teachers know about the value of an integrated curriculum; it is important to practise what we know to be true so that the children can reap the benefits of having a more holistic overview.

14

STORYSEARCH

Children using information technology to interpret texts

Sally Elding and Jennifer Reynolds

Information technology (IT) is taking over, or so it seems. Certainly information is now a powerful resource which permeates many aspects of our daily lives. Yet, as OFSTED recently highlighted, IT is still not a sound enough feature in the primary English curriculum even though many children display a competence superior to that of their teachers. It is important for teachers to recognise the impact of new technologies and to help the children become IT literate by acquiring the necessary skills. A wider definition of literacy, which includes IT, will then see English and information technology working together in a structured and effective way to help children extend their knowledge and ability to use and construct a variety of different texts. Indeed, information technology may now be more properly referred to as information and communications technology (ICT) since new developments make the technology even more interactive. ICT has valuable contributions to make towards children's language development. For instance, through the Internet children now compose and send electronic mail and receive replies. Very young children not only read texts on the screen which combine words, images and sounds but can also take part in the creation of such texts.

Young children searching a CD-ROM for information on minibeasts are using an information source equivalent in size to that of a large encyclopaedia. Pupils are now using numerical graphs and data to answer questions, compile statistics and produce reports from their collected data. As one class of children collect and record rainfall samples from which they will produce graphs, another group are working out from their own collected data the average height of a Year 4 child while others are preparing reports which will include graphs and collected data about traffic flow outside the school. ICT is without doubt creating exciting possibilities for today's young readers and writers. Collaborations at the computer are frequent, the examples are endless, and all are language-rich experiences.

The handling of information is seen as a key element in principal areas of the National Curriculum in England and Wales. History, geography, science and mathematics all have subject matter which lends itself particularly well to this strand of work; all of them have specific factual content which has to be covered. The content of both English and ICT is less easy to pin down. Like English, information and communications technology is both a subject and the means by which learning occurs. It does, however, have a subject matter and, as we describe in this chapter, where ICT skills and capability combine with English content and processes, some interesting and important links can be developed. In 1989 the Cox Report stated that:

> Most interactions with computers are language experiences. [IT has] to do with the storage of information, much of it linguistic. This huge and expanding technology is therefore of great importance to teachers of English. And Information Technology should be seen as a way of encouraging pupils' language development.
>
> (DES 1989: 27)

More recently, the SCAA document *Information Technology and the Use of Language* stated:

> IT can stimulate discussion and help children develop their reading and writing skills;
> IT offers a new medium for exploring and creating texts;
> IT has a particular contribution to make towards developing children's ability to compose, compare, read, manipulate and transform texts in printed and electronic form.
>
> (SCAA 1997: 1)

Even without these indications from official sources, classroom teachers are already becoming aware of the contribution ICT can make to language development and towards learning as a whole. Word processing is perhaps the best-known application but increasingly teachers (spurred on by their pupils who bring experience from home) are making use of simulations, spreadsheets and databases.

The Storysearch database

Storysearch is a questionnaire/database written in PinPoint (a Longman Logotron product) which invites the reader(s) to respond to a range of features in a text and to record these at the computer.[1] The questionnaire was originally written to gather evidence about readers for a classroom project undertaken by Jennifer, who was at that time following an Advanced Diploma course in language and literacy. She quickly recognised that the questionnaire could be used by the children themselves. Once pupils have encountered – read, seen or heard – a story they complete a questionnaire sheet. The sheet can be completed by individuals, but if the information is provided by a pair, group or class the pupils benefit from the interactive talk.

The completed sheets form a database which can then be searched for information about particular authors, texts set in a particular time and place or more complicated searches such as for an animal/adventure story with a first person narrator. So, Storysearch has a dual function in that the children analyse selected features of narrative texts which are recorded on questionnaire sheets, then interpret and classify the collected information. It is worth pointing out that although one particular piece of software was used to develop this database, most data-handling programmes will contain some of the same features and will enhance similar skills.

Storysearch was originally developed for and in collaboration with Year 5 children. In fact it was the pupils who extended the character and genre categories and through discussion made their own suggested headings for technical language: for example, the children changed the wording *omniscient* narrator to *god-like* on the form; it made more sense to them like that. In further trials Years 4, 5 and 6 children have encountered few problems either using the database, coping with the language of the form or selecting and analysing the texts. Teachers themselves have started to adapt the original Storysearch form to suit their own purposes and plans, and the needs of their pupils. This is because they have realised the limiting nature of traditional handwritten book reviews and have been excited by the stored and accessible nature of the database. Teachers are indeed finding Storysearch a useful way of helping pupils to learn about data handling as well as learning about a wider range of texts.

After reading a book, children see Figure 14.1 on screen, onto which they record information about the text.

Making meanings – demonstrating understanding

Teachers who are using Storysearch overhear many examples of pupil discussions as they develop their ICT and literacy skills. Class teacher Jennifer collected evidence from her pupils by listening to them as they talked together at the computer and by tape recording. Here she first describes and reflects on two pupils as they work at the computer together after reading a Martin Waddell book. Later in the chapter she recounts the discussion of a group of children who have read *The Iron Man* by Ted Hughes.

Alice and Sean (Year 4) used Storysearch to interpret *The Hidden House* by Martin Waddell. The reading group which Alice and Sean belong to had read *The Hidden House* at least twice. Afterwards they discussed the text and the pictures but were deliberately steered clear of the Storysearch structure of interpretation and mainly stuck to personal responses to the text. The children had enjoyed the book and were keen to complete a Storysearch on the computer without adult supervision.[2]

Storysearch

Name   Boy or Girl

Title _____

Year published

Author

Illustrator/Animator

Have you read this story?   Have you seen this story?   Have you heard this story?
☐ Yes ☐ No   ☐ Yes ☐ No   ☐ Yes ☐ No

Narrator
☐ adult
☐ child
☐ animal
☐ storyteller
☐ god-like
☐ other

Characters
☐ animal   ☐ adult (male)
☐ object   ☐ adult (female)
☐ orphaned children ☐ child (female)
☐ adult baddies   ☐ child (male)
☐ wizard/witch   ☐ monster

Genre
☐ picture book
☐ adventure
☐ fantasy
☐ science fiction
☐ supernatural
☐ mystery
☐ horror
☐ school
☐ historical
☐ animal/nature
☐ autobiography
☐ journal
☐ romance
☐ true-life
☐ humour
☐ other

Times

Places

Themes
☐ jealousy   ☐ war
☐ love   ☐ growing up
☐ loss   ☐ relationships
☐ change   ☐ coping with problems
☐ sorrow   ☐ conflict
☐ humour   ☐ other
☐ rich and poor

Other images of this text?
☐ music
☐ computer game
☐ games/toys/objects
☐ other

Messages from the text _____

Figure 14.1 Storysearch

Alice has a statement of special educational need. She has problems retaining knowledge, cannot remember events which happen at home or at school and she finds it difficult to formulate sentences in her head. Alice opts out of large group discussions and has to be coaxed into joining in with small group discussions. She has fifteen hours of Learning Support Assistance and since September her LSA has concentrated on involving her in group tasks to help develop her spoken language.

Sean is a bright, articulate and thoughtful child who has a wealth of general knowledge. He has a sound understanding of what he can read and of texts read to him and he is able to respond to and interpret texts to a good level. However, Sean, too, often opts out of group discussions if he is not working with peers who are his friends.

They both knew that they were being taped and were happy for this to happen. If anything, it implied to them that they were expected to talk and share ideas. Both children are familiar with the software and they have worked in groups inputting data. They have also completed Storysearch sheets but they have never gone 'cold' to the computer before. The tape and transcript provided many examples of Sean and Alice supporting each other's reading skills. Not only have they had to read the text of the book in order to understand and interpret the story, but they are having to read the text on the computer screen to complete the task of filling in the data sheet. The text on the Storysearch data sheet is not daunting to the children, but they do come across words which they do not know the meaning of and words which they cannot read. The children help each other to overcome these difficulties.

The following extracts from the tape and transcript illustrate the language and literacy skills the children are developing as they complete the Storysearch sheet on screen.

Identifying the narrative voice

Alice and Sean have completed the information at the top of the sheet and have now to make some informed decisions about the literary features of the book. At first neither of them understands the meaning of the word *narrator*, yet once they have been reminded that it means the person who is telling the story, they are able to act upon this knowledge. Alice tells Sean that the old man is telling the story. In fact the narrator of *The Hidden House* is quite difficult to identify. The narrator is omniscient but expresses opinions, for example 'But I think that they were happy.'

S: She says who's telling the story? [*repeats this twice*]
A: The old man.
S: Is he ?
A: Us two . . . we told the story.
S: The little man . . . God-like . . . yeah, god-like . . .

221

A: *God-like* [*indecipherable*]. It's an adult telling the story. It's an adult.
S: It's god-like . . .
A: OK, OK it's god-like . . . Right let's go on to the next one.

It is clear that Alice sees the narrator initially as the old man in the story but soon Sean decides that the narrator is definitely god-like. Alice gives in to his decision even though she doesn't seem to fully understand the meaning of a god-like narrator. Perhaps she just decides to agree for an easy life. When both children become more experienced with using Storysearch and they fully understand the meaning of a narrator they would be expected to support their opinions with examples from the text. Alice has good reasons for thinking that the narrator is the old man; if adults were analysing the text they might be led to the decision that the house is telling the story.

Understanding genre

One of the benefits of asking two or more children to put data in together is that this necessarily involves discussion and analysis. The children learn how to justify their ideas – to themselves and each other – as they make decisions about what to enter on the Storysearch screen. On tape there are examples of both children substituting their own language for the language on the data sheet. Although they both struggle to pronounce the word *genre* correctly they are able to complete the section about genre with little difficulty. Alice is convinced that the book should belong to the family of picture books. They have an engaging discussion about it when she persuades Sean to agree with this:

A: It's a picture book.
S: Alice can you do it? [*pointing to the mouse*] Look, swap places. Can you do the mouse? *Alice* . . . you do the mouse control.
A: I don't know what to do.
S: OK. What is it? . . . It is an adventure book.
A: I told you it's not . . . Oh God.
S: Picture book? Is it a picture book? No . . .
A: Yes it is.
S: It's got pictures in but it's not just . . . it's not just . . . adventure book?
A: You're supposed to put every single one.
S: You're not . . .
A: Right I've done this before . . . I did . . . Right . . . *Is it a picture book?*
S: No because it's got writing in too.
A: I'll click it.
S: *No because* . . . [*appealing to a friend*] William, Alice thinks it's a picture book.
A: It is a picture book.
S: A picture book is just plain pictures.
A: Click it to say yes.

Apart from the language skills and literacy experience the children are using to think about the genre of the book, Alice is talking far more than ever before in a small group activity. She is having difficulty in justifying why she thinks that the book is a picture book but is convinced that she is correct. Their language is purely their own. Not once do they refer to the word *genre*. However, they are only one step away from linking the word genre to its meaning, as they already understand the concept and with support, before completion of their next Storysearch sheet, they will be able both to read the word and use it in context.

Thinking about characters in the text

The reading demands of the Storysearch sheet lead to some genuine wrestling with the text for all pupils. As their class teacher it showed me something about the strategies they were using to tackle print. Here for instance Alice and Sean try to pronounce the word *characters*:

S: What's this? Char . . . ar . . . [*sounding out*] Char . . . chers . . . [*aside to friends on other computer*] What's a char . . . chers?
A: Oh I know what this is Sean because I've done this before. It means . . . have you . . . what . . . erm . . . what has it got in it?
S: Dolls.
A: No what is it about? [*confusing characters with themes*]
S: There's an object in it.
A: Has it got a monster in?
S: No.
A: Is there an adult male? Yes.
S: Adult male. Yeah.
S: [*appealing to his friend*] William, what is this? What does 'chers' [*characters*] mean?

Here we can see how the children are again making sense of a word which they cannot read. Alice has correctly told Sean what the word means but he does not fully understand and is unwilling to commit himself to any decision. He again asks William who is working on the next computer for help. Later on in the activity they asked me and were told the meaning of the word *characters*. Once explained to them, they were able to identify the characters within the text quite easily:

A: Oh look there it is . . . Child female.
S: There's a little girl, isn't there?
A: Yeah and two little boys.
S: Adult female. Yeah.
A: Put 'cats'.
S: Well where? You can't exactly put 'cats'.

223

A: Animals.
S: Look that's animals I've put down. Look there.
A: Yeah click on animals. What's that?
S: Objects. Is a toy an object?
A: Yeah it's an object.

Alice and Sean demonstrate that their language is developing while they are learning and very quickly show evidence of their understanding. Sean is aware that certain words categorise items together. Alice wants to include the cats as separate characters, but Sean helps her to understand that the word *animals* applies to them. Later, she is able to use this knowledge of grouping when they think about the dolls in the story and she identifies them as objects.

Developing their own opinions

Alice and Sean have to make decisions about the text and in doing so find themselves having different opinions. This is an essential part of interpreting texts in groups. Alice and Sean need opportunities to re-read and think about texts which they have read. As both of them are less experienced readers their previous experiences of texts have been limited to scheme reading books which offer few chances to develop the skills of interpretation and understanding texts. In forming their own opinion about texts and discovering that it differs from that of their partner they automatically justify why they have reached a certain opinion. In doing so they refer to the text to support their opinion:

A: Oh look there it is . . . 'Child female'.
S: There's a little girl, isn't there?
A: Yeah and two little boys.
S: Adult female. Yeah.

And when asked to identify themes in the text Sean clearly justifies decisions with reference to the text:

A: Yes 'cos it does change.
S: And . . . sorrow . . .
A: There's not rich and poor. There's *not* loss.
S: Yeah there's loss . . . remember they lost Bruno?
A: Oh yeah!
S: War . . . No.
A: Growing up? . . . Relationships! [*giggles*]
S: Erm . . . coping with . . . coping with problems.
A: Erm . . .
S: *Yes.* I think . . . 'cos they had bugs all over them, didn't they?
A: Yes. Coping with problems [*entering into computer*].
A: Erm *con* . . . *fl* . . . *ic* . . . *t* . . . conflict?

S: I dunno . . . Not 'other' . . .
S: Sorrow there was sorrow . . . sorrow means they're sad.
A: Yeah they were sad.

Sharing ideas and reaching consensus

Alice and Sean show that they can share ideas and opinions as they discuss the text they read together. In the following example, a larger group of Year 4 pupils have just read together *The Iron Man* by Ted Hughes and have been asked to complete the datafile sheet at the computer. Working together in larger groups, or even as a whole class, offers opportunities for pupils to wrestle with language and concepts. The pupils – two boys and six girls – are trying to decide the genre of the book. The list of suggestions is on the screen in front of them:

LAURA: . . . and the genre is . . .
STACEY: Genre, what's the genre? Adventure?
CHLOE: Fantasy.
LAURA: Horror.
PHILIP: I'm just taking time to think which is the best 'cos we're arguing.
GILLIAN: Yes.
TOM: Right, what do you think?
PHILIP: I think probably . . . probably adventure or fantasy.
CHLOE & VICKY: Adventure or fantasy . . . fantasy.
STACEY & OTHERS: I think it should be science fiction 'cos there isn't such a
      thing as an iron man . . .
TOM: Anything else . . . ?
GILLIAN: Adventure.
LAURA & VICKY: Horror and fantasy.
GILLIAN: Fantasy.
TOM: I think it's fantasy cos it's not real.
VICKY: Definitely adventure though.
TOM: It is a bit of a horror because . . .
VICKY: . . . it's adventure though.
PHILIP: . . . probably is. . . . No I think it's fantasy 'cos it's not real, there's never
      been a monster of iron.
STACEY: Hey you guys we're arguing again.
PHILIP: Fantasy probably.
LAURA & TOM: Horror as well because of the Space Bat Angel . . .
VICKY: Definitely adventure though.
LAURA: Mystery. Why did it come down? *Why* did it come down?
CATHERINE: Yes, mystery.
LAURA: Yeah, 'cos why did it come down, we don't know that . . .
PHILIP: Yeah we did 'cos we read the book yes 'cos he heard all the wars and
      things . . .

This is a really lively discussion in which everybody joined in, sometimes all at the same time! Even though they say they are arguing they are actually engaging in enthusiastic debate; there is no acrimony. They are using each other as sounding boards for ideas – doing some thinking talk and, when challenged, justifying their opinions or offering reasons for their answers. They demonstrate, too, that they clearly understand what *genre* means. They are confident talkers with each other, make some thoughtful responses to the text and their discussion overall demonstrates that reading the book has given them pleasure and that they have understood some of the implications and complexities.

Reflections

All the children who are using Storysearch are learning a great deal not only about texts but how to discuss, justify their opinions, quote from and refer to the texts they are reading. Storysearch provides a contextualised opportunity for children to re-read and reflect on the texts they have read. Like Alice and Sean, many children need this time to pause and think before launching into the next text. Children who are fluent readers find the discussion about the themes within a text most interesting and their discussions show them referring to the text in order to support their opinions. They help each other to make sense of the text and will often return to what they see as important parts. They also change each other's opinions and present intelligent and interesting arguments to support their opinions.

It is possible to achieve all of this so long as the work is carefully planned and the ICT skills gradually introduced to the children as part of a systematic and progressive programme. In many classrooms only one computer is available for most of the time. This should be taken into account as the children have to be introduced to the ICT software and the skills needed to operate it as well as becoming familiar with the Storysearch questionnaire and database. It may be that the best way to approach each aspect of the work is through a class lesson followed by plenty of opportunities for individuals, pairs and groups to have hands-on experience. Not all discussions need to take place around the computer, however. A paper copy of the form can be thought about by individuals before being discussed by pairs or groups; one member of the group can be nominated to complete the questionnaire page of the computer at the earliest opportunity. At regular intervals, the whole class can gather at the computer and search the database for response to specific questions such as:

How many Roald Dahl books have been entered on the database?

Is there a school story with a boy narrator?

Is there a war story with an animal in it?

What books has my friend Tom read?

Children who become familiar with Storysearch take great care over their decisions in response to the questionnaire. Through their serious and (sometimes for them) passionate discussions they show that what they are talking about is important to them and that it is not just *telling the teacher what I think*. Storysearch helps pupils to develop a vocabulary through which to think and talk about texts. It involves them in evaluation and shows them that it is valuable to share thoughts and opinions, and to reflect upon and analyse their reading.

Notes

1 The Storysearch database is available through Logotron, 124 Cambridge Science Park, Milton Road, Cambridge CB4 4ZS.
2 An extract from this part of the chapter has also appeared in E. Bearne, *Making Progress in English*, London: Routledge, 1998.

References

Department for Education and Science (1989) *Report of the English Working Party 5–16* (the Cox Report), London: HMSO.

Hughes, T. (1986) *The Iron Man*, London: Faber & Faber.

SCAA (School Curriculum and Assessment Authority) (1997) *Information Technology and the Use of Language at Key Stages 1 & 2*, Hayes, Middlesex: SCAA Publications.

Waddell, M. and Barrett, A. (1992) *The Hidden House*, London: Walker Books.

15

'I LIKE CLIMING, HOPING AND BIKING'

The language of physical education

Patricia Maude

For many children, movement is a significant factor in the development of language, language is a significant factor in becoming physically educated and physical education is an important medium for enhancing language. From the beginning of their lives, movement and language are interlinked:

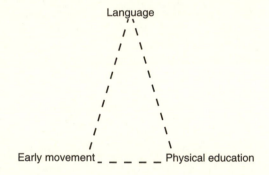

Early movement 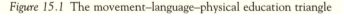 Physical education

Figure 15.1 The movement–language–physical education triangle

The model in Figure 15.1 shows a triangle of learning to illustrate the inter-relatedness of early movement, language and physical education. Both early movement and physical education (PE) provide a medium for developing move-ment and language; language is integral to learning in PE and early movement provides the basis for becoming physically educated.[1]

In this chapter I shall examine the development of language in relation to early movement and motor skill development and will then go on to explore ways in which teaching and learning English can be enhanced through skilful use of language in teaching physical education. Finally, I shall consider ways in which increasing mastery of language contributes significantly to learning in PE by providing communication potential in addition to that exemplified through body language and the communication potential of movement alone. For children to achieve their full potential in physical education they need both knowledge and understanding of movement and a sound command of language.

Early movement and language development

In infancy a great deal of learning is achieved through movement. Moving enables the infant to explore the environment, to gain familiarity with that environment, to find out about the body, to discover the uniqueness of each part of the body and also the interdependence of one part with another for successful movement. Gradually the infant becomes more independent and increasingly able to use movement to learn as well as to learn through movement.

An example of infants discovering the interrelationship of various parts of the body can be seen when a child extends both arms and hands towards a toy near the face, at first swiping at it, then contacting the toy with both hands, grasping it and clawing it forwards, if possible into the mouth. The hands are also used to find out about the rest of the body, such as reaching to grab the toes and put them into the mouth. The participation of the carer in such learning is invariably accompanied by verbal commentary, for example, 'Here's your rattle, take hold of your rattle, clever girl, putting your rattle into your mouth, give it to me.'

Once infants have developed sufficient musculature, they can roll over from back to front when they are lying down. This is usually followed by sitting up, crawling or creeping, pulling up to stand. When eventually they take steps, then walk, the world takes on a whole new challenge, with potential explorations at every turn. These activities are likely to be accompanied by verbal commentary by the carer, such as, '*sit* on your bottom, *hold* on to, *stand, climb* up, *walk* to me'.

Movement itself also provides an early medium of communication, in advance of speech, whereby infants can make their own needs known, can attract attention and make demands on others. Parents and carers can often pick up signals from the children's gestures and other movements which provide communication clues. For example, turning the head away during feeding substitutes for *no more, thank you* and reaching up the arms towards the carer is often a mutually agreed signal to be interpreted as a plea *to be lifted up*.

Not only does the infant's own movement provide a means of communication to others, but many infants are exposed to the almost constant verbal communication of parents and carers, who talk near to, talk at and talk to the child. Much of the speech that infants may hear around them is related to movement, as carers talk through the actions and activities that the child is about to be engaged in, or is already experiencing, and that are subsequently achieved unaided. For example, '*hold* the cup, *put* the spoon into your mouth, let me *wipe* your mouth, *let go* of the spoon, *put on* your socks, *take off* your hat'. Another important aspect of early verbal familiarisation centres around the parts of the body, such as *mouth, head, tummy, bottom, knees, arms, hands, fingers, legs, feet, toes*. These feature constantly in child care and as many are key instruments for movement and learning in early motor development, the labelling of them provides important markers, both for location, for example '*sit* on your *bottom*', and for action: '*lift up* your *foot*'.

According to Asher, 'Children decode language through the intimate integration and subsequent relationship of language and bodily movement' (Asher 1983: 3). Once the child is mobile and can participate in a much wider range of play activity, movement takes on a greater communication significance, both in terms of its own declaration, for example when pushing a doll's pram along, and in terms of the emergent language related to the activity, such as *teddy walkie*. Bruner (1983) suggests that action, play and movement, which constitute 'the culture of childhood', are crucial to language development.

Talking about what they are doing gradually becomes a notable feature of the child's actions and play such that, by the time children attend Nursery and Reception classes, their movement and language should be so inter-related that 'Language is orchestrated to the choreography of the human body' (Asher 1983: 4). An excellent example of this is Emma (whose words form the title for this chapter), who is five years old. She knows both what she can do and what she enjoys doing and can not only tell us but can write down her preferences and read them to us with confidence. She enjoys physical activity and is skilful for her age when she climbs, hops and rides her bicycle. She is also very able in a range of other activities, such as rolls and headstands in gymnastics, rolling, throwing and catching a ball in games, and jumping and skipping in dance.

This tendency to use language as the 'orchestration to the choreography of the human body' is not only observable in children's gross motor functioning but also in their fine motor functioning through such activities as drawing, painting, cutting and sticking, and writing, where talking about what they are doing, explaining what is drawn or painted and describing the activity in which they are involved demonstrates ever increasing breadth of vocabulary and enhanced levels of verbal expression. Bruner (1983: 23) develops this idea further when he suggests that action, play and movement are crucial to language development, believing that within play 'all utterances have relevance, as the game becomes the topic and the situation provides a contextual conversation'. He goes on to note:

> Movement based interactions provide an environment in which the learner is immersed in understandable messages, where language can be placed in context naturally and meaningfully.
>
> (Bruner 1983: 23)

Through physical activity, children gather a wealth of knowledge, understanding and ability for self-expression that provides an excellent springboard for maximising the learning opportunities available in school. It is an equally excellent basis for teachers to capitalise on the movement ability and movement and language experience gained by young children in their pre-school environments. The importance of continuity and progression in movement learning from home into school cannot be overestimated. For some young children the school day may contain too few gross-motor-learning experiences and too many seat-based and fine-motor-functioning tasks, such as writing. For others, regular and frequent PE sessions are provided, but children are encouraged to work without talking and can thereby lose out on the full range of available learning experiences. The challenge for the teacher is to ensure that children learn and use both an ever-increasing vocabulary of movement and an ever-extending vocabulary of language in PE, throughout their school career.

Learning language in physical education

Although it used to be considered that physical education was a 'doing' and not a 'talking' subject, there are and always have been excellent opportunities for developing language and gaining experience in a range of language activities through PE. Translating body language into speech language is a skill in itself and provides a sphere of communication that can be richly developed through PE perhaps in a way that cannot as readily be exploited in other learning situations. In physical education, not only is speech the main medium for task-setting by the teacher, but feedback to improve performance is also most commonly delivered through the medium of speech. Even when tasks are set using demonstration, that demonstration is usually accompanied by a verbal commentary. Listening and interpreting, then, are vital skills for children, in accessing the activities to be undertaken and in improving the quality of their performance. This teaching strategy is not new. Traditional physical training (PT) in the 1940s depended on speech for task-setting and feedback. My own experience of 'drill' during PT lessons in my primary school involved the class standing in lines, following a series of instructions shouted out by the teacher, who always hoped that her commands would result in the whole class of children doing the same thing at the same time. This was considered to be a successful lesson – and we were expected to be silent!

The concept of speech being interpreted in movement is one of the special qualities of PE, unlike any other subject in school, except perhaps drama. This can often prove a challenge for teachers, whose responsibility is to elicit purposeful movement in response to a verbal task from a class of children of varying abilities in interpretation. It can be a challenge for children, too, particularly those who find instructions difficult to understand when the required response is movement, or who prefer to take time to consider an instruction before starting work and who therefore seem to be inactive during the lesson, whilst other children have already responded in movement. If, as teachers of PE, we expect children to spend the majority of the lesson being active, since movement is the main medium for learning, then it is essential that task-setting is clear, succinct and unambiguous, so that the movers can plan, perform and evaluate their performance as they work to select and refine their response to the task and endeavour to produce a quality movement solution to that task.

As Blake says: 'a process of communication needs to be established which guarantees that information is given clearly, concisely and accurately' (Blake 1996: 5).

The teacher's role, then, is both to establish that process of communication and to extend children's listening skills and language understanding through listening, in order to make use of the given information. Another role of the teacher is to extend children's language through talking, for speech is one way of ascertaining the level of knowledge and understanding that children are achieving. Children's talk during their PE sessions should include asking and answering questions, describing movement, explaining their own and others' work, giving feedback to others and increasingly developing the ability to analyse movement, discuss techniques and progressions, articulate their planning and evaluation, as well as their criteria for achieving quality movement.

What is the particular language vocabulary in PE? This is wide-ranging, even at Key Stage 1 when children are following only three areas of the Programmes of Study, and particularly at Key Stage 2 when they are learning all six areas of PE: athletics, dance, games, gymnastics, outdoor and adventurous activities, and swimming, each with its own vocabulary both in language and in movement.

For example, in dance, language has an important role in helping children to interpret and improve the expressive qualities of their actions. The language used should include descriptive words and phrases to which the children can relate, for example *explode suddenly into the air and gently drift down to the ground*. Language can also be used to help children to express feelings and moods as well as to create characters and narrative in dance. Expressive use of the teacher's voice can add clarity and meaning to the words and rhyming words can provide the accompaniment for a rhythmic dance. Another example of the use of language in dance is to ask children to make up a *words dance*, selecting, say, four words from those shown in Figure 15.2 and developing movement vocabulary to express those words:

whirl	shrink	slither	glide	whisk	leap	
	bound	stride	expand	pounce	dart	shake
flutter	stalk	float	dive	jerk	press	
	toss	turn	shake	clap	grow	tiptoe
rock	flop	crouch	shatter	zigzag	dash	
	scatter	plunge	wander	soar	melt	flick

Figure 15.2 Words for dance actions (adapted from *Teaching Physical Education*, Homerton College, 1996)

The use of poetry, such as *The Cataract of Lodore* by Robert Southey, with key words and phrases such as 'eddying and whisking', 'darting and parting', 'threading and spreading', can provide the dancer not only with a stimulus for movement, but also with a challenge to interpret that vocabulary through sequences of expressive movement. Experimentation and exploration of movement around phrases such as these can lead to the planning and performance of dance compositions, using the reading or recitation of the poem as accompaniment to the movement.

Instead of selecting a poem, the language emanating from discussion of a single object can also provide a rich stimulus for dance. Whereas in the preceding example the vocabulary comes from the pen of a poet of the eighteenth century, here the language is emergent and living and the ownership of that language is with the dancers themselves. A class of ten-year-old children were each asked to hold a piece of flint, to feel and describe it to each other. They were asked to create movements that expressed the key words used to describe their flint and then to compose a dance with a verbal accompaniment. One group danced to their chant, *Humps and hollows and bits that stick out* and another group just used the words *Smooth and sharp*.

The teacher took the children on to learn how to record their movement by simple notation or *motif writing*, whereby they selected symbols to represent the key movements in their dance and then wrote these to represent the phrases of the dance (Figures 15.3 and 15.4).

Figure 15.3 Notation for *Humps, hollows and bits that stick out*

Figure 15.4 Notation for *Smooth and sharp*

Taking account of all the areas of the Programmes of Study for PE, their particular specialisms and all the movement opportunities that can be experienced within them, there are at least eight generic categories of vocabulary that can usefully contribute both to the overall language development of children and to children's physical education:

- **body awareness vocabulary**: to include the whole body, the limbs and the joints making up each limb, e.g. *foot, ankle, knee, hip, shoulder, elbow, wrist, hand* and the organs such as the heart and lungs, that facilitate movement learning. This category also includes the vocabulary to support the relationship of the limbs to each other and their positions, in order to achieve the most efficient or the most articulate or aesthetic movement possible, e.g. *arms swung back, shoulder-width apart and legs extended, with feet together;*

- **environment vocabulary**: to include both indoor and outdoor facilities, such as *the hall, the playground, the field* or *the swimming pool*;
- **resource, apparatus, equipment vocabulary**: whether of the *bat, ball, racket, goal*-type used in games; the *mat, box, rope, bench*-type used in gymnastics; the *cymbal, tambourine, piano*-type which accompanies dance; the *stop-watch* in athletics, the *compass* in outdoor and adventurous activities or the float in swimming;
- **spatial vocabulary**: by which children learn directions in movement, for example, *forwards, sideways*; or levels in movement such as *high, medium, low, up, down*; or aspects of personal and general space such as *near to, far from, around, under, over*;
- **temporal vocabulary**: enabling learning about *going slowly* or *quickly* and about *accelerating, decelerating, starting* and *stopping*;
- **motor skill vocabulary**: the infinite number of verbs that make up the movement vocabulary, such as *jump, catch, roll, throw, run, aim, go, stop, pull, kick, spin, balance, climb*;
- **quality of movement vocabulary**: the adverbs that add quality to the verbs, such as *lightly, strongly, powerfully*;
- **physical education vocabulary**: such as vocabulary to help with the core abilities to *plan* and *evaluate* performance and the vocabulary to ensure that appropriate risk assessment has been undertaken and that safety has been taken into account in the setting up, doing and clearing away of every activity. The language of safe practice can greatly enhance safe practice in movement;
- **specific activity vocabulary**: whether the language specific to each of the areas of PE in the primary school such as *dance, games, gymnastics*, or the specific vocabulary related to sport and dance such as *recreation*, or the language of *health-related exercise* and *fitness*. This language also represents the language of culture, since dance and sport are an inextricable part of our culture.

With the introduction of the National Curriculum for Physical Education came a formal acknowledgement of the importance of language in learning PE and the importance of teaching language through PE. Within the National Curriculum, one of the Common Requirements is to ensure that children express themselves clearly in speech. One of the General Requirements states that children should be taught to respond readily to instructions. Within the End of Key Stage Descriptions in both Key Stage 1 and Key Stage 2, there are several language-related requirements, including:

> They talk about what they and others have done and are able to make simple judgements. They describe the changes to their bodies during exercise. (Key Stage 1)

> They make simple judgements about their own and others' performance
> . . . and demonstrate that they understand what is happening to their
> bodies during exercise. (Key Stage 2)
>
> (DfE 1995: 11)

Even before embarking upon the National Curriculum, the pre-school
curriculum contains clear indications for using language to explain activities
involving movement.

The SCAA publication *Nursery Education: Desirable Learning Outcomes* states
that 'Children are encouraged to talk about their learning', and says that
'Approaches to teaching include recognition of the value of . . . giving clear
explanations, and of using play and talk as a medium for learning' (SCAA 1996:
6). It is play which underpins the PE curriculum and from which children draw
their movement vocabulary during PE sessions. If children have learned to talk
about their play, then when they start school they will also bring a valuable
speech vocabulary and skills of communication to enhance their learning in PE.
Fulfilling the language elements of the National Curriculum for PE (above), is
therefore a natural element of continuity and progression and not a new piece of
learning. For example, in each unit of work there should be a language
development target, whether to enable children to demonstrate knowledge of the
appropriate technical language of the activity or to describe or judge the quality
of their own or another's work, or to improve the quality of listening to the
teacher or a partner, in order to interpret speech-set tasks in movement. For
children in Key Stages 1 and 2 for whom English is an alternative language, PE
has much to offer by way of access to participation, since the medium of learning
is not language, but movement, and is immediately accessible by means of
watching other children and modelling their movement. At the same time, the
teacher's and other children's use of language relating to the physical activity
gives an opportunity for learning language in a context which has meaning.

In addition to capitalising on physical education to develop speaking and
listening, PE can also provide opportunities for enhancing reading and writing.
Using task cards to provide learning opportunities is a common practice in
sessions where children are able to read and understand the task. Reading back
records made during a practical session, perhaps to develop a database of athletics
results or rules of created games, is a useful way of developing writing skills
through PE. Written records are very valuable in PE where, otherwise, learning is
transitory, since, unless recorded on video, it happens only on the one occasion
and can rarely be repeated in exactly the same way.

The rich potential of PE for developing reading and writing, as well as the
more obvious area of speaking and listening, raises some important questions
about the relationship between physical education and language in the
curriculum. The National Curriculum had already been in place for over two
years before the following key questions were posed by SCAA:

- In what ways can work in physical education help to develop speaking and listening skills?
- How can children's understanding of physical education be enhanced by developing these skills?

The challenge now, in relation to the first question, is to re-examine past practice and to set new targets for the future enhancement of both the language of movement and the language of speech. One way forward would be to ask and answer some further questions, such as the following:

> In what ways does your PE curriculum maximise opportunities to develop children's language and particularly their speaking and listening skills? Is there more that could be achieved, either through curriculum planning or through curriculum delivery, whilst also enhancing the quality of the children's movement vocabulary and its use in all areas of the PE curriculum?[2]

The following section attempts to provide some answers.

Learning physical education through language

Having a command of the language that informs movement learning is fundamental to achieving potential in that learning. Quality movement is dependent on the refinement of motor skill knowledge and its applications, as well as on an understanding of the quality of movement required for every physical activity. Much of this can be achieved through experiential learning, through feedback gained using video, or by observing a performance of superior quality and attempting to match that model. These can also be enhanced through verbal feedback, reference to literature on the topic and through analysis and discussion of performance. Collaboration with others involved in similar learning experiences can add other dimensions to the learning, can provide comparative or contrasting data and help to embed the learning.

Unlike other subjects, movement work cannot be collected for marking, since it is transitory. Peer tutoring, therefore, is a valuable tool in PE as it is impossible for the teacher to observe the fleeting movement of every child in the class at the same time. However there is a need to develop progressive evaluation of movement learning and children themselves can provide evidence of progress which informs both them and their teacher. For example, children can keep written records of their movement learning for themselves – on the computer, by drawing or in writing.

Once children have sufficient technical vocabulary to describe what they have seen and sufficient knowledge of the task to provide feedback on the performance, their description, analysis or judgement can provide instant information for the mover to evaluate and then plan the next practice, refinement or performance.

Several interesting, examples of peer tutoring can be seen in the video *The Gym Kit* (Maude 1994). The first example is of peer tutoring in Year 4, to facilitate rope climbing:

> Ricki is helping me to climb a rope and he says that you should keep your hands about 10 centimetres apart, you need upper body strength and you need to keep practising. Practice makes perfect.

The second example is of children in Years 5 and 6 in another school who are observing a partner and giving feedback to improve the performance of a sequence. Emily is told by her partner, John: 'When you do your arabesque, you wobble like this. Can you keep still like this?' The video shows John's accompanying demonstrations and Emily's next practice of her arabesque balance. This is an excellent example of the use of language to focus the learner on the precise element to be improved; John's verbal feedback is beautifully orchestrated with the choreography of his movement vocabulary.

The final example is of David (Year 6), who knows clearly that he has benefited from the verbal feedback of his friends, in their group sequence. When interviewed about his achievements in gymnastics, he reports:

> I've had a lot of feedback from Laura and Anna to help me . . . how to keep my legs together and keep them straight, because they used to be all over the place when I did a cartwheel.

Self-evaluations in PE can be recorded by even the youngest children. The following examples are of children in Reception and Year 1 who have been given the opportunity of recording their achievements. Figure 15.5 is by Stacey (aged five), who assessed her achievements by recording her knowledge and experience in gymnastics during a unit of work on body awareness and particularly of learning about the extension of the knees and ankles, to show pointed feet. Peter (aged six) wrote an evaluation as a written record of his gymnastics (Figure 15.6). These examples aptly demonstrate both the importance of language in developing movement and the importance of movement in developing language.

Dean and Gross claim that 'movement-based lessons have the capacity to generate empowering environments' for the learning of language (in Gildenhuys 1996: 105). The integration of movement and language in movement development and, as a complement, the integration of movement and language in becoming physically educated and in developing rich language mastery, cannot be overstated. The central role of language in learning movement is indisputable as is the central role of teachers to give explicit attention to language in their physical education teaching.

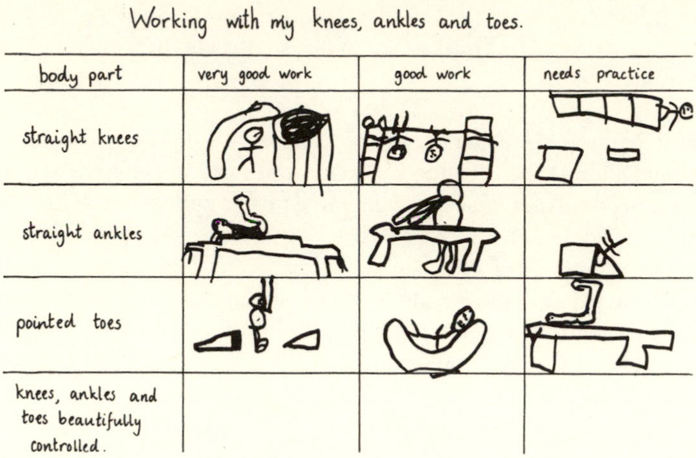

Working with my knees, ankles and toes.

body part	very good work	good work	needs practice
straight knees			
straight ankles			
pointed toes			
knees, ankles and toes beautifully controlled.			

Figure 15.5 'Working with my knees, ankles and toes'

Peter

Evaluate your gymnastics.

1. What do you enjoy most? Going on the spring-boards.

2. What are you best at? Swot-on

3. What do you need to practise? Forwd rolls, bacwd rolls, hand stans

4. Do you like working
on your own? Yes
with a partner? yes
in a group? yes
Why? Because its fun

Figure 15.6 Evaluate your gymnastics

Notes

1 The undoubted contribution of early movement learning to planning and teaching in physical education must not be overlooked, but will not be discussed in this chapter. Further information and guidance can be found in P. Maude, 'From Movement Development into Early Years Physical Education', in D. Whitebread (ed.) *Teaching and Learning in the Early Years*, London: Routledge, 1996.

2 For further reflections on these questions and for some specific suggestions of activities to provide more answers, reference should be made to the document *Physical Education and the Use of Language* (SCAA 1997).

References

Asher, J.J. (1983) *Learning Another Language through Actions*, Los Angeles, CA: Sky Oaks.

Blake, B. (1996) *Use of Language within the National Curriculum for Physical Education*, Nafferton: BAALPE (British Association of Advisers and Lecturers in Physical Education).

Bruner, J. (1983) *Child's Talk: Learning to Use Language*, Oxford: Oxford University Press.

Department for Education (1995) *Physical Education in the National Curriculum*, London: HMSO.

Gildenhuys, C.A. (1996) 'Movement and Second Language Acquisition', *Sport, Education and Society* 1 (2): 12–16.

Homerton College PE Department (1996) *Teaching Primary Physical Education*, Cambridge: Homerton College.

Maude, P.M. (1994) *The Gym Kit* (video and handbook), Albion Television, The Health Promotion Research Trust. Obtainable from Homerton College, Cambridge.

SCAA (1996) *Nursery Education: Desirable Learning Outcomes*, Hayes, Middlesex: SCAA.

SCAA (1997) *Physical Education and the Use of Language*, Hayes, Middlesex: SCAA.

Part 6

A COMMON APPROACH TO LANGUAGE DEVELOPMENT

The SCAA core document *Use of Language: a Common Approach* summarises the principles which should guide a whole school approach:

- developing a shared understanding between all staff of the role of language in pupils' learning and how work in different subjects can contribute to and benefit from the development of pupils' ability to communicate effectively;
- helping teachers be clear about the ways in which their work with pupils contributes to the development of pupils' communication skills;
- knowing and understanding pupils' standards of achievement in speaking and listening, writing and reading, and the identification of any areas of strength and weakness;
- taking account of the needs of all pupils, including the more able, those with special educational needs and pupils for whom English is an additional language;
- structuring lessons appropriately in ways that support and stimulate language development and showing how learning objectives for pupils are to be achieved;
- recognising how resources will be organised and used to support this teaching;
- monitoring and evaluating the impact of common goals and having clear, shared expectations of pupils' developing ability to talk, read and write effectively, and, specifically, establishing whether targets have been achieved.

The first point in this list is the key. Once shared understandings are reached about the role of language in learning, then the regular practices of school will follow. However, this is not as straightforward as it sounds; if it were, then there would be no need for this book or for the work which has been undertaken by major national projects. In the last ten years the National Writing Project, the

241

Arts in Schools Project, the National Oracy Project, the Language in the National Curriculum Project and, most recently, the National Literacy Project have worked with teachers specifically to develop shared understandings about the important role language plays in learning throughout the curriculum. The Bullock Report, worth revisiting for its breadth and scope of thoughtful knowledge about language (despite some obvious signs of age), offered a great opportunity for getting to grips with *Language across the Curriculum*. None of these major initiatives have found the task easy. This is not because of the recalcitrance of teachers; much the opposite. One of the main difficulties in developing shared understandings about the role of language in learning is that language is forever changing. The kinds of texts which children meet today are very different from those met by children only ten years ago and so the language demands made on children constantly shift. This has its impact on the responsibilities carried by teachers who are trying to provide a full and challenging language and literacy curriculum.

There are other reasons, of course. The burden on teachers over the past decade has been immense; the model of English (not *language*) promoted through government documents is problematic, as this book has already shown. The model of learning which increasingly permeates official requirements is also a matter of debate. Whilst this book emphasises the processes of using language and the importance of seeing language and learning as *a process of production*, current educational practice tends to lay more stress on the products, measured by SATs and summarised in league tables. Whilst SCAA documents recognise the value of language for constructing knowledge, their focus is on pupils being

> taught to express themselves clearly in both speech and writing, and to develop their reading skills. They should be taught to use grammatically correct sentences and to spell and punctuate in order to communicate effectively in written English.
>
> (SCAA 1997: 2)

As has been made very clear throughout, the contributors to this book would not disagree with any of that. The reservation about such a requirement is that its scope is narrow, threatening to restrict any shared understanding about language to *language as effective communication*, more valued for accuracy than for conviction, critical awareness or opinion. It also lays much more emphasis on teaching than on learning, suggesting a straightforward delivery model of curriculum content. If teachers are genuinely to reach shared understanding about the role of language in learning they will need to have a more complex interactive model of the construction of learning.

This part of the book suggests ways in which colleagues might reach that shared understanding, following the development of policy into an examination of practice. It offers activities for curriculum development, in this case to ensure common policy and practice about the use of language throughout the curriculum.

The frameworks and suggestions for activities offered here are founded on the view that one of the most effective starting points in any process of development is to identify current good practice and work from there. Another foundation stone is a definition of policy as *what happens in practice*. There are schools throughout the UK where policy documents gather dust on the shelves, only to be brought out when OFSTED come to call. This is emphatically not the kind of policy development suggested here. This part of the book is about policy-in-practice evident from what teachers do in the classroom and accessible through the document which informs parents, governors and others about *what we do in this school*. The paper version of the policy should act as a source of reference for teachers and a means of informing others about practice. Just as important, however, is the enacted version of the policy which takes place in the classroom. This section covers a range of ways in which policy can be established, or reviewed, by considering:

- how to develop shared understanding about the role of language in learning;
- ways of identifying current (good) practice;
- where language fits into learning;
- teachers' own knowledge about English   – at text or discourse level,
         – at word and sentence level,
         – processes;
- audits of reading, writing, speaking and listening;
- issues of correctness;
- the environment for using language – school and classroom;
- organisation for learning;
- using information and communications technology;
- planning and structuring learning;
- assessing progress;
- monitoring, evaluating and target-setting.

Developing shared understanding about the role of language in learning

As many teachers know, the process of development of any policy is just as valuable as the final product; this returns to the idea of a synthesised *process of production* rather than separating the two elements. The greatest contribution to the establishment of shared understanding lies in the discussions which take place, the negotiations and sharing of ideas as teachers work on curriculum development. A group of colleagues might feel that they all mean the same when they talk about *drafting writing*, for example, but open discussion can often reveal significant – and sometimes worrying – differences in approach. The production of a policy about language in use, therefore, should take place as a result of long-term discussion. Much of this may already have happened while putting together the English policy, but it would be dangerous to assume that because the school has an English policy which has been collaboratively developed, the staff have cracked *language in use*. There is a shift of emphasis from simply thinking about the content of English towards seeing learning as a built-in component of the English curriculum as well as an important orientation towards the relationship of other subject areas with English teaching. As this book shows, these relationships can save teachers time; many of the requirements of the English curriculum can be approached through art or design and technology, through geography, history, information and communications technology, mathematics, music, PE, science . . . One of the first steps is to establish how language enters learning; but before that, it is important to reach a group view of what learning involves. This, of course, has been meat for many thousands of books and billions of words, so it is unrealistic to expect colleagues to come up with any definitive or particularly learned answers. Nevertheless, since learning is the business of teachers, it should be possible to reach some kind of working definition, composed of a series of statements.

Where does language fit into learning?

When asked *What is learning?* one group of teachers came up with the following ideas:

- putting existing experience or knowledge alongside new knowledge, experience, facts . . . ;
- finding things out, making discoveries;
- increasing awareness;
- continually updating ideas;
- reflecting on experience;
- learning *how* as well as *what* and *why*;
- having curiosity and satisfying it . . .

(Bearne 1996: 245)

Activity: Colleagues might be asked the following question as a brief group brainstorm activity and a preparation to the following activity:

What would you add to/amend/delete from the above list?

The next question, *Where does language fit into learning?*, starts to link language with learning. Some answers might be:

- preparation; getting ideas going, framing questions;
- gathering, organising or categorising information;

- exploring ideas: hypothesising, predicting, explaining, describing, persuading, arguing;
- giving information to others, communicating ideas;
- reflecting on and evaluating learning, reviewing progress;
- demonstrating that something has been learned.

Activity: Taking one subject area – say mathematics – colleagues could compile examples of how these language processes are currently used in that subject (see Figure A).

This could be done again as a group brainstorm but might yield more information to be shared if done individually at first then used to make a composite list. The oral feedback after individual thought for a few minutes should raise some interesting areas of common and disparate practice.

Any significant gaps should be noted to build towards a set of targets for future work on language in use. You may want to use Figure Q to note relevant points (see p. 281).

Language processes	Current practice
Preparation; getting ideas going, framing questions.	
Gathering, organising or categorising information.	
Exploring ideas: hypothesising, predicting, explaining, describing, persuading, arguing.	
Giving information to others, communicating ideas.	
Reflecting on, evaluating learning, reviewing progress.	
Demonstrating that something has been learned.	

Figure A Grid for discussing 'Where does language fit into learning?'

Establishing current (good) practice in using language for learning

The next step is just a short one – looking at the language demands of different subjects. This job has been done for teachers through the SCAA *Use of Language* documents which give some examples from the programmes of study for English indicating subject areas where those aspects of English can be developed. The examples are very close to the list above; the main difference is that they separate out the processes of language for learning into the attainment targets for English – Speaking and Listening, Reading and Writing (see Figures B–D). These summary sheets can be used as a means of beginning to identify current practice across curriculum areas.

Activity: This might be carried out in small groups or, building on the last activity, focused on one subject at a time, with subject co-ordinators leading discussion. Using one of the attainment targets (Figures B–D) as a reference point (or groups taking one each) colleagues could consider the following:

What could you add to the English Attainment Target summary lists as they stand?

For example:

- What other subject areas cover the Attainment Targets?
  What other aspects of speaking and listening, reading or writing not listed here have you covered in geography (for instance) recently?

Activities such as these not only begin to establish shared understanding through exchanges of ideas, approaches and activities, they also build a foundation of current practice which allows identification of gaps in practice.

Teachers' own knowledge about English

One of the SCAA principles relates to teachers being assured about how their classroom work 'contributes to the development of pupils' communication skills'. The previous activities will have begun to make this clear, but, as earlier sections of this book have shown, learning language is a complex business which goes beyond the kinds of descriptions in the attainment targets for English. These list the kinds of experiences children should be given and some of the skills they should be taught. They certainly cover the process of getting and conveying information; they also include some of the range of text types children need to encounter. However, because the National Curriculum is a generalised document, it cannot adequately cover the full range and repertoire relevant to

English Attainment Target *Speaking and listening*	Subject
Talk to different audiences and for a variety of purposes including telling stories, describing, predicting, explaining, reporting.	
Listen carefully, remember and respond. Ask and answer questions.	
Participate in dramatic activities, e.g. role play and performances of different kinds.	
Describe observations and experiences; make simple, clear explanations of choices; give reasons for opinions and actions.	
Explore, develop and clarify ideas.	
Plan, predict and investigate.	
Learn by heart, speak with confidence and with clear diction and appropriate intonation.	

Figure B Examples of language in use in different curriculum areas – speaking and listening

English Attainment Target *Reading*	Subject
Find information in books and computer-based sources by using organisational devices to help decide which parts of the material to read closely.	
Read for different purposes from a range of sources, including reference material and stories, to gather information and stimulate imagination and enthusiasm.	
Use various approaches to word identification and recognition.	
Read IT-based reference materials with a variety of structural and organisational features; represent information in different forms and evaluate texts.	
Make use of patterned and predictable language	
Adopt an appropriate range of skills and strategies for the task in hand	
Read from a range of genres and from a variety of cultures and traditions.	
Read with fluency, accuracy, understanding and enjoyment.	

Figure C Examples of language in use in different curriculum areas – reading

English Attainment Target *Writing*	Subject
Write about classroom experience for a variety of audiences; match style, format and vocabulary to the intended audience.	
Organise and present writing in different ways, helpful to the purpose.	
Write as a means of developing, organising and communicating ideas.	
Write in response to a variety of stimuli including personal experience.	
Plan and review writing, plan, draft and improve work, assembling ideas on paper and on screen.	
Understand the value of writing.	
Use writing with appropriate vocabulary to aid remembering and to report experiences, observations and factual information	

Figure D Examples of language in use in different curriculum areas – writing

each group of pupils in individual schools, nor does it fully take into account those less tangible areas – the behaviours associated with language use: the process of developing discrimination, choice and independence; of sensitivity, versatility or commitment to a personal view founded on reason. More particularly, by separating out the attainment targets into speaking and listening, reading and writing, it gives an apparently fragmented picture of language which may not help when considering the role of language in learning.

The model of English outlined on p. 12 puts together the areas of language covered in the National Literacy Strategy and the National Curriculum. Figure E, an augmented model, makes this explicit.

National Literacy Strategy	National Curriculum
Texts	**Processes**
Study of language: (includes standard English) at sentence and word level.	*Getting and conveying information and ideas in reading, writing, speaking and listening.*
Study of the structure of texts: includes media texts, ICT, spoken texts and aspects of standard English, fiction and non-fiction.	*Developing discrimination as readers, writers, speakers and listeners.*

Figure E Augmented model of the English curriculum

It represents the texts and processes which make up English as integrated components. The texts are what the National Literacy Strategy is all about. The processes involve the modes of language in the National Curriculum. This model covers the content of both documents. The texts, or discourses, into which language is organised for specific purposes need not simply be those which are traditionally associated with English. The National Literacy materials specifically include non-fiction, ICT, media texts – often the resources for learning in curriculum areas other than English. The processes on the right-hand side similarly happen throughout the curriculum – including English lessons. As the different chapters in this book show, however, study of language and study of texts can enter any subject area.

Teachers' own knowledge about language – at text or discourse level

The model in Figure E offers an integrated picture of the word, sentence and whole texts (or discourses) which children need to experience and the processes

250

which will help them to use their knowledge. In developing a shared approach towards language in use, besides helping children through the processes of getting and conveying information and ideas and supporting them as they gradually develop discrimination and critical sense, teachers also need to be clear about the language structures which contribute to those processes.

The range and repertoire might include reading, writing, speaking and listening activities based on:

Fiction genres – picture books, short stories, videos and novels of:

- traditional stories from different cultures – folktales, fairy stories, fables, myths, legends
- contemporary stories from different cultures
- fantasy
- science fiction
- human interest stories
- animal stories
- adventure and mystery stories
- long-established children's fiction
- historical fiction

Plays – traditional and modern; for radio, screen or stage

Poetry – traditional and modern, narrative and descriptive etc., from different cultures

Non-fiction might include pictorial and print text such as:

- biography, autobiography and reference material on the lives or backgrounds of authors
- newspapers and magazines – persuasive, argumentative, reportage, analysis
- television documentaries and video information films
- environmental print
- information books
- travel writing
- journals
- letters

Activity: Figure F offers a checklist for noting when you have used any of the texts listed above in a specific subject area over the past term. This can be completed individually or in year groups or Key Stage groups.

The completed grids for each year group can be used to compile a picture of progression in using texts across the curriculum (see Figure G).

Any gaps in practice might be noted on Figure Q: 'Setting targets for developing use of language' at the end of this part (p. 281).

Texts	Fiction, picture books, poetry, drama, media	Non-fiction, including media
Art		
Design and technology		
Geography		
History		
Maths		
Music		
Physical education		
Science		
Religious education		

Figure F A checklist for texts used throughout the curriculum over a specified period of time

	Reception	Year 1	Year 2	Year 3	Year 4	Year 5	Year 6
Term One							
Term Two							
Term Three							

Figure G Example of grid for recording progression of use of texts throughout the curriculum

Teachers' knowledge about English – word and sentence level

Several of the chapters in this book have stressed the need for teachers to help children develop a vocabulary to talk about concepts encountered in different subject areas. This may consist of phrases or individual words which have specific meaning within art, mathematics or physical education – the word *form* for example. If teachers are to reach shared understandings about language use, there should be consistency and coherence about what technical language is relevant and when it should be introduced.

Activity: Figure H offers a framework for recording specific terms used for different subject areas. This activity is probably best carried out in groups – either Key Stage or whole staff so that colleagues can discuss the staged introduction of specific subject terminology.

It may be useful to allow time after the discussion for the groups to continue to add to the lists. You might put them (perhaps enlarged) on the staff room noticeboard so that whenever a word or phrase occurs to someone they can note it immediately.

After a period of time (perhaps when looking at the activity related to units of work) the compiled list can be revisited.

Any gaps in practice might be noted on Figure Q: 'Setting targets for developing use of language' at the end of this part (p. 281).

Subject area	Technical terms	When introduced
Art	e.g. figure, shading . . .	
Design and technology		
Geography		
History		
Mathematics		
Music		
Physical education		
Religious education		
Science		

Figure H Towards a progressive glossary of technical terms used in different subject areas

Attention to language at word and sentence level does not just involve the specific language of different subject areas, however. It also implies a common approach to introducing terminology used to talk about language. There are many examples where language is used specifically in different curriculum areas and it is important to consider the vocabulary of the subject. It is often claimed that the technical aspects of language – grammar, punctuation and spelling – are no longer part of what teachers teach. If you take a moment to list the terminology you and colleagues use in the classroom, what quickly becomes clear is that, contrary to popular myth, grammar *is* being taught and language *is* being carefully studied. Whether at Key Stage 1 or 2 teachers continually teach and reinforce reflective language about language.

The next step is to ensure that these aspects of language are being addressed equally in music, science and D & T as in English lessons.

Activity: In English, the specific vocabulary is to do with texts or words, and teachers use a wide variety of technical terms in the course of a teaching day or week. For example:

letter, word, phrase, sentence, noun, verb, adjective, adverb, capital letter, full stop, comma, question mark, speech marks, exclamation mark, colon, semicolon, apostrophe, paragraph, punctuation, plural, connective, upper case, lower case, consonant, vowel, brackets, caption, heading, description, explanation, account, narrative, notes, tense, beginning/opening, middle, end/conclusion, rhyme, rhythm, alliteration, dialogue, discuss, predict . . .

Ask colleagues to brainstorm a list of the language they have used to talk about language in the past week. How many of the above list were included? What gaps are there?

You might want to develop a similar progression list to the one used in the previous activity.

(Figure H could be easily adapted to track the gradual introduction of the metalanguage used to talk about grammar, punctuation and text structure.)

Any gaps in practice might be noted on Figure Q: 'Setting targets for developing use of language' at the end of this part (p. 281).

Teachers' own knowledge about language – processes

Some of the processes of getting and conveying information and developing discrimination and choice will have been touched on in the activity looking at the role of language in learning and in considering the SCAA examples of English as represented in different areas of the curriculum. These were largely group activities, however, and did not ask for closely observed detail of practice.

Activity: This is designed first of all to help individual teachers identify their current good practice and focus on any areas which need extra thought. The audit in Figure I should be completed over a week's teaching, allowing teachers to note where, in the different subject areas, the processes are catered for.

Alternatively, this format could be used as a prompt for planning (see 'Planning and structuring learning' on p. 265).

If individuals identify any gaps in practice these might be noted on Figure Q: 'Setting targets for developing use of language' (p. 281) or they might form part of the teacher's own target-setting.

Processes:	Getting and conveying information: researching, skimming, scanning, listening, note-making, informing, explaining		
	Developing independence and discrimination: drafting, choosing reading material, varying texts for purpose and audience		
	Reading	Writing	Speaking and listening
Art			
Design technology			
Geography			
History			
Maths			
Music			
Physical education			
Science			
Religious education			

Figure I A checklist for auditing the processes of English throughout the curriculum

Auditing reading, writing, speaking and listening

Before trying to improve reading across the curriculum or writing or speaking and listening, it's worth finding out just what kinds of reading go on throughout the school in order to build on a steadily accumulating repertoire of strategies for getting meaning out of print in all sorts of forms and for a range of purposes.

Activity: The audit of reading opportunities/challenges (Figure J) should first of all be completed individually. This can be done in about 15 minutes or so. It can then form the basis for sharing between colleagues in year groups or Key Stage groups. They might consider the following:

- What kinds of reading are not represented?
- What might be added to responses to the last two questions?
- Do these practices ensure continuity for the children as they move from class to class and from Key Stage to Key Stage?

After colleagues have had time to consider these, you may want to ask one person from each group to identify key areas for discussion which arose from the activity.

Figures K and L give examples of two teachers' audits of reading across the curriculum, one at Key Stage 1 and one at Key Stage 2.

Any gaps in practice might be noted on Figure Q: 'Setting targets for developing use of language' (p. 281) or individuals might want to use issues arising from these discussions as part of their own target-setting.

Audit of reading opportunities/challenges

(not including reading in 'English' sessions)

- List the different kinds of reading that your class has done over the last few days

- How were these linked to writing?

  . . . and talking?

- How did the children learn to read these different types of text?

- What activities do you use to teach children to get information from texts?

Figure J Audit of reading throughout the curriculum

READING ACROSS THE CURRICULUM

There may be more reading going on in your classroom than you imagine.

Before trying to improve reading across the curriculum, it's worth finding out just what kinds of reading go on throughout the school so that you can be assured that you're building on a steadily accumulating repertoire of strategies for getting meaning out of print in all sorts of forms and for a range of purposes.

Audit of reading opportunities/challenges
(other than reading in 'English' areas of the curriculum)

List the different kinds of reading your class has done in the course of a few days:

cereal packets. Reference. Poetry, own writing, Graphs, charts, co-ordinates, T.V. Read music. Board instructions spellings. Read with a friend. hymn practice words. Labels, computer, each others work. Maps.

Consider these questions:

How were these linked to writing?

Poetry → . Reading writing journals, topic work; book reviews, graphs.

. . . and talking? Intervenes at all parts. discussed book reviews & friends recommendations. discussed nutritional value of cornflake packets. discussed P.S.E. Verification of instructions. Getting meaning.

How did the children learn to read in these different ways?

adults as models,
Opportunities.
Support of other chn. } gain confidence.
 " " adults

Need to follow instructions.

Experience.
Intervention of planned practice — one to one matching
— phonic awareness
— sentence building
— using pictures
— discussion of how books work

Figure K Reading across the curriculum: first teacher's audit

READING ACROSS THE CURRICULUM

There may be more reading going on in your classroom than you imagine.

Before trying to improve reading across the curriculum, it's worth finding out just what kinds of reading go on throughout the school so that you can be assured that you're building on a steadily accumulating repertoire of strategies for getting meaning out of print in all sorts of forms and for a range of purposes.

Audit of reading opportunities/challenges
(other than reading in 'English' areas of the curriculum)

List the different kinds of reading your class has done in the course of a few days:

Reading instructions from board or worksheets.
Looking at topic related information books to retrieve information.
Stories. free choice.
Reading scheme books.
Class displays - Explanations of display - Information contained.
Computer programmes - Following instructions, finding information.
Maths books - instructions etc.
Newspapers/magazines/comics
Lists eg seating plan for lunch. / class rules.
Newsletters / Messages sent to parents.
Road signs & Information signs all around us.

Consider these questions:

How were these linked to writing?

children see information & stories in print & in writing around the room.
Often this writing will necessitate reading for information to use in their reports etc.
Other stories might be a stimulus for their own writing of stories.

. . . and talking?

i) Discussions about stories/reading on 1-1 basis with adult
ii)   "   with other children about content.
iii) Beginning to question & admit not understanding certain words
iv) Extending vocabulary.

How did the children learn to read in these different ways?

Saturation - helping to motivate children to want to learn to read in seeing the importance that is given to the printed word & how it is a vital link to the outside world.

Figure L Reading across the curriculum: second teacher's audit

Activity: Similar audits can be made of writing and speaking and listening. For example:

Audit of writing opportunities/challenges (not including writing in 'English' sessions)

- List the different kinds of writing that your class has done over the last few days:
- How were these linked to reading?
- . . . and talking?
- How did the children learn to construct these different types of text?
- What activities do you use to teach children to organise information?

Audit of speaking and listening opportunities/challenges (not including talk in 'English' sessions)

- List the different kinds of speaking and listening that your class has done over the last few days:
- How were these linked to reading?
- . . . and writing?
- How did the children learn to use these different types of talk text?
- What activities do you use to teach children to listen attentively for information/use talk for learning?

Issues of correctness

Correctness in writing is an issue which causes perennial problems. If the school has a spelling and handwriting policy then there may be no need to consider how colleagues introduce these aspects of writing throughout the curriculum. However, the staff may need to reach common understanding about *when* they consider it important to get children to produce correctly spelt and carefully handwritten texts – whether short or more extended pieces. For example, do you ask children to redraft notes made during science experiments or to use as prompts for a brief talk about an aspect of topic work? There is not always a clear-cut approach to drafting written work and a brief auditing session can help establish shared practice and understanding, identify areas of overlap or gaps in practice.

The environment for using language – school and classroom

The environment for learning is more than just the physical provision of books, materials and nicely mounted displays. The school and classroom environment reveals the value placed on language and literacy and this in turn reflects the

Activity: Figure M uses the stages of drafting from the National Curriculum for English to identify key areas of practice. Ask colleagues to complete sheets individually or in year groups then to pair up with teachers from the next class in age (Reception/Year 1 pairs with Year 1/2; Year 2 with Year 3, etc.). These pairs or small groups should then feed back to the whole group starting with the youngest age range. As the feedback continues the discussion builds towards a very clear view of shared practice in teaching children progressively how to structure texts.

The sheets can also be used to make a document which describes progression. An example of this can be found in *Making Progress in English* (Bearne 1998).

Any gaps in practice might be noted on Figure Q: 'Setting targets for developing use of language' (p. 281) or individuals might want to use issues arising from these discussions as part of their own target-setting.

Successful strategies for drafting

What types of writing would you expect children to redraft?

How do you help them to

* plan (note and develop initial ideas);

* draft (develop ideas from the plan into structured written text);

* revise (alter and improve the draft);

* proof-read (check for errors, omissions or repetitions);

* present (prepare a neat, correct and final copy)?

When did you last follow through the whole drafting process in an activity other than for English?

Figure M Building a progressive programme of teaching children how to structure texts

inner environment of the teacher's mind. A rich and inventive mind will create a stimulating visual and material environment. The empty noticeboard or dog-eared display tells a visitor – and the children – a great deal about the teachers' minds and the expectations and opportunities which are (or are not) on offer for the children. It is worth taking another look at the school and classroom environment.

Activity: This is a brief audit of the school environment for language. The headteacher or the staff as a whole might consider the following:

By walking down the corridors, what messages would a visitor receive about the value the school places on language and literacy? For example:

- what languages are represented in the notices around the school?
- do the displays represent all subjects of the curriculum?
- what kinds of reading material are evident?
- does the library look inviting as a resource area for general enquiry?

Any gaps in practice might be noted on Figure Q: 'Setting targets for developing use of language' at the end of this part (p. 281).

Activity: This is intended as a personal classroom audit, not necessarily for sharing with colleagues. Individual teachers might ask themselves:

What messages does my classroom give about the value I place on developing language throughout the curriculum?

Points to consider might be:

- are there special areas for reading, writing, speaking and listening?
- texts and materials: are they varied? do they draw on different subject areas?
- walls, displays and notices – do they reflect language used in all areas of the curriculum?
- reflections of diversity – different cultures, gender images . . .

Individual teachers might want to note any gaps or areas for improvement as part of their own target-setting.

Organisation for learning

Many of the chapters in this book show the value of group work for developing use of language. However, working with groups is not necessarily a straightforward matter. For a start, just what is a group? It's rather like asking 'How long is a piece of string?' Even more challenging is the question 'What is effective group work?' – in other words, 'What will really get the learning done?' These questions might have many answers, depending on the context, the task, the individual teacher and so on. The whole subject of group work is complex and diffuse, but certainly bears scrutiny if organising for learning is to be as effective as possible. Just putting learners into groups doesn't guarantee that learning will happen; there has to be rather more focus than simply rearranging the furniture! Also, roles within groups can be different or can vary during the process of a group's work; the person who is an information giver in one grouping, or at one stage in a group's work, may be the scribe or a silent appreciator in another group or at another stage of the group's work. While it can be easy to slip into routines about who works with whom, there are distinct advantages to varying groupings, particularly when considering issues of equal opportunities, gender, special needs, and pupils who have English as an additional language.

Some ways of varying groupings can be through:

- single sex grouping
- organising roles within groups
- listening triangles
- using group observers
- pair building
- jigsawing
- envoying

(See Bearne 1998 and National Oracy Project 1990.)

There are, of course, many other ways in which groups can be organised effectively. The key point is to consider the range and extent of variation you want to provide over a specified period of time. Once children get into the way of working with flexible groupings, the management can be much more relaxed.

The organisation of groups will have an impact both on the effectiveness of the learning and on the role of language in developing effective communicators. Group organisation also feeds into considerations of differentiation and diversity (see Bearne 1996).

Using information and communications technology

One of the most significant developments in classroom resourcing has come about through the greater availability of computers. ICT can contribute to English teaching and learning in a range of ways. What are the benefits of using ICT in English? Perhaps the most universally accepted form of computer application for English is word processing. Desktop publishing packages mean that books, pamphlets and newspapers can be produced to a professional standard. In terms of reading, the advent of the CD-ROM is probably the most

Activity: As part of a personal classroom audit, individuals might like to consider their organisation for language learning in terms of:

- types or groupings/group activities;
- varying activities and groupings: how much variety is there in the course of any one week?
- the range of resources – human and material. Does this represent language use in all areas of the curriculum?
- what provision is made for the language development of:
  - less fluent and confident learners?
  - children who are very assured and fluent learners?
  - children who have statements of special educational need?

Individual teachers might want to note any gaps or areas for improvement as part of their own target-setting.

significant shift, enabling quick referencing and, importantly, the capacity for several children to research at once. The added value of discussion can enhance their learning and shift information gathering very quickly towards genuine understanding. Databases can be used to store and retrieve information about texts. In other curriculum areas, the requirement to input data in abbreviated form also means attention to language and more genuine comprehension of information texts. (Chapter 14, pp. 217–27 gives a detailed case study of using databases.)

Information and communications technology needs to be introduced into all aspects of work in the classroom. It is an ideal way of promoting and developing explanatory, predictive and hypothesising talk as well as encouraging negotiation and collaborative practices. Also, of course, it allows individuals to find pleasure in their own expertise. Computers provide very good opportunities for children to work independently of the teacher and although you may need to manage the timetabling of use (and to monitor boy/girl use) once routines have been established it can be a site for fruitful observation of collaborative talk. Word processing can give a chance for pupils to draft, revise, edit and proof-read writing together. Databases involve a great deal of discussion about what should be entered and how it can best be entered. CD-ROMs offer opportunities for explanations, questions and the display of a pupil's knowledge which the teacher may not have known about. The discussions might not even have to take place around the computer; work for databases can be discussed in groups before entering the information on the machine, as in the following example.

Activity: Discussion amongst colleagues could discover the extent to which ICT is being fully exploited to develop language. Questions to consider would be:

How many of the following types of texts are available to the pupils in an electronic form in the school?

Fiction	Non-fiction
Drama texts	Newspapers
Magazines	Reference books
Encyclopaedias	Dictionaries

How many of the following IT resources are available to the pupils?

Word processors	Desktop publishing
Simulations/adventures	Language development software
Talking books	Databases
CD-ROM	Internet and e-mail
Overlay (concept) keyboards	

Individuals may want to consider the following questions about classroom-based ICT:

- Approximately how often do pupils have opportunities to use ICT to develop their reading, writing, speaking and listening – daily/weekly/termly/yearly?
- How do you use ICT in developing language and literacy?
- Do all the children have equal access to computers?
- How might you make more use of ICT to support language and literacy?

Any gaps in practice might be noted on Figure Q: 'Setting targets for developing use of language' (p. 281) or individuals might want to use issues arising from these discussions as part of their own target-setting.

Planning and structuring learning

The SCAA principles outlined on p. 241 emphasise provision for language in planning. It is worth running a quick audit of schemes of work (long-term plans) and Units of Work (termly or half-termly plans) and teachers' weekly (or fortnightly) and daily planning to check the inclusion of language in all subject areas. Looking at medium-term plans or Units of Work is the best route towards compiling a list of language objectives which can be checked against long-term plans in each subject area. Starting with the medium term can also lead to thinking about the level of detail needed for weekly or daily plans. All the activities so far in this part should have contributed towards identifying some areas which staff do well besides finding gaps in practice. The following activity should add to those areas.

Activity: This audit might be done by subject co-ordinators on behalf of colleagues or through members of staff checking out their own topic planning.

Check each termly or half-termly Unit of Work for provision of:

- **learning objectives** – experiences, concepts/knowledge, conventions/ skills, strategies and behaviours
- **resources/materials** – remembering that people can be resources, too
- **provision for Use of Language** – subject specific
  - texts
  - processes
- **tasks/activities**
- **groupings** and provision for **differentiation**
- **links with National Curriculum Programmes of Study**
- **assessment criteria** – what will be used as evidence of progress (see activity on p. 267)
- **evaluation to inform future learning**

Any major gaps might form the basis for future meetings about language. Other activities in this section may be useful in identifying areas for future work. Subject co-ordinators or individuals might want to use issues arising from these audits as part of their own target-setting.

Assessing progress

Progress in teaching will be monitored at subject and class level through evaluation at the end of every Unit of Work. Every school should have an assessment framework for each subject. It would be worth identifying within that framework the ways in which language development is to be assessed. One of the more challenging aspects of assessment is to establish a sense of continuity and progression in the criteria used to judge individual children's progress. How are parents to be informed of children's progress? How do you measure and compare the performance of boys and girls? How do you describe progress in reading, writing, speaking and listening? How can you be sure that learning objectives for language have been met? The documents about baseline assessment, particularly *Baseline Assessment Scales* (SCAA 1997: 4–5), suggest some starting points for assessing progress in language in the following categories: reading: for meaning and enjoyment, letter knowledge, phonological awareness; writing; and speaking and listening.

Where do you go from there? These broad areas do not give much guidance. Figures N–P (pp. 268–80) give a set of progression statements for reading, writing, speaking and listening which are more detailed. They are organised to match the four components of the model of English on p. 250:

- the process of getting and conveying information;
- the process of developing independence and discrimination;
- the study of language at sentence and word level;
- the study of texts – fiction and non-fiction.

These could equally be used as part of baseline assessment and then be built on as the child goes through the school.

Activity: In order to see how these progression statements can be used, individual teachers should have in mind one child in the class who is motoring along nicely, who doesn't cause them any major concern. Using a highlighter pen they should then mark on copies of Figures N–P those statements which match what the children can do as readers, writers, speakers and listeners.

Highlighting statements for all the children will immediately show up any areas for attention, but the statements are most useful as longer-term records. After two terms, using a different colour of highlighter, teachers should mark those statements which then match what the child can do. This will immediately provide a visual indication of progress.

Alternatively, teachers might simply want to note on a class register the category which best represents the child's current achievement (A, B, C/D, etc.). Six months later they can go through the register again and similarly note progress (see Bearne 1998 for a fuller explanation of how these records might be used).

These statements may form the basis for gathering information on pupil performance in preparation for target-setting.

Reading	Getting and conveying information	Developing discrimination and choice	Knowledge of language at sentence and word level	Knowledge of texts – fiction and non-fiction
A a reader in the early stages of learning	• may not yet have made the connection between meaning and print • recognises some environmental print, logos etc. • can read pictorial text but needs others to read print aloud	• can express a response to the written word • can behave like a reader: turning pages, holding the book the right way up etc. • tends to choose known texts for shared/paired reading	• can identify own name, familiar signs or symbols	• understands stories, rhymes and information read aloud by a more experienced reader • knows about how a book works (e.g. the cover, back, front, beginning, end of a book . . .)
B a reader who is gaining experience and fluency	• can read and use classroom notices, labels, captions • still needs support in reading reference or informational material	• can express an opinion or preference for a particular book/story • shows greater assurance with familiar texts but still needs help with new or unknown text • chooses reading material with more pictorial than printed text	• may depend on one strategy more than another when reading aloud • shows evidence of drawing on several strategies when attempting to read unfamiliar material (e.g. picture cues, initial sounds, memory of similar word shapes . . .) • reads own dictated 'emergent' text with some assurance and accuracy	• can use some vocabulary to talk about books (e.g. word, letter, page, cover, title . . .) • can predict events of stories read aloud by or shared with a more experienced reader • shows understanding of behaviour of characters in fiction • knows the difference between fiction and non-fiction

C a more assured reader, growing in experience	• can use some reference material with assurance • is beginning to skim/scan for familiar words or phrases	• reads some texts with developing accuracy, fluency and expression • reads silently at times • browses purposefully • chooses a wider range of types of reading and some unfamiliar material but returns to the known for independent reading	• uses a range of strategies when reading aloud (e.g. picture cues, shape and sound of words, one-to-one matching ...) • is beginning to read own text critically	• shows understanding of the main points of a story/passage • usually talks appropriately about books using relevant vocabulary (e.g. author, illustrator, characters ...) • can discuss structure of texts with a more experienced reader • uses different reading strategies to get meaning from fiction and non-fiction
D a more experienced and independent reader	• readily uses information and reference material • can locate information through contents, indexes, glossaries	• shows increasing assurance with books and with a greater range of reading activities • is beginning to use inference and deduction when talking about written text • usually reads silently and for more sustained periods • is prepared to 'have a go' with more complex material	• reads a range of print and pictorial texts with assurance, accuracy, fluency, expression and understanding, but may still occasionally need help • reads own text critically	• talks readily about books and other types of text (e.g. poetry, pictorial and media) using relevant vocabulary • identifies differences in structure between various fiction and non-fiction texts

Figure N Progression statements for reading (continues pp. 270–1)

Reading	Getting and conveying information	Developing discrimination and choice	Knowledge of language at sentence and word level	Knowledge of texts – fiction and non-fiction
D cont.		• chooses books purposefully and offers opinions about types of preferred texts		
E an experienced and almost independent reader	• can find information from a variety of sources for own purposes • is beginning to draw inferences from books, read independently and make thoughtful observations about content • can distinguish between and discuss fact and opinion	• is confident with a wide range of print and pictorial texts and reading activities • can justify opinions about texts • is prepared to persevere with complex texts • chooses material confidently and can decide whether to read silently or aloud for own purposes	• shows accuracy and some versatility when reading aloud • reads a range of texts critically	• can compare and discuss different types of text using technical vocabulary (e.g. reference, narrative, drama, information . . .) • can comment on structure of texts (e.g. climaxes, complications . . .)

F a very experienced and independent reader	• can follow instructions independently from a range of procedural texts • is able to sort, classify and use evidence from a range of material • reads between the lines well; can sift ideas and understands inference and allusion	• reads accurately, fluently, thoughtfully and with understanding from a wide range of texts for a wide range of purposes • can make choices from a wide range of reading material for pleasure and research • has established tastes in fiction and/or non-fiction • can give reasons for preferences in reading • shows development of a personal response to literature • can vary pace, pitch and expression when reading aloud	• draws on a wide range of reading styles for different reading tasks	• shows critical awareness of the structures of a wide range of texts • can discuss how language is used to create particular effects, using relevant terminology (e.g. to persuade, excite, depict character . . .)

Writing	Getting and conveying information	Developing discrimination and choice	Knowledge of language at sentence and word level	Knowledge of texts – fiction and non-fiction
Pre-writer	• uses writing to communicate during play/role play	• experiments with writing	• imitates symbols and word shapes in play writing	• knows that adults write lists, notes, letters etc.
A a writer in the early stages of learning	• knows that writing communicates meaning • writes for an audience even though needing help with technical conventions	• is keen to write and will experiment • can comment orally on own writing	• knows about direction and orientation of writing and can form some letters correctly • can construct a simple sentence	• has ideas for extended writing but needs teacher or other adult as scribe • can represent ideas pictorially, sometimes with related phrase or words • can tackle captions, lists, greetings . . .
B a writer who is gaining experience and fluency	• can compile lists/charts, organise writing into separate pages • writes accounts of experience in chronological order	• demonstrates some enthusiasm for writing • writes some texts independently but still needs help at times • can comment on own work orally and in writing	• varies chosen vocabulary and experiments with newly discovered words • writes in sentences showing some use of capital letters and full stops • forms letters correctly, joining letters if appropriate • attempts spellings using some rules and phonic awareness	• is beginning to write stories with a character/event • knows about beginning, middle and end in stories • uses some genre knowledge when writing (e.g. *once upon a time*)

C a more assured writer, growing in experience	• has experience of a variety of types of writing and a variety of forms (e.g. accounts of science experiments, observations) • can tell the difference between writing a list, report, notes	• shows some confidence in experiments with content and technicalities of writing • is maintaining enthusiasm for writing • is developing sustained concentration • drafts and redrafts with help • is beginning to comment independently on own and peers' work	• uses more varied connectives and description more often • uses generally accurate sentence construction • tries a wider range of punctuation more often (e.g. commas, question marks, exclamation marks …) • spells more key words correctly • uses cursive writing	• writes poetry which shows attention to form, rhyme and rhythm • is increasing the complexity of events/characters in story • uses models drawn from reading for fiction and non-fiction writing
D a more experienced and independent writer	• can produce non-chronological writing independently • makes notes from reference material with guidance • can use different planning formats • uses writing to organise thoughts	• is learning to collaborate over writing • can write extensively and with enthusiasm at times • is developing strategies for redrafting writing independently, using thesaurus and dictionary more often • is becoming more selective about publishing and increasingly able to comment critically on own work and that of others	• varies sentence openers and connectives • experiments with more varied punctuation (e.g. brackets, hyphens …) • draws on a range of strategies to get spelling right and uses standard spelling more consistently	• can use paragraphs • has experience of a variety of types of writing and a variety of forms • is beginning to use different genres and experiments with developing new genres • includes character and setting in story writing

Figure O Progression statements for writing (continues pp. 274–5)

Writing	Getting and conveying information	Developing discrimination and choice	Knowledge of language at sentence and word level	Knowledge of texts – fiction and non-fiction
E an experienced and almost independent writer	• can write extensive pieces of non-narrative writing • can make notes, identifying key words/phrases without help	• will collaborate over writing • usually chooses an appropriate style for the writing purpose and readership • shows assurance and commitment in writing independently • drafts, redrafts and proof-reads more independently or in collaboration with other pupils • responds helpfully to other people's writing	• varies sentence structures for particular effect • punctuates all kinds of writing with increasing accuracy and consistency • can punctuate direct speech • achieves standard spelling most of the time	• structures lengthy narrative logically • writes direct and reported speech • can depict setting, atmosphere, character, and motivation in fiction • varies the style of poetry writing according to the mood/content • can write in different genres and forms (e.g. adventure story, news article, play, poem, report)

F a very experienced and almost independent writer	• selects from a range of non-narrative forms for own purposes • selects from a range of appropriate models for planning	• makes appropriate choices about collaborative/ independent writing activities • gains satisfaction from writing • is able to work to deadline/set own deadlines • when redrafting looks more for content/style/ vocabulary rather than technical features alone • chooses and sustains an appropriate register for writing • shows a greater range of critical comment in writing (e.g. in response to books read)	• uses a wide range of vocabulary for specific effect • sets out direct speech correctly after opportunities to self-edit • can achieve standard spelling and accurate punctuation most of the time	• uses a range of narrative sequencing (e.g. starting at the end and using flashback; fracturing a narrative for effect; leaving a story hanging) • uses a variety of genres showing awareness of the structural elements involved • can write in standard and non-standard forms for chosen purposes • draws on a wide range of reading in order to explore other writers' techniques

Speaking and listening	Getting and conveying information	Developing discrimination and choice	Knowledge of language at sentence and word level	Knowledge of texts – fiction and non-fiction
A a beginner speaker/ listener	• indicates a range of simple needs using a range of methods of communication • communicates enjoyment of familiar stories read aloud to a group/individual • understands an instruction to carry a message and returns with an answer with an answer (written, verbal or signed; a single word is appropriate) • answers simple questions about her/himself • listens to teacher's instructions in a one-to-one situation when asked to do so	• joins in familiar action songs/rhymes in a group situation	• uses simple rhythms (e.g. clapping the syllables of own name) • experiments with sound and words	• anticipates a known pattern in a familiar or repetitive story • shows understanding of the difference between role play and real life

B a speaker/listener who is gaining experience	• conveys a simple or familiar message or a written message which requires remembering a straightforward verbal answer • remembers, tells and answers questions about an area of personal knowledge or experience • begins to ask other people questions • listens to teacher's instructions when asked to • asks for things or gets friends to ask	• joins in a whole-class/group story led by the teacher • talks with others spontaneously (during play for example) but might not respond to conversational cues	• uses rhythmic or rhymed patterns to help read aloud • shows an interest in the sound of words in own speech and that of others	• tells a story from given pictures and picture books in a simple sequence • plays in role for lengthy periods • talks about parts of books read and enjoyed
C a more assured speaker/listener, growing in experience	• conveys a verbal message and brings verbal reply independently • listens to instructions without being reminded • remembers, and tells in sequence, an event of personal significance • explains own work to another (child or adult) • asks own questions in response to other people's ideas	• joins in a whole-class/group story without adult prompting • shows a sense of audience – waiting for quiet, speaking to be heard • talks with enthusiasm about books read, commenting beyond the literal • uses reasons in discussion • listens and responds in	• creates a rhythm and notices rhyme when reading aloud • enjoys using the sound of new or complex words	• tells a story from own pictures or recounts an event with a beginning, middle and end • structures situations in role play activities • refers to/quotes from books read, films/videos seen

Figure P Progression statements for speaking and listening (continues pp. 278–80)

Speaking and listening	Getting and conveying information	Developing discrimination and choice	Knowledge of language at sentence and word level	Knowledge of texts – fiction and non-fiction
C cont.		• conversation with a friend • discusses familiar issues (e.g. classroom rules) with a known group		
D a more experienced speaker/listener	• explains personal preferences for reading material • with support or collaboration, presents and explains work to a large audience (e.g. assembly) • retells events selecting significant points with detail for a group/class audience • asks and responds to questions with some assurance • makes up questionnaires or questions	• uses different forms of talk for different people (e.g. teacher, friend, doctor, visitor . . .) and different situations (incl. use of standard English) • copes (verbally) with peers who present awkward behaviour in discussion groups • listens to and is tolerant of others' points of view • has an established concept of turn-taking (even if not always doing it) • organises group activities and delegates tasks	• gives attention to rhyme and rhythm in discussion and performance • uses different and specific language and/or vocabulary relating to interest and activities	• explains an extended storyboard sequence • can convey character in enacting role play or reading from play text • can switch from non-standard to standard English as necessary • can comment on narrative/informational structures of oral texts, films/videos, reading material

E an experienced speaker/listener			
• retells someone else's ideas accurately • gives opinions about experiences, things known or learned about • can give a sustained talk to the class/group • debates and discusses ideas found in research materials • makes appropriate and relevant (brief) comments in large-group/whole-class discussion • talks about own work and partner's or collaborative work using specific vocabulary and giving adequate explanations and reasons	• discusses books (films, TV, video, poetry, plays) giving reasons for choice, enjoyment or dissatisfaction • acts as enabler as well as contributor in group discussion • shows empathy with others' points of view • indicates awareness of others' conversational needs	• has a vocabulary with which to talk about language (e.g. about dialect, elements of grammar, rhythm and rhyme) • uses new vocabulary adventurously	• explains ideas/tells stories in clear sequence • uses role play to create different characters, genres, situations and to talk about how or why events happen in dramatic representations (incl. use of standard English) • can vary oral presentation of text according to genre (e.g. poem, informational text, story)

Speaking and listening	Getting and conveying information	Developing discrimination and choice	Knowledge of language at sentence and word level	Knowledge of texts – fiction and non-fiction
F a very experienced speaker/listener	• can describe, present and evaluate a piece of work or activity to a group • listens actively and attentively, responding perceptively to ideas • understands complex ideas presented orally (e.g. when read aloud or in a lecture or talk) and shows this understanding in the responses made • makes sustained (or brief, as appropriate) contributions to large-group/whole-class discussion	• confidently (or apparently so) initiates questions and makes contributions or offers opinions in a range of contexts • varies tone and formality according to context and subject (incl. use of standard English) • discusses literature, music, ideas with balance and conviction • initiates and leads discussion, extending and elaborating on others' ideas when necessary • engages in discussion as a contributor and listens autonomously without reminders about turn-taking • empathises and sees the points of view of others and articulates them in a range of settings (familiar/ unfamiliar; pairs/ groups/whole class; with peers/adults; known/unknown)	• uses technical or subject-specific vocabulary appropriately and accurately • uses vocabulary to talk about language with assurance and accuracy	• varies tone and formality according to context, subject and genre (incl. use of standard English) • takes on character, creates atmosphere, sustains suspense in drama or role play

Monitoring, evaluating and target-setting

Each school will have its own arrangements for monitoring and evaluating teaching and learning. (The final section of *Making Progress in English* (Bearne 1998) covers this fully.) Target-setting is an extension of such monitoring and evaluation. Targets can be set at whole-school level, at the level of the classroom and in terms of pupil performance. The notes made on Figure Q offer a good basis for setting targets at school and individual classroom levels. Once targets have been set, there needs to be a plan of action – and working out a programme for implementation, monitoring and evaluation. It is important that sufficient time is allowed for discussion and development of any initiatives, and then time for implementation within the classroom before their effectiveness is evaluated. A three-year programme is usually workable.

It is important to make sure that any targets identified as a result of any of the activities undertaken in this part of the book are built into the school development plan. Successful development of language in use cannot be taken on in fits and starts, nor is it appropriate to begin to overload teachers with additional burdens. It is essential to set priorities. Targets can be dealt with in plans for specific subject areas in line with the programme outlined in the school development plan. Shifts in language or teaching approaches in mathematics, for example, will necessarily have their impact on other areas of the curriculum, as the material in this book shows. The central point to hold on to when attempting to develop curriculum practice in language is the holistic nature of English. All of

Setting targets for use of language: record			
Date	Activity	Area to be developed	Proposed action/time-scale

Figure Q Setting targets for developing use of language

281

the issues covered in this part of the book can be approached either through English or through any other area of the curriculum. That is the advantage of teachers having a model of language development which is interactive and based on a view of language (and learning) development as recursive, continually looping back on itself, revisiting past learning in the light of new ideas and so widening its scope. The contributors to this book hope that their work will aid that process.

References

Bearne, E. (1996) *Differentiation and Diversity in the Primary School*, London: Routledge.

Bearne, E. (1998) *Making Progress in English*, London: Routledge.

National Oracy Project (1990) *Teaching Talking and Learning in Key Stage One* and *Teaching Talking and Learning in Key Stage Two*, York: National Curriculum Council.

SCAA (School Curriculum and Assessment Authority) (1997a) *Use of Language: a Common Approach*, Hayes, Middlesex: SCAA.

SCAA (1997b) *Baseline Assessment Scales*, Hayes, Middlesex: SCAA.

INDEX

NOTES

NOTES